THE
POLITICS
OF
U.S.
INTERNATIONAL
TRADE

PROTECTION,
EXPANSION
AND
ESCAPE

STEFANIE
ANN
LENWAY

UNIVERSITY OF MINNESOTA

Pitman
Boston · London · Melbourne · Toronto

Pitman Publishing Inc.
1020 Plain Street
Marshfield, Massachusetts 02050
Pitman Publishing Limited
128 Long Acre
London WC2E 9AN

Associated Companies
Pitman Publishing Pty. Ltd., Melbourne
Pitman Publishing New Zealand Ltd., Wellington
Copp Clark Pitman, Toronto

Library of Congress Cataloguing in Publication Data

Lenway, Stefanie Ann.
  The politics of U.S. international trade.

  Bibliography: p. 252
  Includes index.
  1. United States—Commercial policy. I. Title.
HF1455.L43 1985   382'.3'0973   84-25395
ISBN 0-273-02250-4

Manufactured in the United States of America
10 9 8 7 6 5 4 3 2 1

PITMAN SERIES IN
BUSINESS AND PUBLIC POLICY

CONSULTING EDITOR
EDWIN M. EPSTEIN
University of California, Berkeley

CURRENT BOOKS IN THE SERIES:

John D. Aram, *Managing Business and Public Policy: Concepts, Issues and Cases*

R. Edward Freeman, *Strategic Management: A Stakeholder Approach*

S. Prakash Sethi, Nobuaki Namiki and Carl L. Swanson, *The False Promise of the Japanese Miracle: Illusions and Realities of the Japanese Management System*

Charles S. McCoy, *Management of Values: The Ethical Difference in Corporate Policy and Performance*

Stefanie Ann Lenway: *The Politics of U.S. International Trade: Protection, Expansion and Escape*

CONTENTS

LIST OF ACRONYMS   vii

PREFACE   ix

1 INTRODUCTION: THE POLITICS OF
   U.S. INTERNATIONAL TRADE POLICY   1

   The GATT as an International Regime   5
   The Cases   7
   Trade Protection versus Adjustment   9
   The Organization of the Study   11
   Notes   16

2 DOMESTIC INTERESTS AND U.S. TRADE POLICY:
   A CRITIQUE   21

   Introduction   21
   The Economic Basis of Political Coalitions   23
   The Conspicuous Absence of Consumers   26
   The Autonomous Congress   30
   The Interest Group Model   32
   The Principal-Agent Perspective   33
   Notes   39

3   THE NATIONAL INTEREST AND INTERNATIONAL
    COLLABORATION IN INTERNATIONAL TRADE
    POLICY   43

    Introduction   43
    Political Autonomy versus Economic Interdependence   45
    State Strength and International Trade   46
    The International Regime as a Reflection
        of the National Interest   55
    Notes   58

4   U.S. TRADE POLICY IN RETROSPECT   59

    American Trade Policy: 1922−34   61
    The International Trade Organization   68
    The General Agreement on Tariffs and Trade   71
    The Trade Agreements Program: 1947−58   75
    The Trade Expansion Act of 1962   79
    The Kennedy Round   82
    The Trade Act of 1974   82
    The Tokyo Round   85
    Notes   88

5   TEXTILES: THE POLITICS OF PROTECTION   93

    Introduction   93
    Why Import Restraint?   97
    Trade Policy in the Textile and Apparel Industry   100
    The Textile White Paper   107
    Epilogue   118
    Implementation   119
    Conclusion   121
    Notes   122

6   AUTOS: THE POLITICS OF ESCAPE   125

    Introduction   125
    The Development of the U.S. Auto Industry   128
    Pre-ITC: The Executive Branch and Congress   134
    The UAW and Ford Petitions   139

The ITC Proceedings   143
Postscript   156
Conclusion   158
Notes   160

7   TELECOMMUNICATIONS: THE POLITICS
    OF EXPANSION   165

    Introduction   165
    The Telecommunications Industry   169
    The Government Procurement Code   171
    Nippon Telephone and Telegraph   175
    The Network of Interests: Japan, the United States,
        and the European Community   177
    How NTT Was Isolated   179
    The Negotiations over the Bilateral   185
    The Agreement   187
    Industry and Labor Reaction   189
    Epilogue   190
    Conclusion   191
    Notes   194

8   BEYOND DOMESTIC INTERESTS   199

    Interest Group Pressures and Trade Policy:
        Schattschneider's View   200
    The Transactional Model: The Basis for
        Congressional Autonomy   202
    The State as an Autonomous Actor   203
    Pragmatic Liberalism in U.S. International Trade Policy   205
    Industrial Policy in the United States   207
    U.S. Foreign Policy and International Trade   210
    Notes   212

BIBLIOGRAPHY   214

INDEX   221

LIST OF ACRONYMS

AT&T	American Telephone and Telegraph
CAFE	Corporate Average Fuel Economy
CEA	Council of Economic Advisors
CWA	Communications Workers of America
DOT	Department of Transportation
EEC	European Economic Community
EIA	Electronic Industries Association
FCC	Federal Communications Commission
GATT	General Agreement on Tariffs and Trade
GM	General Motors
GTE	General Telephone and Electronics
IBM	International Business Machines
ISAC	Industry Sector Advisory Committee
ITC	International Trade Commission
ITO	International Trade Organization
ITT	International Telephone & Telegraph
LDP	Liberal Democratic Party
LTA	Long-Term Arrangement
MCI	Microwave Communications Incorporated
MFA	Multifiber Arrangement
MFN	most-favored nation
MITI	Ministry of International Trade and Industry
MNC	multi-national corporation
MTN	multilateral trade negotiations

NTB	nontariff barrier
NTT	Nippon Telephone and Telegraph
OECD	Organization for Economic Cooperation and Development
OMA	orderly marketing agreement
PBXs	private branch exchanges
R&D	research and development
RFP	request for a proposal
STA	Short-Term Arrangement
STR	Special Trade Representative
TSB	Textile Surveillance Board
UAW	United Automobile Workers
VRA	voluntary restraint agreement

PREFACE

In the United States, international trade has often been considered to be a purely domestic political issue in which vocal interest groups vying for trade protection define policy. This book suggests that to understand American trade policy in both its economic and political dimensions U.S. policy process cannot be considered in isolation from international politics and international political organizations.

Specifically, this study explores the way in which the General Agreement on Tariffs and Trade (GATT) is embedded in the U.S. trade policy process. Three case studies illustrate the influence of the GATT: namely, case studies of the textile and apparel, automobile, and telecommunications industries. Each case supports the contention that U.S. adherence to the GATT makes it difficult for industry interest groups to influence the trade policy process.

This book raises questions for academic analysts of international trade as well as for both corporate and governmental policymakers. Each case study attempts to answer two theoretical questions. First, What is the role of interest groups, primarily from the business sector, in defining U.S. national interest in the area of trade policy? Second, Does membership in the GATT compel the United States to pursue a trade policy that does not reflect its national interest? Together these questions provide the foundation for an analysis of the tension between the liberal and protectionist forces within the U.S. trade policy process.

Analysis of these cases suggests that a significant source of constraint on the ability of interest groups within the three sectors to influence U.S. trade policy comes from American commitment to sustain a liberal trading order through adherence to GATT norms, rules, and procedures. Underlying this commitment is the belief that an open international trading system reflects U.S. national interest, although the open system also requires that specific sectors adjust to foreign competition and can intensify the process of industrial decline in sectors of the economy not competitive internationally.

For corporate managers this analysis raises questions about how best to respond to international competitive pressures. It suggests that a strategy for dealing with international competition based on the expectation that the government will impose import restraints is unlikely to be effective. Despite the fact that management—in each case study—portrayed increased foreign competition as a force likely to undermine the U.S. economy through the destruction of American firms and jobs, both Congress and the executive responded with some skepticism. While the government did negotiate some increase in trade protection in the textile and apparel and auto cases, the increase proved insufficient to insulate U.S. firms from international competitive pressures. In the telecommunications case, to divert industry pressure for protection the United States negotiated increased access to the Japanese telecommunications market.

Finally, for policymakers this study raises questions about the options open to the government in responding to sectors of the U.S. economy that request import protection. The GATT does offer Congress some leverage with which to resist industry pressure. Yet congressional representatives cannot afford to alienate their constituents if they hope to be reelected; so they are often constrained to act pragmatically. Their activity frequently involves providing the industry with some form of trade protection to diffuse the political pressure of industry interest groups. Although the cases suggest that these stopgap measures amount to sufficiently less than industry interest groups request, they still impose significant costs on the U.S. economy. In conclusion, this analysis raises the question, If these costs of protection were measured against the costs of a policy that would promote industrial adjustment to international competitive pressures, could the government offer less costly alternatives to politically important sectors of the U.S. economy? This concern is based on the belief that to sustain the stability of the international economy the United States needs to find alternatives to trade protection to mitigate the social costs that result from the shifting patterns of trade.

This work has been a collaborative effort. I would especially like to thank Edwin Epstein for his advice on how to make this a study in business and public policy and for his encouragement throughout all phases of this research. Ernst Haas helped me to think about the interaction among states in international organizations and about the way in which trade is a part of international politics. Stephen Kohlhagen offered insight into both the economics of international trade and the workings of the trade policy process. Dow Votaw, David Vogel, and Robert Harris challenged me to consider more carefully the structure of the argument presented here. Jeanne Logsdon, David Palmer, and Paul Tiffany aided this effort tremendously by always being willing to read and help make sense out of various drafts of this study.

The themes around which the cases in this version of the study are structured emerged from conversations with Beverly Crawford, whom I would especially like to thank for her patience and willingness to listen when I was struggling with this material. Yair Aharoni and Stephen Haggard also contributed constructive criticisms improving this revision. The assistance of Carol Jacobson was invaluable in completing the final revision. I would also like to thank Michael Weinstein, the Production Manager at Pitman Publishing for his patience in making sense out of the corrections. The copyediting assistance of Susan Badger helped to improve the quality of the manuscript.

This book would not have been possible without the willingness of numerous government and industry officials to explain the intricacies of the trade policy process. Without the help of Mieyko Kosobayashi and Kenneth Oye I would never have been able to locate them. The American Association of University Women, the Brookings Institution, and the Haas Fund for the Study of Business and Public Policy at the University of California–Berkeley provided financial support, which gave me time to both think about and carry out this research. The preparation of the manuscript would not have been possible without the help of Lynda Wambles, Linda Young, Mary Blair, and Phyllis Koerner in the word-processing group at Washington University, who graciously tolerated my erratic work pace.

Finally, I would like to thank my mother, Ann Lenway, who always assumed this project would be completed. I dedicate this book to the memory of my father, Fred H. Lenway, who made international trade a part of my life.

1

INTRODUCTION
The Politics of U.S. International Trade Policy

This study brings into play both the domestic and the international dimensions of contemporary U.S. international trade policy.[1] The analysis focuses on the tension between the domestic and the international political institutions within which trade policy is formulated. The domestic dimension of this policy process in the United States involves negotiations between various sectors of U.S. industry and the government as well as the dynamics of intragovernmental negotiations. The international dimension involves both bilateral and multilateral negotiations among nation-states. The focus of both the domestic and the international negotiations is the level of import restraints and the manner in which imports are regulated.[2]

This analysis differs from previous studies of the impact of business interest groups on U.S. trade policy in that it places the domestic policy debate and process in an international political context.[3] The point of departure for this study is that trade policy has an impact on both domestic and international politics and in turn is affected by both. So to explain U.S. trade policy outcomes, one must take into account both the domestic and the international institutional context in which this policy is formulated.

Four alternative explanations, each of which specifies a different political dynamic that informs the policy adopted by the United States, provide the basic framework for this analysis. The four explanations are complementary, and they are not analytically distinct. The first two rely primarily on Congress to explain U.S. trade policy. Whereas the first sees congressional decisions as being the result of interest group political pressures, the second suggests that congressional representatives are autonomous and able to choose the interest groups to which they respond. The third explanation is based on a perspective on trade that stems from international politics and considers state autonomy to be the most important determinant of a state's international trade policy. The fourth—the basis of this study—takes into account the tension between the economic incentives to engage in trade and the domestic and international political constraints that create the need for states to maintain some degree of policy autonomy.

The first two are primarily domestic in scope. Both assume that the U.S. Congress determines the definition of the *national interest* in trade policy. The first contends that interest groups determine trade policy. Here, interest groups use their resources to persuade congressional representatives that their industry needs to be protected from foreign competition, and the representatives respond to maximize their chances of reelection. The model for this approach to trade policy is E. E. Schattschneider's analysis of the 1930 Smoot-Hawley Tariff Act.[4] Congress compiled this tariff legislation, and it did not involve negotiations with any of the countries whose exports were reduced by the tariff increases.

The second explanation also focuses on Congress. Here, Congress is able to resist political pressure from interest groups in the formulation of trade policy. Instead of reflecting the policy preferences of dominant interest groups, congressional representatives determine U.S. trade policy autonomously. Representatives choose the interest groups that influence their decisions. This characterization of congressional behavior is based on Raymond Bauer, Ithiel de Sola Pool, and Lewis Dexter's notion of "transactional politics."[5]

The international political aspects of U.S. trade policy provide the primary basis for the third and fourth explanations. They share a concern with the effect that trade has on the political power of one state relative to others. The third approach considers trade policy to be determined primarily by considerations of international politics. From this perspective the goal of trade policy is to maximize the political power of the state by maintaining a high degree of autonomy from trading partners. States can then use this autonomy to manipulate trade policy—both to achieve foreign policy goals and to maintain domestic social stability.[6]

To emphasize national autonomy as the primary goal of trade policy assumes that states are willing to trade off the economic benefits of trade for the political benefits of autonomy. In contrast, the fourth explanation takes into account both the economic benefits that states realize by agreeing to conduct trade along the lines of comparative advantage and the need for states to maintain some degree of policy autonomy to respond to domestic political pressures. This autonomy is used both to mitigate the disruptive social effects of a rapid influx of low-cost imports and to accommodate powerful domestic interest groups. This explanation, the basis for this study, is termed *pragmatic liberalism*.

This perspective on U.S. trade policy is similar to John Ruggie's contention that the U.S. emphasis on aggregate economic efficiencies has been historically embedded in a domestic social policy that provides limits on the degree to which the market can lead to economic and social dislocation. Ruggie defines this combination of state intervention to secure domestic stability with the liberal international economic order created after World War II as "embedded liberalism." He suggests:

> The essence of embedded liberalism is to devise a form of multilateralism that is compatible with the requirements of domestic stability. Presumably, then, governments so committed would seek to encourage an international division of labor which, while multilateral in form and reflecting *some* notion of comparative advantage (and therefore gains from trade), *also* promised to minimize socially disruptive domestic adjustment costs as well as any national economic and political vulnerabilities that might accrue from international functional differentiation.[7]

In contrast, the notion of *pragmatic liberalism* used here includes the possibility that trade policy can be used as a political mechanism to redistribute wealth to the owners of protected industries as well as to "minimize socially disruptive domestic adjustment costs."

A major task of this study will be to separate those policy proposals that reflect interest group pressures to redistribute wealth from those conceived to reduce the inequities (in the domestic market) of "unfettered" market forces. Ultimately, however, one must recognize that at some point the two are indistinguishable and that to a large extent *pragmatic liberalism* reflects a recognition on the part of the state of what is a politically acceptable compromise between domestic pressures for protection and the need for progressive trade liberalization to sustain an open trading system.

Considered individually, none of the first three explanations can account for the mixture of trade liberalization and protection that is characteristic of postwar U.S. trade policy. The fourth explanation, however, can accommodate the tension between trade liberalization and protection inherent in postwar U.S. trade policy because it takes into account both the domestic and the international dimensions of trade. The *international dimension of trade* refers specifically to the General Agreement on Tariffs and Trade (GATT).[8] The GATT was created in 1947 to be an international political framework within which states could negotiate to conduct trade along the lines of comparative advantage.

The constraints imposed by the principles, norms, rules, and decision-making procedures set up by the international trade regime, the GATT, as embedded in the U.S. policy process, has an influence on U.S. trade policy. Thus, a politically acceptable compromise on trade issues within the United States is less protectionist than it would be in the absence of the GATT. The GATT wields an influence because the U.S. Congress and departments in the executive branch choose to take the constraints in its charter seriously. The GATT does not have supra national authority over its members. The influence of the GATT on U.S. trade policy does not involve relinquishing any U.S. sovereignty to this international organization. Instead the liberal norms of the GATT are embedded in the domestic policy process, as will be shown later. These norms play a significant role in U.S. trade policy because they act as a counterweight to domestic interest group pressures for protection. The commitment of the U.S. government to support these norms is especially important because the widespread benefits of a liberal trade policy to consumers do not evoke significant countervailing interest group activity in response to industry and labor pressure for trade protection.

THE GATT AS AN INTERNATIONAL REGIME

The international regime that provides the international institutional context for U.S. trade policy is the GATT. The definition of *regime* used here to describe the GATT is that developed by Stephen Krasner.

> Regimes can be defined as sets of implicit or explicit principles, norms, rules, and decision-making procedures around which actors' expectations converge in a given area of international relations. Principles are beliefs of fact, causation, and rectitude. Norms are standards of behavior defined in terms of rights and obligations. Rules are specific prescriptions or proscriptions for actions. Decision-making procedures are prevailing practices for making and implementing collective choice.[9]

Principles

The principles upon which the GATT is based are derived from the theory of comparative advantage formulated by David Ricardo in 1817. The theory of comparative advantage is a generalization of the theory of absolute advantage developed by Adam Smith. Smith argued, "If a foreign country can supply us with a commodity cheaper than we ourselves can make it, better buy it from them with some part of the produce of our own industry, employed in a way in which we have some advantage."[10]

Ricardo demonstrated that two countries could benefit from trade when the amount of labor embodied in the entire volume of one country's exports is less than the total labor that would be necessary to replace its imports with domestic production.[11] Ricardo's insight is based on a comparison between two countries of the number of labor units necessary for the production of one commodity relative to another. By way of this comparison he demonstrates that there are mutually beneficial gains from trade by focusing on the ability of one country to produce one product (wine) relative to another (cloth) rather than on absolute differences in productivity.

E. Heckscher and Goran Ohlin extended the theory of comparative advantage to include two factors: capital and labor, both of which are embedded in different products in varying proportions. Their theory suggests that countries with an abundance of capital will export capital-intensive products, whereas countries endowed with more labor relative to capital will export products that are labor-intensive.[12] Raymond Vernon in his application of the product life cycle to the factor proportions model of international trade added a third factor "that comprises a host of special skills on the part of labor or of capital equipment."[13] This third factor is important in the production of new products that require the use of new technology. It gives advanced industrial countries a comparative advantage in the production of these new products in spite of high labor costs. Once the production process becomes standardized, labor costs again determine the type of country in which a particular product is likely to be produced.

Stephen Magee, in reviewing the theory of international trade, suggests that the incentive for states to engage in trade is based on both production and consumption gains from trade. The production gains of trade result from an economy switching the factors of production into those goods in which it has the greatest comparative advantage. The consumption gains result from the ability of consumers to purchase products on world markets that are less expensive than similar goods produced domestically.[14]

Norms

The central norms upon which the GATT regime is based include nondiscrimination, multilateralism, reciprocity, and a commitment to the progressive liberalization of trade. Nondiscrimination involves the use of the same tariff level for all imports regardless of origin.[15] Multilateralism is accomplished by the generalization of tariff concessions offered to one country to all member states. Reciprocity implies that the offer of any one member to reduce tariff levels is contingent upon tariff reductions by other members. In addition, through its collection of data the GATT provides a high degree of transparency of trade restrictions.[16] It further provides member states with the right to impose temporary import restraints against sudden increases in imports of a specific product from a specific country.[17]

Rules

These norms are embodied in rules that compose the GATT Charter. The norms of the GATT attempt to create political conditions under which trade can follow the pattern of comparative advantage.[18] The GATT rules pertain primarily to the conditions under which a member state can raise tariffs or unilaterally impose import restraints. They also specify conditions under which an exporting state can retaliate if its exports have been restrained.

These rules are implemented through decision-making procedures that consist of periodic multilateral negotiations to reduce tariffs and other forms of trade barriers, dispute settlement procedures written into the charter that can be evoked at the request of a member state, and ongoing meetings of national representatives to deal with the daily business of the GATT. The decision-making procedures rely primarily on consensus and emphasize a pragmatic resolution to conflicts that arise among member states.

These principles, norms, rules, and procedures exert an important effect on U.S. trade policy. Three case studies, each of which involves attempts on the part of a significant proportion of the industry to obtain trade protection from the government, illustrate this effect. Each case illustrates the way in which the GATT framework acted as a constraint on the ability of industrial sectors (both business and labor) to influence the ultimate policy taken by the American government. The measure of the effect of this constraint is the difference between what the industry asked for and what the government, both the executive and Congress, was willing to offer.

This is not to say that other factors such as the influence of domestic interest groups are not also important variables in explaining U.S. trade policy. While each of the three cases emphasizes the influence of the GATT, the case study methodology does not allow one to determine with any precision the extent to which the GATT both as an agreement and as an organization influences outcomes relative to other factors.

THE CASES

Each case study focuses on a trade decision which deals with a specific sector of the U.S. economy. The first case involves an attempt by the U.S. textile and apparel industry to insulate the domestic market from future increases in import competition during the Tokyo Round negotiations of the GATT. The analysis focuses specifically on the negotiations between the industry and the U.S. government over the Carter Administration's "Program for Textiles," which was made public in March 1979. This policy statement was put together in order to obtain the support of the textile and apparel industries for the ratification of the Tokyo Round multilateral trade negotiations. The international context for this analysis is the Multifiber Arrangement (MFA).[19]

The second case concerns the auto industry, focusing on an attempt by the Ford Motor Company and the United Automobile Workers (UAW) to obtain temporary import relief from Japanese imports during the 1978-80 period. The GATT context for this request to limit imports is Article 19 of the charter, the escape clause.[20] Congress delegated to the International Trade Commission (ITC) the authority to hold hearings on the escape clause after it became a part of U.S. trade agreements.

The third case, which deals with the telecommunications industry, differs from the first two in that it does not involve a direct request for trade protection. Instead, it looks at pressure on the U.S. government brought by U.S. telecommunications producers to pry open the Japanese telecommunications equipment market. The GATT context for this case is the government procurement code negotiated during the Tokyo Round.[21] This case, although explicitly concerned with the question of trade expansion, raises two issues with respect to trade protection. First, the industry was prepared to ask the government for import restraints in the absence of concrete possibilities for increased access to foreign markets. Second, for the United States to maintain the political viability of its support for an open trade policy, it needs to obtain increased access to foreign markets for those goods in which it has a comparative advantage.

Vernon's product life cycle approach to international trade provides a criterion with which to evaluate the relative ability of the United States to compete in each of these sectors. In Vernon's terms the basis of the comparative advantage of the United States is in capital and the "third factor," which includes skilled labor and technology. It is losing its comparative advantage in those products involving a uniform production process, which can easily be exported to low-wage countries. In addition, the United States possesses a declining, but not irreversible, comparative advantage in "mature industries" such as autos and steel owing to obsolete plants and equipment and the continuation of a managerial strategy formulated when U.S. markets for these products were effectively insulated from international competition.

The three industries considered in this study correspond to these three levels of comparative advantage. Textiles and apparel are labor-intensive. Because of the high labor content involved in the production of these products and the high cost of U.S. labor, the United States is losing its comparative advantage to low-wage producers in developing countries.

Autos, in contrast, are capital-intensive, although labor costs also make a difference. U.S. automobile producers became aware of the difference between U.S. and Japanese labor costs in the late 1970s when gasoline shortages in the United States led to a dramatic increase in the demand for fuel-efficient Japanese automobiles. In spite of a massive investment on the part of U.S. automakers to build the capacity they need to make fuel-efficient automobiles, U.S. producers still do not foresee themselves being able to produce some small-car lines at a profit and currently are opting to market small cars built in Japan.[22] With this investment U.S. producers hope to become competitive once again in some lines of fuel-efficient cars.

The telecommunications sector is primarily capital-intensive, and it is characterized by rapid changes in technology. The United States has a comparative advantage in this sector provided by Vernon's "third factor," and U.S. firms have been prominent in the development and production of the computerized telephone switching systems. To maintain their competitive edge some industry.representatives argue that they need access to bidding opportunities for sales in foreign markets. Without foreign sales to allow for increased production runs, they argue that U.S. industry will have to restrict its market in telecommunications equipment in order to remain viable.

TRADE PROTECTION VERSUS ADJUSTMENT

The political tension that pervades U.S. trade policy emerges from (1) the divergence between the policy prescriptions that involve the continual adaptation of the U.S. industrial structure to the requirements of international trade based on comparative advantage and (2) the restrictive policy that results from pressure group politics. In the arena of pressure group politics there is little emphasis on the need for industrial adjustment in response to changes in import competition. Rather, the debate is dominated by requests on the part of industries in which the United States is losing its comparative advantage to reduce the need for this adjustment by insulating the U.S. market from foreign imports to save American jobs. This insulation of sectors of U.S. industry from international competition often results in the financial benefit of those industries successful in receiving import restraints. Owing to the reduction in supply, domestic producers can raise their price (depending on the price elasticity of the product), thereby enhancing their profitability. This price increase, however, can only be implemented at a considerable economic loss to society.

In 1972 Stephen Magee estimated that the average annual cost of U.S. import restrictions was between $3.3 and $5.0 billion.[23] Dale Larsen updated this study in 1979. He found that the net cost of import restraints to the United States in 1978 was between $4.1 and $8.1 billion.[24] Michael Munger, in a study that measured the total transfer costs from consumers to producers, found that the tariffs and quotas in place in 1980 cost U.S. consumers $58.451 billion for that year.[25]

Ilse Mintz breaks these costs down into four components. The first two of these components are deadweight losses to the economy, whereas the second two are resource transfers from consumers to producers. The first component involves production costs that result from the use of resources to produce a good that could be imported more cheaply from abroad. These resources could be used more productively if they were allocated to sectors of the economy in which the United States had a comparative advantage. The second component, the consumption cost, arises when consumers have to switch to less desirable substitutes because of the higher cost caused by the quota. The third component reflects the increased price of foreign goods due to the restriction. This "import cost" is a wealth transfer to foreign producers. The fourth component is the "transfer cost," which involves the transfer of wealth from consumers to producers who would have supplied the product at a lower price without the quota. Mintz argues, "Such redistribution is usually the main intended effect of quotas, whether those who impose them look at the effect in this fashion or not."[26]

The commitment of the United States to the GATT is in part motivated by a desire in Congress and the executive branch to minimize these costs of trade protection. The commitment of the United States to the GATT, in turn, reduces the ability of industry groups to influence trade policy. This effectively constrains the political influence of business.

THE ORGANIZATION OF THE STUDY

This study is divided into two sections. The first part deals primarily with a theoretical and historical overview. The second section consists of an application of the theoretical framework to the three case studies. The evidence upon which the case studies are based comes primarily from (1) government documents; (2) press reports; and (3) interviews conducted both in the United States and in Western Europe with representatives from the U.S. private sector, including industry, labor, and trade association officials; government officials in the Departments of the Treasury, State, Labor, and Commerce and the Office of the Special Trade Representative; and officials at the GATT.

Chapter 2 reviews prior studies of U.S. trade policy that focus on the domestic political interaction between government and business in the formulation of U.S. trade legislation. This literature assumes U.S. trade policy to be the outcome of interest group politics. These studies further use the policy results embedded in different pieces of trade legislation to refine assumptions about the power of interest groups in the American political process.

The main dilemma raised by this literature stems from the expectation derived from Mancur Olson's work on the logic of collective action. While Olson would lead one to expect that interest groups are more likely to organize around trade protection than trade liberalization, the reality is that the international trade regime is relatively open.[27] The concentrated benefits of trade protection to declining industrial sectors provide greater incentives to or-ganize than the diffuse costs of this trade protection to consumers. In addition, industries injured by imports are more likely to lobby to persuade the government that increased barriers to imports are necessary than are industries likely to benefit from the reduction of foreign barriers to trade. If the incentives for interest groups to organize for trade protection is so strong, why then has the United States been able to maintain a relatively open trade policy during the postwar period? Some analysts have used this divergence between the expectation that political pressures will lead to trade protection and the actual relatively open trade policy of the United States to argue that domestic interest groups do not have access to many resources and lack power.[28]

In contrast, this research suggests that the crucial variable re-quired to explain the lack of success on the part of domestic interest groups to obtain import restraints is not a change in their power but the change in the international institutional framework within which U.S. trade policy is negotiated. Specifically, membership in the GATT provides the U.S. government with leverage with which to resist interest group demands for protection.

Chapter 3 focuses on how the constraints imposed by the GATT on the U.S. policy process can be reconciled with an evolv-ing definition of the *national interest*. In order to define the *U.S. national interest* in terms of its membership in the GATT, the major part of this chapter will consist of a discussion of both the political and economic costs and benefits of maintaining an open trade regime.

There are two dimensions to the political costs of this policy. The first is international. A policy stance that maintains openness in trade precludes the use of trade relationships as a means to influence the foreign (or domestic) policy of another state. States that pursue an open trade policy also forego the opportunity to make unilateral changes in the level of import restraint and may come to rely on both imports and access to export markets. Thus, the second cost of openness is a loss of domestic policy autonomy. Politicans, who do not support import restraints, may lose credibil-ity and future constituency support, especially in regions of the country where dominant industries are declining and clamor for protection.

The economic costs of trade policy are a function of the degree to which a state chooses to forego potential increases in foreign trade. These costs have both a domestic and an international dimension. To the extent that wealth contributes to a state's strength, the economic gains from an open trading system can result in an increase in state strength vis-à-vis other states in the international system. The domestic economic benefits of the choice to engage in trade are derived from the static and dynamic gains from trade.[29] Whereas the static benefits are derived from the theory of comparative advantage, the dynamic benefits from trade consist of technological innovations that result from increased competition.

Chapter 3 suggests that to the extent U.S. trade policy is oriented toward the gains from trade, it is in the national interest to accept the policy discipline imposed by membership in the GATT. This definition of the *national interest* may, however, diverge from one defined by an industry in which the United States is losing its comparative advantage. In the debate that surrounds the attempts of industry groups to redefine the *national interest* as one of protection, the GATT as an organization can compel a government to consider explicitly the economic costs involved in the restriction of foreign trade. It also serves as a forum within which national representatives are subject to considerable peer pressure to oppose policies that would lead to increased closure of the trading system. The GATT, however, possesses no legal sanctions with which to prevent the United States, or any other member state, from imposing trade restrictions once a policy of trade restraint has been defined to be in the national interest. It can only threaten that protectionist policies will bring about the demise of the international economic order and remind member states of the devastating economic and political consequences that international economic nationalism had in the 1930s and could have potentially in the present.

Chapter 4 consists of a basic overview of the principles and practice of U.S. international trade policy. This discussion intends to provide some background on the major concepts upon which U.S. trade policy is based. These include nondiscrimination, reciprocity, multilateralism, and escape clause actions. The Reciprocal Trade Act of 1934 will serve as the point of departure for this discussion, as it provided the legislative basis for contemporary U.S. trade policy as well as the congressional authority for U.S. participation in the first round of the GATT negotiations. The chapter goes on to consider the U.S. domestic political debate over the proposed International Trade Organization (ITO) and the role intended for the ITO in the postwar international economic order. An account follows of how the GATT—the commerical policy section of the ITO Charter—emerged as the basic framework for the regulation of international trade after the ITO Charter failed to receive ratification by the U.S. Senate. The concluding section explains the role of Congress and the executive branch agencies in the trade policy process. This discussion also includes a description of the constituencies of the different executive branch agencies and the impact these constituencies have on the trade policy process.

With this background providing an analytical framework, the three case studies follow. The cases use the GATT framework to provide perspective on the arguments of the three industrial sectors for import protection. The overarching hypothesis put forward in each of the three cases is that when international agreements are in force, they can act as leverage with which the United States can resist interest group demands for trade protection. The cases are used specifically to demonstrate how an international collaborative framework—that is, the GATT—can deflect internally generated political forces. An analysis of the domestic political forces that actively supported the creation of the GATT regime is beyond the scope of this study. In addition, no predictions are made here with respect to whether the United States will continue to adhere to the rules of the regime. The definition of the *national interest* remains in continual flux. The major hypothesis suggests only that as long as the United States is a member of the GATT, it will be difficult for specific protectionist sectoral interests to prevail over that commitment.

Initially, each case explains the economic basis for the industry's perception that import competition has increased substantially and that the national interest will be furthered by some kind of trade restriction. These arguments are then filtered through the procedures internalized within the U.S. government designed to keep U.S. trade policy in conformity with the GATT. The cases are structured to illustrate the interplay between the international agreements and domestic political pressures. In each instance the ultimate action taken by the United States involved a significant reduction of the industry's request and did not contravene an international agreement.

The political tension inherent in each of the cases is well characterized by Robert Reich, who suggests that the tension involved in trade policy debate results from the dual role that trade plays in the economy and society. While trade enhances the level of economic growth, at the same time it intensifies the process of "creative destruction" rendered by the market upon society.[30] Reich argues that international trade provides U.S. firms with access to larger markets and a wider range of resources and technology with which to work than they would have if their activities were limited strictly to the U.S. market. He further points out that the international market provides firms with an opportunity to reduce their unit costs, thus allowing for faster economic growth. In addition, Reich notes that foreign trade can exacerbate problems of adjustment in a slowly growing economy. While providing economic benefits, trade also creates conditions in which "domestic labor is left behind within vast regional pockets of unemployment from which escape is costly and psychologically difficult, while domestic industries that have high fixed costs gradually lose their market share to their foreign rivals."[31] The political problems and the policy dilemma posed in each of the three cases stem from this tension between the economic benefits and the social costs that result from international trade.

Although this study is international in scope, the emphasis of the discussion ultimately returns to a concern with the domestic economy and the varying roles that industrial sectors play in attempting to slow the rate of industrial adjustment through the restriction of trade. The primary concern in this analysis is not with how the United States can manipulate trade flows to obtain foreign policy objectives.[32]

This all suggests important limits to the degree to which this analysis can be generalized to U.S. trade policy as a whole. Specifically, in order to isolate the political tension between domestic interest group pressure for protection and the need for industrial adjustment to promote aggregate economic growth, the book focuses on trade primarily among industrialized countries. Thus the strategic military issues raised by East-West trade as well as the debate over the question of resource transfer and the relationship of trade to development, which dominates much of the discussion of North-South trade, are not addressed. In addition, the cases all deal with trade in manufactured products and not with strategic commodities, raw materials, or agricultural goods. Trade in strategic commodities such as oil and other raw materials—for example, tin, bauxite, and copper—involves questions of security of supply, a consideration not central to the debate over trade in manufactured goods.[33] Trade in agricultural goods also poses different problems from trade in manufactured goods because the political strength of European and Japanese agriculture has made negotiations over the reduction of tariffs almost impossible. International markets for agricultural commodities are also much more volatile than they are for manufactured goods.

Within these limits, however, there still remain important questions with respect to the role of foreign trade in U.S. economic policy and the kinds of political pressures involved in the trade policy process, both domestic and international. To the extent that foreign trade policy deals with phasing out industries in which the United States is losing its comparative advantage together with the promotion of those in which the United States has the potential of being competitive on an international scale, the politics of U.S. trade policy relates to the larger question of industrial policy.[34] Chapter 8, the final chapter, discusses the U.S. commitment to the GATT as a de facto component of U.S. industrial policy and suggests some implications that the lack of a coherent American industrial policy has for the future of U.S. economic development.

NOTES

1. The primary backdrop for this study is the Multilateral Trade Negotiations (MTN) held at the General Agreement on Tariffs and Trade. These negotiations, known as the Tokyo Round, began in 1973 and were concluded in April 1979. The specific cases at issue in this analysis were decided between 1978 and 1980.

2. The level of import restraint here refers primarily to tariffs, whereas the way in which imports are restrained refers to the use of quotas as well as various nontariff barriers (NTBs). These include government procurement policies and

other domestic regulatory policies that discriminate against foreign products in the process of promoting domestic policy objectives.

3. The most well-known of these studies are E. E. Schattschneider, *Politics, Pressures and the Tariff* (Hamden, Conn.: Archon Books, 1963); and Raymond Bauer, Ithiel de Sola Pool, and Lewis Anthony Dexter, *American Business and Public Policy: The Politics of Foreign Trade* (Chicago: Aldine, 1972). Schattschneider's study, first published in 1935, is an analysis of the 1930 Smoot-Hawley Tariff Act. Bauer, Pool, and Dexter's study focused on postwar trade legislation. Although after World War II the United States was a member of the GATT, the focus of their analysis is on Congress. This work was a part of a larger series of studies on communications and foreign policy, first published in 1963.

4. Schattschneider, *Politics*.

5. Bauer, Pool, and Dexter, *American Business and Public Policy*.

6. Albert O. Hirschman, *National Power and the Structure of Foreign Trade* (Berkeley: University of California Press, 1945).

7. John Ruggie, "International Regimes, Transactions, and Change: Embedded Liberalism in the Postwar Economic Order," *International Organization* 36 (Spring 1982): 399.

8. The GATT was created in 1947 to provide a legal framework within which the first postwar multilateral tariff negotiations were conducted. The charter for the GATT was based on the commercial policy chapter of the ITO. The GATT was to become a part of this more comprehensive organization after the ITO had been ratified by member states. When the ITO failed to receive congressional ratification, the GATT emerged as the primary organizational and legal framework within which trade is regulated on an international basis. For a discussion of the failure of the ITO and the creation of the GATT, see Chapter 4.

9. Stephen Krasner, "Structural Causes and Regime Consequences: Regimes as Intervening Variables," *International Organization* 36 (Summer 1982): 186. Krasner notes that this definition is consistent with other recent discussions of regimes. A consensus on this definition was arrived at during a conference on international regimes held in Los Angeles in October 1980.

10. David Ricardo, *The Principles of Political Economy and Taxation,* (New York: E.P. Dutton, 1948). First published in 1817, Adam Smith, *An Inquiry into the Nature and Causes of the Wealth of Nations*, ed. Edwin Cannan (Chicago: University of Chicago Press, 1976), pp. 478–79.

11. The specifications of Ricardo's model included one input—labor; two commodities—wine and cloth; and two countries—England and Portugal. It is based on three assumptions: free mobility of goods, domestic mobility of factors of production, and no international mobility of factors of production. This discussion is based on William Allen, *International Trade Theory: Hume to Ohlin* (New York: Random House, 1965), p. 9.

12. For a discussion of the factor proportions model developed by E. Heckscher (1919), Goran Ohlin (1933), and more recently by Paul Samuelson (1948), see Gerald Meier, *International Economics: The Theory of Policy* (New York: Oxford University Press, 1980), pp. 29–36. The point of departure for this model is that countries are endowed with many factors but in different proportions. The

difference in relative factor endowments then provides the basis for international specialization.

13. Ronald W. Jones, "The Role of Technology in the Theory of International Trade," in *The Technology Factor in International Trade*, ed. Raymond Vernon (New York: Columbia University Press, 1970), p. 84.

14. Stephen Magee, "International Trade" (Working Paper no. 79–10, University of Texas at Austin, Bureau of Business Research, Austin, Texas, 1979), p. 10.

15. Included in this is a preference for restricting trade through tariffs as opposed to quotas.

16. Here *transparency* refers to both the multilateral surveillance and the publication of all trade restraints.

17. This is based on a discussion of the attributes of the GATT regime by Charles Lipson, "The Transformation of Trade: The Sources and Effects of Regime Change," *International Organization* 36 (Spring 1982): 417–56.

18. Governments need an international organization to sustain an open trade regime because domestic political pressures for trade protection overwhelm those for trade expansion. For a discussion of this point see Chapter 2.

19. The Multifiber Arrangement was first negotiated in 1973. A Protocol of Extension was signed in 1977.

20. Article 19 states that if a government can demonstrate that imports of a specific product are entering the country in sufficient quantities to cause, or threaten to cause, serious injury to domestic producers of like or directly competitive products, it can impose temporary import restraints on a nondiscriminatory basis. There is also provision for prior notification and consultation and for retaliatory action by the country against whose exports this "safeguard" action has been taken. This discussion of Article 19 is taken from *The Tokyo Round of Multilateral Trade Negotiations* (Geneva: General Agreement on Tariffs and Trade, 1979), p. 90.

21. Negotiations over the government procurement code began in 1976 when a subgroup was formed at the multilateral trade negotiations. Multilateral negotiations over the substance of the code were concluded in April 1979. The bilateral discussions between the United States and Japan over those departments of the government that were to be included under the code continued through the end of 1980.

22. For a discussion of the decision by General Motors (GM) to import 200,000 subcompacts from Isuzu Motors Ltd. of Tokyo per year, see "GM Shakes Up the Auto Industry," *Wall Street Journal*, May 26, 1982, p. 30. The article indicates that GM made this decision based on the belief that U.S. factories cannot compete with the Japanese in the production of subcompacts for at least the next decade.

23. Stephen Magee, "The Welfare Effect of Restrictions on U.S. Trade," *Brookings Papers on Economic Activity*, (9) 1972, pp. 645–708.

24. Dale Larsen, "Costs of Import Protection in the United States," mimeographed (May 10, 1979), p. 20.

25. Michael Munger, "The Costs of Protectionism: Estimates of the Hidden

Tax of Trade Restraint" (Working Paper no. 80, Washington University, Center for the Study of American Business, St. Louis, July 1983), p. 4.

26. Ilse Mintz, *U.S. Import Quotas: Costs and Consequences* (Washington, D.C.: American Enterprise Institute for Public Policy Research, 1973), p. 28.

27. This point is based on Mancur Olson, *The Logic of Collective Action* (Cambridge, Mass.: Harvard University Press, 1975).

28. This argument is made by Bauer, Pool, and Dexter, *American Business and Public Policy*.

29. For a discussion of the difference between the static and dynamic gains from trade, see Meier, *International Economics*, pp. 72–75. Meier notes that the first statement of the dynamic gains from trade was made by John Stuart Mill. In *The Principles of Political Economy* (New York: Appleton-Century-Crofts, Inc., 1848) Mill states: "The tendency of every extension of the market [is] to improve the processes of production. A country which produces for a larger market than its own, can introduce a more extended division of labor, can make greater use of machinery, and is more likely to make inventions and improvements in the processes of production." This passage is quoted in Meier, p. 72.

30. The term *creative destruction* is taken from Joseph Schumpeter's *Capitalism, Socialism, and Democracy* 5th edition: (London: Allen and Unwin, 1976). Here Schumpeter states, "The opening (up) of new markets, foreign or domestic, and the organizational development from the craft shop and factory to such concerns as U.S. Steel illustrate the same process of industrial mutation . . . that incessantly revolutionizes the economic structure *from within*, incessantly destroying the old one, incessantly creating a new one. This process of Creative Destruction is the essential fact about capitalism (p. 83). *Capitalism, Socialism, and Democracy* was first published in 1943.

31. Robert B. Reich, "Making Industrial Policy," *Foreign Affairs* 60 (Spring 1982): 852.

32. For an account of how the United States uses export controls as an instrument of foreign policy, see "Unreliable Supplier: U.S. Trade Restrictions in Recent Years Are Said to Cost Billions in Lost Business," *Wall Street Journal*, May 26, 1982 (p. 156). This article mentions U.S. grain embargoes affecting the Soviet Union in 1975 and 1980, the ban on sales of high-technology equipment to the Soviet Union in 1978, Carter's "human rights" export limits in 1978, the freeze on Iranian assets held in the United States in 1978, and President Ronald Reagan's ban on the sale of turbine rotors and pipe-layers for the Soviet gas pipeline to Western Europe in 1981 as examples of decisions that have cost the United States billions of dollars in lost export sales. The article further comments that many of these actions have cost the United States more than the country against which these actions were initially aimed.

33. For a discussion of U.S. trade policy in raw materials see Stephen D. Krasner, *Defending the National Interest, Raw Material Investments and U.S. Foreign Policy* (Princeton, N.J.: Princeton University Press, 1978).

34. Economists suggest that industrial policy should consist of adjustment assistance to facilitate the movement of resources out of the industry that is losing its comparative advantage. This adjustment assistance can take various forms.

Gerald Meier lists direct compensation to workers and firms in industries suffering serious injury from imports, retraining and relocation allowances for displaced workers, employment and marketing information, technical assistance, financial assistance, and tax relief to firms among the policies that the government can employ to enhance "social stability." He further suggests that these measures can be accompanied by the negotiation of a market safeguard arrangement, that is, an orderly marketing agreement, a voluntary export restraint, or a temporary quota, if it can be demonstrated that "the adjustment cost can be reduced by extending the transformation process in time." The rationale for these measures is that the United States would be better off by pursuing a liberal trade policy and "compensating the losers," that is, those industries injured by imports, than it would if it imposed permanent trade restraints whenever a domestic industry was threatened by international competition. Stephen Magee found that the cost of adjustment assistance to affected workers and firms is smaller than the benefits of reduced prices for consumers. (See Magee, "The Welfare Effects of Restrictions on U.S. Trade") This is based on Meier's discussion of adjustment assistance in *International Economics*, pp. 114–16.

2

DOMESTIC INTERESTS AND
U.S. TRADE POLICY
A Critique

INTRODUCTION

In this chapter we focus on the literature that treats U.S. trade policy as if it is determined solely within the domestic political process. All of the literature covered here shares the implicit assumption that U.S. tariff levels can be explained in terms of interest group pressure either for trade protection or for expansion.

This perspective may have been appropriate when E. E. Schattschneider wrote the first major work on the politics of U.S. trade policy.[1] This study was written when the U.S. tariff was nonnegotiable and determined entirely within the confines of domestic political arenas. The passage of the 1934 Reciprocal Trade Agreements Act, however, made the American tariff negotiable and introduced both the interests of American exporters and the interests of states that exported to the United States into the trade policy process. This legislation delegated to the executive branch the authority to reduce U.S. tariff levels on a bilateral basis in exchange for the reduction of foreign tariffs on goods exported by the United States. This negotiating authority later provided the basis for the first round of multilateral trade negotiations held in 1947 under the auspices of the GATT.[2] In these negotiations the reduction in the

U.S. tariff was offered in exchange for reductions negotiated by the United States with other countries as well as reductions negotiated in other sets of bilateral negotiations.

Thus the tariff levels in the United States are not only a function of pressure group activity; they are also determined by what U.S. negotiators perceive to be necessary in order to obtain increased access to foreign markets. This process involves the rejection of requests for increased protection by powerful domestic interest groups to prevent international trade negotiations and trade agreements from unraveling.

Since the level of U.S. protection is ultimately the result of negotiations among states, we need to consider the international institutional context of the policy process to explain why interest groups are not more effective in influencing U.S. trade agreements. This international dimension of the trade policy process provides the U.S. government with leverage with which to resist domestic interest group pressure for protection. This interaction among states in the formulation of trade policy helps to explain why trade agreements do not entirely reflect demands made by industry interest groups.

The literature that focuses on trade policy as a domestic political issue offers several alternative explanations as to why U.S. trade agreements do not correspond with interest group preferences. Raymond Bauer, Ithiel de Sola Pool, and Lewis Dexter argue that interest groups are not very influential and that congressional representatives act autonomously from interest group pressure. Theodore Lowi, in a review of Bauer, Pool, and Dexter's study, suggests that U.S. trade policy results from conflict among interest groups that negates the impact each group has on Congress. Michael Hayes, in a rejoinder to Lowi, offers yet a third explanation. He contends that the crucial question that analysts of interest group influence need to ask is when—not whether—interest groups are powerful.[3] His argument is that the political arena in which a specific policy is decided determines the degree to which interest groups will be able to affect the final policy. Hayes attributes the apparent inability of interest groups to influence trade policy in Congress to the irrelevance of Congress to the trade policy process (after 1934). In looking beyond the Congress to other political arenas, Hayes, however, does not look to any political institutions outside the scope of the U.S. government.[4]

In contrast to Hayes and Bauer, Pool, and Dexter, I assume (like Schattschneider) that Congress is not autonomous from interest group pressure for protection. To maximize their chances of reelection, congressional representatives need to be responsive to constituency preferences. To explain the relative inability of powerful industry groups to receive protection from the government, the international institutional context of trade, specifically the GATT, needs careful consideration. Whereas Hayes sees the major turning point in U.S. trade policy to be the passage of the 1934 Reciprocal Trade Agreements Act, the research here indicates that the creation of the GATT in 1947 involved a more critical change. The influence of the GATT in the U.S. trade policy process is especially important given that interest groups are more likely to organize in support of trade protection than trade expansion.

I will begin with a discussion of the theoretical basis for the asymmetry in interest group activity in support of trade protection based on Mancur Olson's analysis of the formation of interest groups. I will go on to discuss the way in which Schattschneider; Bauer, Pool and Dexter; Lowi; and Hayes explain why pressure groups that lobby for increased trade protection have not been more successful. In conclusion I will suggest that a political analysis of U.S. trade policy cannot be confined to the domain of domestic politics and that an explanation of why interest groups are not more influential must be sought within the wider context of the international trade regime.

THE ECONOMIC BASIS OF POLITICAL COALITIONS

Mancur Olson, in *The Logic of Collective Action*, questions three major assumptions made in classical interest group theory. These assumptions are embedded in David Truman's *The Governmental Process: Political Interests and Public Opinion*.[5] The three assumptions with which Olson takes issue are:

1. When groups share a common interest, they will organize and become politically active.

2. Potential interest groups are always present to act as countervailing pressure against dominant interest groups.
3. The size of an interest group does not make a difference in terms of the ability of different groups to organize around a specific issue.

In his analysis Olson questions these assumptions and then goes on to specify conditions under which interest groups will organize. His analysis is based on assumptions about rationality taken from economic theory. The point of departure for his analysis is that "organizations typically exist to further the common interest of groups of people."[6] This common interest consists for the most part of the provision of "public" or collective goods for the members of the group.[7] He goes on to argue that although all the members of the group "have an interest in obtaining this collective benefit, they have no common interest in paying the cost of providing the collective good."[8]

This observation raises the question, Under what conditions will groups organize to request that the government provide this collective good? In answer, Olson evokes the notion of rational self-interest, which suggests that a rational individual will be willing to contribute voluntarily to an organization only if this individual believes the public good to be obtained by the organization will be worth at least as much as the amount of the voluntary contribution. Thus, Olson argues:

> The necessary condition for the optimal provision of a collective good, through voluntary and independent action of the members of a group, can . . . be stated very simply. The marginal cost of additional units of the collective good must be shared in exactly the same proportion as the additional benefits. Only if this is done will each member find that his own marginal costs and benefits are equal at the same time that the total marginal cost equals the total or aggregate marginal benefit.[9]

Olson notes that situations that conform to these conditions are rare and that to explain the provision of collective goods one needs to take into account the size of the interest groups. Relatively small interest groups, he suggests, have an easier time in obtaining collective goods from the government because it is likely that at least one member "will find that his personal gain from having the collective good exceeds the total cost of providing some amount of that collective good."[10] So in small groups one member may bear all the costs involved in obtaining the collective good because he or she expects that the benefits will exceed the initial outlay of funds. In contrast, Olson argues that large groups have a far more difficult time in obtaining collective goods based on voluntary interest group activity. Furthermore, in very large groups there is no incentive to bear the costs of collective action because all the members receive the benefits whether or not they pay; and no one individual can make a "noticeable contribution." In these large groups members have little or no incentive to participate because "if one member does or does not help provide the collective good, no other one member will be significantly affected and therefore no one has any reason to react."[11]

Based on this analysis Olson argues, "however beneficial the function large voluntary associations [also known as latent groups] are expected to perform, there is no incentive for any individual to join such an organization."[12] He concludes that the difference in size is crucial to an understanding of interest group formation.

> For the small privileged group one can expect that its collective needs will probably be met one way or another, and that voluntary action will solve its collective problems, but the large latent group cannot act in accordance with its common interests so long as the members of the group are free to further their individual interests.[13]

As a result Olson suggests that there is no reason to believe that latent groups will coalesce around an issue and prevent policies from becoming overly biased in favor of certain interest groups. In contrast, classical pluralist theory has held that these large "latent groups" are always on the verge of political action. Truman writes:

> The interests of the potential groups are usually widespread, though momentarily weak, and as such serve to limit in a general way the behavior of the more apparent participants in politics. The unacknowledged power of such unorganized interests lies in the possibility that if these wide, weak interests are too flagrantly ignored, they may be stimulated to organize for aggressive counteraction.[14]

Olson takes issue with the pluralist notion that potential interest groups serve to provide balance within the political system. In contrast to Truman, he suggests:

> The distinction between the privileged and intermediate groups, on the one hand, and the latent group, on the other, also damages the pluralistic view that any outrageous demands of one pressure group will be counterbalanced by the demands of other pressure groups, so that the outcome will be reasonably just and satisfactory. Since relatively small groups will frequently be able voluntarily to organize and act in support of their common interests, and since large groups normally will not be able to do so, the outcome of the political struggle among the various groups in society will not be symmetrical.[15]

Olson's analysis of the dynamics of interest group formation provides a framework with which to analyze interest group activity in the trade policy process. Those sectors threatened by import competition fall into Olson's category of privileged (small) or intermediate groups.[16] The collective good these groups are attempting to obtain from the government is a tariff increase or the imposition of another kind of trade barrier, that is, a quota. The economic benefits of this increase in trade protection are sufficiently high to producer groups to provide incentives for members to contribute toward the costs of maintaining an organization to further their interests. Thus Olson's analysis suggests that producer groups are likely to organize in order to obtain trade protection, owing to their relatively small size.

THE CONSPICUOUS ABSENCE OF CONSUMERS

The group with the greatest interest in opposing increased trade protection consists of all consumers. They have an economic interest in opposing trade protection because of higher prices and less product choice owing to trade restraints. Consumers, however, fall into Olson's category of latent groups, which suggests that there is little basis upon which to expect consumers to organize in opposition to industry pressure for protection.[17]

Schattschneider observed this asymmetry in interest group

activity in his analysis of the Smoot-Hawley Tariff Act. He argues "that broadly speaking, any one item in the legislation may make so little difference to an economic group that it will not react at all.[18] He suggests in the Smoot-Hawley tariff revision that the costs imposed on consumers by the new tariff increases were too thinly spread to evoke a political response from the groups affected and goes on to conclude:

> Thus it is possible to impose burdens which taken as a whole are great without provoking general opposition. The political agitation concerning the tariff is profoundly influenced by the fact that, in many instances, the benefits of the legislation to an individual producer are obvious while many of the costs are obscure.[19]

The Smoot-Hawley tariff revision, the basis for Schattschneider's study, was the last American tariff set unilaterally by Congress. In determining tariff rates no consideration was given to the potential adverse affects on foreign economies that would result from closing off the American market or to the probable impact of foreign retaliation on the U.S. economy.[20]

The rationale underlying the determination of tariff levels for each product was the equalization of foreign and domestic prices. Schattschneider notes that both the Democrats and the Republicans believed that the "actual difference in the cost of production at home and abroad, with adequate safeguards for the wage of the American laborer, must be the extreme measure of every tariff rate."[21]

Schattschneider makes two assumptions about the role of interest groups in his analysis of the Smoot-Hawley tariff revision. The first is that there is a connection between economic interest and political behavior. He then notes, however, that it is not necessarily true that there is a direct correspondence between interest group political activity and the economic interest of a specific group.

> The hypothesis is, therefore, that the connection of interest and political behavior, though real, bears close scrutiny. The task is to measure the strength of this drive in politics, to observe its direction and variability, and to note the manner in which it is deflected and controlled.[22]

Schattschneider's second assumption concerns the nature of public policy. He argues that the substance of the actual legislation is the result of effective demands on government. Here, Schattschneider shares with pluralist theory the assumption that the content of public policy is determined by pressure groups that formulate their policy goals independently and then go on to pressure the government to incorporate these goals into actual legislation. In contrast to the pluralist assumption that the interests of all groups are represented in policy process, Schattschneider contends that only some interest groups are able to make "effective demands" of government.

The notion of effective demands for Schattschneider implies that "many of the claims urged upon the government are ineffective."[23] He argues that the structure of the political process in which a policy is made will largely determine which economic interest groups are likely to be effective and which demands will be incorporated into the resulting legislation. Schattschneider suggests, "If it is true that demands largely determine public policy, it follows that policies can be explained in terms of the processes by which pressures are shaped and modified."[24]

In the case of the Smoot-Hawley tariff revision, Schattschneider argues that the preference for protectionism on the part of Congress was the main factor that determined which economic interest groups were active and ultimately successful. This preference was especially pronounced in the congressional committees in charge of determining the tariff rates: the House Ways and Means Committee and the Senate Finance Committee. Thus the majority of the political activity focused around those groups seeking increased tariffs. Schattschneider observes, "Men came to the hearings to ask for things that had been promised to them by a political group which sought to make the legislation extremely hospitable to all who might be induced to come within its ever broadening terms. The committee did not have the time to hear the evidence called for in the formula [the difference between foreign and domestic production costs]."[25]

The bias in the political process toward trade protection led Schattschneider to question the quality of the policy in the resulting legislation. This concern with the quality of U.S. trade policy was motivated by the divergence between the stated intent of

Congress and the actual policy eventually included in the legislation. For the legislation to be consistent with the stated intent of Congress, the committees had to make two kinds of calculations. First, they had to determine which industries or products were eligible to receive tariff increases. It was not possible simply to assume that all foreign products were cheaper than those produced in the United States and required a tariff increase to equalize the foreign and domestic cost of a particular product. The second determination centered around the amount of increase in the tariff required to equalize the two costs.

Schattschneider found in his investigation of the hearings on the Smoot-Hawley tariff that the committees raised the tariff rates for all groups that petitioned for a rate increase. This interest group pressure resulted in the failure of Congress to distinguish between those industries that did or did not need protection. The resulting legislation was so indiscriminately broad "as to destroy the logic and the sense of the policy."[26] He attributes this erosion of any coherence to U.S. tariff policy to the absence of countervailing interest groups in the policy process. The finding that there was little evidence of countervailing interest group activity did not support his initial expectation that the interest groups in support of and in opposition to the legislation should also be about the same. In principle he expected that interest group political activity on both sides of the issue would ensure the coherence of this policy.

Yet in practice Schattschneider found the pressures exerted upon Congress to be extremely unbalanced.

> Although the benefits and costs of the protective tariff, viewed in their totality, are probably very nearly equal, and theoretically the interests supporting and opposed to the legislation are, therefore, likewise approximately equal, the pressures exerted upon Congress are extremely unbalanced.[27]

This imbalance in political activity then allowed those groups that were politically active to overwhelm the legislative process, thereby leaving the United States with an economically disastrous trade policy that was not even informed by the criteria that Congress had established for itself.

THE AUTONOMOUS CONGRESS

Like Schattschneider, Bauer, Pool, and Dexter also focus their analysis of American politics on trade legislation. They base their study on the renewals of the Trade Agreements Act beginning in 1953 and ending with the passage of the Kennedy Trade Expansion Act in 1962. The Trade Agreements Act—in part as a response to congressional dissatisfaction with the Smoot-Hawley tariff revision—was first passed in 1934. The 1934 act authorized the president to lower duties by as much as 50 percent of the Smoot-Hawley levels through the negotiation of bilateral trade agreements. As a result not only did the American tariff become negotiable, but the tariff rate was fixed in a trade agreement that did not require ratification by the Senate. Although after the Trade Agreements Act was passed Congress no longer had direct control over the tariff rates, it retained a potential veto over the trade agreements program. This veto was based on a provision in the act that required Congress to renew the program every three years. This work is essentially an analysis of these renewals of the Trade Agreements Act.

Bauer, Pool, and Dexter introduce their study as "a dissent from Schattschneider's position."[28] They disagree with his findings about the power of interest groups as well as the absence of countervailing interest groups. In contrast to Schattschneider, they describe interest groups as "on the whole poorly financed, ill-managed, out of contact with Congress and at best only marginally effective in supporting tendencies and measures which already had behind them considerable Congressional impetus from other sources."[29] They also assume countervailing interest groups to be involved in the policy process and argue: "We are quite certain that, whatever the outcome, it would have been quite different if all the organized interest groups on one side had been silenced while all those on the other had remained vocal. . . . It is in the nature of the democratic struggle that this does not happen."[30]

These two observations led Bauer, Pool, and Dexter to question not only Schattschneider's conclusions but also the pressure group model of American political behavior. Although they do acknowledge that some difference in the degree of pressure group influence during the Reciprocal Trade Agreements Act renewals may have been a result of the delegation of the authority to set specific tariff rates from Congress to the executive, they do not believe this to be an adequate explanation and go on to question the validity of the pressure group model of the congressional process.

> But, if pressure politics no longer satisfies as an explanation of what happened regarding reciprocal trade, this is not just because of a change in the times. We are probably also reflecting a characteristic stage in the discipline. The pressure group model was a sophisticated refinement of the previously naive views of the Congressional process. It may now be time for a still more complicated view of the process of influence on and in Congresss.[31]

They call this still more complicated model of the congressional process the *transactional model of political influence*. In the transactional model the direction of pressure between the congressional representative and the pressure group is reciprocal. In contrast to the pressure group model in which the congressional response is considered to be a reflection of interest group pressure, Bauer, Pool, and Dexter argue:

> A Congressman very largely gets back what he puts out. In his limited time, he associates more with some kinds of people than with others, listens to some kinds of messages more than to others, and as a result hears from some kinds of people more than from others. He controls what he hears both by his attention and by his attitudes. He makes the world to which he thinks he is responding.[32]

Bauer, Pool, and Dexter go on to assert that the transactional model renders Schattschneider's pressure response model obsolete. They conclude: "For the case which we have studied, it [their analysis] tends to cast doubt on the stereotype of pressure politics, of special interests effectively expressing themselves and forcing politicians either to bow to their dictates or to fight back vigorously."[33]

Unlike Schattschneider, Bauer, Pool, and Dexter do not attempt to evaluate the quality of the policy that resulted from the renewals of the Trade Agreements Act. Instead, they contend that a more realistic understanding of the American political process (the transactional model) will allow for more effective political actions on the part of "those communicators striving for important social goals."[34]

THE INTEREST GROUP MODEL

These apparent inconsistencies between the conclusions of Bauer, Pool, and Dexter and Schattschneider have led to several attempts to develop models of the political process that could incorporate both explanations. The most prominent of these efforts is a book review by Theodore Lowi of *American Business and Public Policy*.[35] In this review Lowi argues that the transactional analysis of American politics need not supersede the pressure group model. Instead, he suggests that both "theories" are appropriate for explaining certain classes of cases. Lowi further contends that Schattschneider and Bauer, Pool, and Dexter arrived at contradictory conclusions with respect to the role that pressure groups play in American politics because they were looking at different kinds of political issues, even though both studies analyzed the politics of U.S. trade legislation.

Lowi identifies three categories of issues in American politics: distributive, regulatory, and redistributive.[36] He argues that Bauer, Pool, and Dexter reach conclusions different from those of Schattschneider because while the Smoot-Hawley tariff was a case of distributive politics, the renewals of the Trade Agreements Act involved regulatory politics. Lowi differentiates distributive from regulatory policies along two dimensions. The first involves the perceived distribution of costs and benefits of a specific policy among interest groups, whereas the second specifies the political arena in which the policy is made. A *distributive policy* is one that can be made without regard to economic resource constraints and is usually formulated in a congressional committee. In contrast, a *regulatory policy* is one that does involve a direct confrontation between the indulged and the deprived owing to the existence of tangible resource constraints.[37] Lowi argues that since the conflict inherent in these policies cannot be contained in a governing committee or regulatory agency, the political arena for these issues is the floor of Congress.

These two categories of issues also serve as the basis for

different types of political coalitions. Lowi contends that the political coalitions for distributive issues are formed through logrolling and consist of individual firms. For regulatory issues the basic political alliance is at the sector level.[38] In contrast to distributive policies in which conflict is eliminated through expanding the coalition by way of logrolling, regulatory politics involves conflict among various sectors of the U.S. economy. Regulatory politics is essentially pluralist in which the ultimate policy "tends to be a residue of the interplay of group conflict."[39]

Lowi reconciles the findings of Schattschneider and Bauer, Pool, and Dexter by arguing that the politics of trade policy had changed from a distributive to a regulatory issue during the time between the Smoot-Hawley tariff in 1930 and the Kennedy Trade Expansion Act in 1962. Schattschneider's characterization of the politics of the Smoot-Hawley tariff revision is consistent with what one would expect from a distributive policy in which the costs are not clearly apparent to the group that would bear them. In contrast, Bauer, Pool, and Dexter's study focused on trade legislation in which there was conflict among sectors over the policy. Their analysis represents, for Lowi, a case of classical pluralism, so he was not surprised to find that pressure groups did not dominate the policy process.

Lowi's identification of Bauer, Pool, and Dexter's study as a case of classical pluralism appears, however, to be inconsistent with their findings regarding the role of interest groups in the policy process. While they retain the pluralist assumption that countervailing interest groups do exist for most political issues, their transactional model does not assume the ultimate policy to be a result of the conflict between these groups. Instead, the multiplicity of interest groups provides Congress with the autonomy to choose which group will be influential on any given issue.

THE PRINCIPAL-AGENT PERSPECTIVE

Michael Hayes offers yet another explanation of the politics of U.S. trade policy in an attempt to reconcile the inconsistency between Bauer, Pool, and Dexter's belief that their study lends support for the transactional model and Lowi's contention that this study is another case of classical pluralism. He argues, "What Bauer, Pool, and Dexter observe as the virtual irrelevance of groups on the tariff issue in the contemporary era may more properly be understood as the virtual irrelevance of Congress to the tariff issue in this period."[40] With the passage of the Reciprocal Trade Agreements Act in 1934, Congress did become irrelevant to the extent that it no longer set tariffs on specific commodities. These were set in bilateral negotiations.

Hayes goes on to argue that in addition to obscuring the limited role that Congress plays in the trade policy process, Lowi's typology also cannot incorporate the way in which trade policy is actually formulated. This confusion is especially apparent in Lowi's contention that Congress did not give up the tariff. He argues that the major change in U.S. trade policy between 1930 and 1962 was that the arena for settling conflict over trade issues changed from the committees to the floor of Congress.

> Congress did not give up the tariff; as the tariff became a matter of regulation, committee elites lost their power to contain the participants because obscure decisions became interrelated, therefore less obscure, and more controversy became built in and unavoidable.[41]

In fact, however, Congress did give up the authority to set individual tariff rates in 1934 when it delegated to the executive the authority to negotiate reciprocal tariff reductions. Robert Pastor, in a study of the role of Congress in foreign economic policy, states that the "law was the first time that the Congress as a whole recognized that it was not suited to set tariffs itself on an item-by-item basis; and for the first time, Congress delegated advance power to the President to raise or lower by as much as 50% all rates on agricultural as well as industrial goods, subject to no check other than a consultative one."[42] Within the context of trade negotiations, Congress only retained the authority to determine general guidelines within which the executive would conduct U.S. trade policy.[43]

Lowi is also ambiguous with respect to precisely which interest groups were involved in the conflict that could no longer be contained in committee. Lowi's identification of trade policy as regulatory in 1962 implies that different sectors of American industry opposed one another in policy process. Bauer, Pool, and Dexter found, however, that firms or sectors did not oppose other sectors when it came to stating their interests. Instead, they asked to be exempted from the overall policy of linear tariff reductions. Bauer, Pool, and Dexter write, "More often than not one hears the advocate of protection begin his statement as follows: 'Of course I am for increasing trade and believe in lowering trade barriers, but . . .' "[44]

Lowi never explicitly clarifies exactly which aspect of the 1962 trade legislation made it regulatory and not distributive. In describing this transition, he states: "The final shift came with the 1962 Trade Expansion Act, which enabled the President for the first time to deal with broad categories [to the sector] rather than individual commodities."[45] This statement seems to refer to the shift in U.S. policy from item-by-item tariff reductions to across-the-board linear reductions. Linear tariff reductions, however, involve tariff cuts across sectors, with exceptions for individual products, and do not imply conflict at the sector level.

In contrast to Lowi, for whom the crucial change in trade policy came in 1962, Hayes believes that the decisive shift was in 1934 when the authority to determine the actual tariff rates on specific products was transferred from Congress to the executive branch of the government. Congress delegated this negotiating authority to the executive in response to the frustration about the influence of pressure groups experienced by those representatives involved in formulating the Smoot-Hawley tariff. In light of this rationale for delegating the negotiating authority to the executive, Hayes comments that "it should come as no surprise that such groups do seem less important in the passage of subsequent tariff legislation."[46] Hayes then suggests that "what is needed is a typology of the policy process that will distinguish those processes under which interest groups are likely to exercise influence from those for which they are largely irrelevant."[47]

In order to determine when to expect effective interest group activity on a particular issue, Hayes offers a two dimensional framework. The first dimension, the demand pattern, indicates whether the policy involves countervailing interest groups or whether it is largely unopposed. He labels these two types of interest group pressure *conflictual* and *consensual*. The second dimension, the supply pattern, characterizes the response of Congress to interest group pressure. Hayes suggests Congress can respond in three ways: it can do nothing (no bill); it can delegate the actual decision to a regulatory agency (delegation or policy without law); or it can pass a law in which Congress explicitly takes responsibility for the allocation of costs and benefits (rule of law).

Like Lowi, Hayes identifies the demand pattern for trade policy to be conflictual. To determine which supply pattern legislators would be likely to choose, he uses the *public choice theory* of legislative behavior. This theory views congressional representatives as being primarily concerned with maximizing the probability that they will be reelected. On the basis of this assumption, Hayes suggests that the supply pattern for trade policy is delegated because Congress has decided it is not in its self-interest to resolve the political conflict that arises in this issue area. Hayes notes that in determining trade policy "Congress could avoid making a clear choice through the delegation of rate-setting authority to the Tariff Commission [now the International Trade Commission]."[48] Implicit in his characterization of regulatory policy is the assumption that the competing interest groups will continue to battle one another within the regulatory arena.[49] Hayes then points to this delegation of rate-setting authority to the Tariff Commission to explain why congressmen appear to be free to vote as they please on trade legislation.

Since the 1934 Reciprocal Trade Agreements Act, however, the Tariff Commission has never been designated to negotiate tariff rates. Until the 1962 trade legislation, the level of the U.S. tariff was determined through negotiations administered by the Department of State.[50] Until 1962 the Tariff Commission could recommend to the negotiators maximum tariff reductions for specific commodities. The law, however, did not require that negotiators follow these recommendations. In 1947 the Tariff Commission was also designated by Congress to hold escape clause hearings to determine whether an industry was "injured" by imports. If the commission finds that the industry is injured, it recommends relief measures to the president.[51] The president, however, need not accept these recommendations.

In explaining the apparent autonomy of legislators, Hayes is specifically referring to the renewals of the 1934 Reciprocal Trade

Agreements Act. In this discussion, he is not referring to special exceptions for specific industries injured by imports. Thus his analysis does not include the kind of trade policy issues that in fact are delegated to the Tariff Commission. Yet he argues that the relative independence of legislators is due to the "delegation of negotiating authority to the Tariff Commission."[52] He concludes, "Thus it was not the multiplicity of interests per se that gave Congressmen considerable latitude on this issue [trade legislation]; it was . . . the availability of delegation, with its potential for obfuscating the outcome."[53]

This suggests that Hayes misunderstands the role of the Tariff Commission in the U.S. trade policy process. George Bronz, a former trade official in the Treasury Department, notes, "While usually regarded as one of the regulatory agencies, the Tariff Commission has no authority to regulate. It issues no orders, except procedural ones, such as those requiring the submission of information or the attendance of witnesses, and the conclusion of its deliberations results, typically, in a recommendation to the President, rather than a decision with operative force of its own."[54]

In addition to misunderstanding the role of the Tariff Commission, Hayes also overestimates the extent to which the commission's deliberations involve an extension of interest group conflict. Escape clause hearings do not evoke much organized opposition. Yet they also do not uniformly result in the industry's favor. The main countervailing force to the industry in question is also not, as Hayes would suggest, the presence of other countervailing interest groups.[55] Instead, industries are not always successful in obtaining protection from the Tariff Commission because they fail to meet the criteria for import relief stipulated by Congress.[56] This criteria, in turn, is informed by the escape clause in the GATT (Article 19). To maintain the integrity of the escape clause, the United States chooses not to interpret it in such a way that industries are guaranteed relief from import competition.

While the political activity of interest groups in escape clause hearings appears to be consensual because of the lopsided political activity in support of import relief, the decisions made by the Tariff Commission would suggest that the interaction among interest groups is indeed conflictual.[57] The contention here is that the politics of U.S. trade policy appears to be conflictual—not because interest groups directly opposed to one another participate in the decision-making process but because the GATT norms embedded in the U.S. policy process (through the activities of the U.S. Tariff Commission) make it difficult for industries to obtain the protection they believe to be necessary. U.S. membership in the GATT makes it appear as if there is strong interest group pressure against protection, even though in fact interest group activity is more indicative of consensual politics.

To make the actual trade policy process consistent with Hayes's analysis, the delegation of negotiating authority to the executive branch would have to be seen as the outcome of a conflictual demand for trade policy. This would imply that the major interest groups in conflict would be those that perceive themselves to be threatened by import protection and those that would benefit from increased access to foreign markets. Yet the argument that the progressive reduction of the U.S. tariff since 1934 is a function of the political dominance of export-oriented industries is not supported by empirical evidence. Bauer, Pool, and Dexter found:

> Businessmen do not often take the same kind of political action to force a particular commodity into a particular foreign market as they do to keep out one that is injuring their established position. Rationally or irrationally, rightly or wrongly, foreign competition is seen as a specific problem, to which for years the letter to Congress has been the appropriate remedy, whereas the extension of export markets is seen as a matter of broad national policy in which every citizen's voice is as relevant as any other's.[58]

This suggests that in addition to interest group support for trade expansion, other forces in the American policy process must be present to act as a countervailing force against industry pressure for protection and to push for increased access to foreign markets. In the United States this pressure for increased openness in international trade comes primarily from the executive branch. Bauer, Pool, and Dexter indicate, "In the past decades it has traditionally been the executive branch that for a variety of reasons, including the fact that it saw commercial policy as an integral part of foreign policy, has carried the banner of liberal trade."[59] Reinforcement for those agencies in the executive branch that support liberal trade policy is provided by the GATT.[60] The GATT also provides Congress with leverage with which to resist political pressures for trade protection. Since the negotiating authority of the executive is delegated by Congress, the executive branch preference for a liberal trade policy must reflect congressional preferences.

The next chapter addresses why the evolving definition of the *U.S. national interest* includes a commitment to the GATT.

NOTES

1. E. E. Schattschneider, *Politics, Pressures and the Tariff* (Hamden, Conn.: Archon Books, 1963).

2. For a discussion of the creation of the GATT, see Chapter 3.

3. Raymond Bauer, Ithiel de Sola Pool, and Lewis Anthony Dexter, *American Business and Public Policy: The Politics of Foreign Trade* (Chicago: Aldine, 1972); Theodore J. Lowi, "American Business, Public Policy, Case Studies, and Political Theory," 16 *World Politics* (July 1964): pp. 677–93; and Michael Hayes, *Lobbyists and Legislators: A Theory of Political Markets* (New Brunswick, N.J.: Rutgers University Press, 1981), p. 19.

4. Here, I am referring specifically to international organizations.

5. Mancur Olson, *The Logic of Collective Action: Public Goods and the Theory of Groups* (Cambridge, Mass.: Harvard University Press, 1975); and David Truman, *The Governmental Process: Political Interests and Public Opinion* (New York: Alfred A. Knopf, 1951).

6. Olson, *Logic of Collective Action*, p. 7.

7. *Public goods* are defined to be those goods provided by the state from which no person can be excluded. The most common example of a public good is defense. In the context of trade policy a tariff increase would be considered to be a public good by the industry receiving the increase in trade protection.

8. Olson, *Logic of Collective Action*, p. 21.

9. Ibid., p. 30.

10. Ibid., p. 34.

11. Ibid., p. 50.

12. Ibid., p. 58.

13. Ibid., p. 58.

14. Truman, *Governmental Process*, p. 114.

15. Olson, *Logic of Collective Action*, p. 127.

16. Olson defines a "privileged" group to be one in which at least one member has an incentive to provide the collective good. In an intermediate-sized group, no single member has sufficient incentive to provide the good, but it is small enough so that the public good can be provided through a minimum of group coordination or organization.

17. If a major exporting country affected by the imposition of a U.S. trade barrier chooses to retaliate against the United States, then those industries whose export markets are cut off constitute yet another pressure group with an economic interest in opposing increased U.S. trade restraints. These industry groups would also fall into Olson's category of small or intermediate interest groups. There is not, however, much empirical evidence in the history of U.S. trade policy to suggest that one industry directly opposes the position on trade restraints taken by another. Yet another possible countervailing interest group, users of imported inputs, typically ask for increased tariffs to cover their increased costs. Schattschneider calls this phenomenon "reciprocal noninterference." He found, "Compensatory duties are used to implement a strategy of reciprocal noninterference in which each industry is encouraged to seek duties of its own and induced to accept the incidental burdens of the system without protest." Schattschneider, *Politics*, p. 284.

18. Ibid., p. 127. The final bill included specific tariff schedules for over 20,000 items.

19. Ibid., p. 27.

20. "By the end of 1931, twenty-six countries had enacted quantitative restrictions and exchange controls, and by 1932, the United Kingdom abandoned free trade and established the Ottawa system of Imperial tariff preferences. . . . Evidence of the adverse effect this had on the U.S. economy can be seen in the following. From 1929 to 1933, U.S. exports fell from $488 million to $120 million; imports fell from $368 million to $96 million. World trade fell from $35 billion to $12 billion." Robert Pastor, *Congress and the Politics of U.S. Foreign Economic Policy: 1929–1976* (Berkeley: University of California Press, 1980), p. 79.

21. Schattschneider, *Politics*, p. 8.

22. Ibid., p. 4.

23. Ibid., p. 4.

24. Ibid., p. 5.

25. Ibid., p. 99.

26. Ibid., p. 283.

27. Ibid., p. 285.

28. Bauer, Pool, and Dexter, *American Business and Public Policy*, p. 25.

29. Ibid., p. 324.

30. Ibid., p. 324.

31. Ibid., p. 456.

32. Ibid., p. 420.

33. Ibid., p. 484.

34. Ibid., p. 490.

35. Theodore J. Lowi, "American Business, Public Policy, Case Studies, and Political Theory."

36. The following discussion will focus on distributive and regulatory issues, as Lowi's analysis of trade policy only concerns these two categories. Redistributive issues involve the explicit transfer of resources from one social class to another.

37. Lowi, "American Business, Public Policy, Case Studies, and Political Theory," page 695. In economic terms trade policy has always been regulatory. Trade barriers involve the distribution of income from consumers to producers. Politically, however, it has appeared to be redistributive because the interest group upon which the costs of the policy are imposed (consumers) are typically not aware that they are paying them.

38. Lowi defines a *sector* as any set of common or substitutable commodities or services or any other form of established economic interaction.

39. Lowi, "American Business, Public Policy, Case Studies, and Political Theory," p. 695.

40. Michael Hayes, "The Semi-Sovereign Pressure Groups: A Critique of Current Theory and an Alternate Typology," 40 *Journal of Politics* (February 1978): 141.

41. Lowi, "American Business, Public Policy, Case Studies, and Political Theory," p. 695.

42. Pastor, *Congress*, p. 92.

43. Even after the Reciprocal Trade Agreements Act, Congress did retain the authority to legislate trade restraints. This authority, however, is rarely used. It is also not relevant to the analysis here because the trade legislation at issue for (1) Schattschneider, (2) Bauer, Pool, and Dexter, (3) Lowi, and (4) Hayes involves tariff changes across a broad array of products included in one piece of legislation, not special legislation to protect one industry.

44. Bauer, Pool, and Dexter, *American Business and Public Policy*, p. 147.

45. Lowi, "American Business, Public Policy, Case Studies, and Political Theory," p. 699.

46. Hayes, "Semi-Sovereign Pressure Groups," p. 141.

47. Hayes, *Lobbyists and Legislators*, p. 25.

48. Ibid., p. 31.

49. The subheading for regulation in his matrix is the extension of group conflict.

50. In the Trade Expansion Act of 1962, the primary responsibility for U.S. trade negotiations was transferred from the State Department to the newly formed Office of the Special Trade Representative.

51. These consist of temporary tariff increases or quotas imposed on the commodity in question.

52. Hayes, *Lobbyists and Legislators*, p. 29.

53. Ibid., p. 29.

54. George Bronz, "The Tariff Commission as a Regulatory Agency," *Columbia Law Review* 61(1961):463.

55. The major political coalitions that arise around escape clause hearings consist of the industry claiming injury, which lobbies in favor of protectionist measures, importers, and occasionally foreign suppliers that oppose import relief. Ibid., p. 409.

56. This criterion was liberalized in the Trade Act of 1974 that made it unnecessary for an industry to demonstrate that the increase in imports was the

result of trade concessions. It also reduced the amount of injury that must be attributed to increased imports.

57. Crucial to consensual policy for Hayes is not that there is a consensus about the distribution of economic goods resulting from a policy decision but that the costs of the reallocation of resources involved in the decision are pushed on to inactive political groups (in this case, consumers).

58. Bauer, Pool, and Dexter, *American Business and Public Policy*, p. 222.

59. Ibid., p. xiv.

60. The executive branch can be disaggregated into those agencies that typically support trade liberalization—Treasury, State, and the Office of the Special Trade Representative—and those that are protectionist by reputation—Commerce and Labor.

3

THE NATIONAL INTEREST
AND INTERNATIONAL
COLLABORATION IN INTERNATIONAL
TRADE POLICY

INTRODUCTION

This chapter deals with the question of state strength and the national interest with respect to international trade policy. The chapter explicates the political and economic costs and benefits of collaboration in international trade to suggest why the United States perceives adherence to the rules of the GATT to be in its national interest. From a political perspective relinquishing policy autonomy through GATT membership can be seen as negative if *state strength* is defined in terms of the ability of states to act autonomously. Here, international trade is perceived to be a constraint on autonomy. In contrast, the theory of comparative advantage suggests that insofar as trade allows for relatively higher rates of economic growth and efficiency than does autarky (self-sufficiency), increased trade can be considered to contribute to the economic component of state strength. From an economic perspective state power is enhanced by a thriving economy, and economic autonomy is not critical to the definition of *state strength*. Thus, while from an economic perspective international trade is seen as enhancing economic growth and thereby contributing to state strength, from a political perspective trade is seen more in terms of introducing a constraint on state autonomy, thereby reducing state strength.

International trade poses a dilemma for policymakers: While it may provide long-run economic benefits, the short-run dislocation within an industry creates immediate political costs. In an attempt to capture some of the economic benefits from trade while at the same time minimizing the political costs, the United States, after World War II, chose to collaborate over the regulation of international trade. This choice reflected a decision that the economic benefits of trade were greater than the political costs resulting from the loss of state autonomy.

This chapter first considers the tension between the economic benefits and the political costs of trade on the basis of a comparison of Albert Hirschman's *National Power and the Structure of Foreign Trade*[1] and Stephen Krasner's "State Power and the Structure of International Trade."[2] Hirschman emphasizes the economic gains as well as the international political costs and benefits from trade expressed in terms of relative state strength. His analysis intends to explain the political and economic factors that allow states to manipulate trade relationships to achieve foreign policy goals. In contrast, Krasner does not emphasize the economic component of state strength and assumes economic autonomy to be its primary determinant. He further argues that international trade can bring with it unacceptable domestic political costs that result from intensifying pressure for economic adjustment within declining sectors of the economy. This comparison illustrates how Krasner's neomercantilist perspective on trade neglects the economic costs involved in forgoing trade. To the degree that state strength is a function of economic growth, forgoing the economic benefits of trade can contribute to the weakening of the state.

In contrast to these two neomercantile positions is the liberal argument, which provides the conceptual basis for the international trade regime. This perspective takes as its point of departure the assumption that states cannot afford to forgo the economic benefits of international trade. The economic benefits of trade create incentives for states to cooperate. The theoretical basis for this liberal international economic order is developed in the work of Jan Tumlir.[3] Whereas Hirschman specifies the international political costs of trade, Krasner adds the domestic political costs. In contrast, Tumlir argues that international collaboration in international trade involves neither international nor domestic political costs. It provides only economic benefits through the provison of rules that reduce political uncertainty and thereby allow trade patterns to reflect considerations of comparative advantage.

POLITICAL AUTONOMY VERSUS ECONOMIC INTERDEPENDENCE

The tension between the neomercantile and the liberal vision of the international economic order results from the need for states to relinquish some policy autonomy to reduce the political uncertainty involved in trade. One way to reduce this uncertainty is not to trade—autarky. States, however, found autarky to involve unacceptable economic costs. In looking back upon the collapse of the liberal trade norms in the 1930s and the economic dislocation wrought by beggar-thy-neighbor trade policies such as exporting unemployment, Western states found the opportunity cost of forgoing trade to be excessive. During World War II, policymakers in the United States and Europe decided that they were willing to collaborate over the rules that would reduce uncertainty to capture the gains from trade.[4] Certainty takes the form of stable expectations about the policies of the member states in the international trade regime.

States collaborate to generate stable expectations about the degree of openness of the international economy because firms require the reduction of uncertainty in order to undertake production for the international market. A highly uncertain international economic environment increases the level of risk, making investment geared toward international trade prohibitively costly. When states agree to reduce the political uncertainty in trade policy, however, they face increased domestic economic uncertainty. This economic uncertainty stems from increased competitive pressures in conjunction with the agreement not to restrict international trade. The increase in this uncertainty is part of the price of participation in the international economic order.

The GATT is based on the perception of member states that

collaboration over the norms of international trade reduces uncertainty and furthers the national interest. Ernst Haas argues, "The need for collaboration arises from the recognition that the costs of national self-reliance are usually excessive."[5] Haas further explains that international collaboration "is an attempt to reduce uncertainty when a multiplicity of values are at stake and the simplest strategy for reducing uncertainty—autarky—is not practicable."[6] Thus to the extent that states define the reduction of uncertainty to be in the national interest and find the economic costs of their preferred policy—autarky—to be excessive, they will collaborate.

STATE STRENGTH AND INTERNATIONAL TRADE

Hirschman concerns himself with the relationship between international trade and state power. His major analytic assumption is that the ability of a sovereign state to regulate trade flows is a key component of a state's national power policy. By *national power policy* he means "the power of coercion which one nation may bring to bear upon other nations."[7]

Hirschman looks at trade in terms of the impact it has upon the distribution of power among states and from the perspective of comparative advantage. The theory of comparative advantage suggests that international trade provides economic benefits for all participants owing to the expanded opportunities for specialization within individual states and increased efficiencies in international resource allocation. These economic gains translate directly into gains in the political power of both the exporting and the importing states.[8]

In contrast to liberal trade theory, Hirschman does not see trade solely as providing mutual gains to both trading partners. Instead, he analyzes trade in terms of the gain in power of one state relative to another. Although Hirschman's analysis considers trade to be a source of the gain in the relative power of a state and is reminiscent of mercantilism, he is not a classical mercantilist. Classical mercantilists argue that any level of imports were a sign of weakness and drained the power of the state through the reduction in the gold supply. But Hirschman considers imports to be a source of economic gain "by providing a more plentiful supply of goods or by replacing goods wanted less with goods wanted more."[9] For Hirschman, imports also increase the political power of the importing state relative to the exporting state. In this respect his analysis again differs fundamentally from classical mercantilism, which considered exports to be the basis for state strength because they were purchased with gold.

By including considerations of both economic benefits and political power in his analysis of trade policy, Hirschman brings out the tension between the economic and political dimensions of trade. The political dimension of trade that he considers to be the power concept is called the "dependence on trade." To distinguish this from the economic dimension that he adopts from the theory of comparative advantage, Hirschman introduces the notion of the "gains from trade."

Hirschman derives the power concept—the dependence on trade—from an analysis of the degree to which a state would be impoverished if its trade were cut off. This impoverishment is in inverse proportion to the level of economic gains that states realize through trade. Hirschman suggests that "the classical concept, the gain from trade, and the power concept, dependence on trade . . . , are seen to be two aspects of the same phenomenon."[10]

This double-edged quality of international trade is central to Hirschman's analysis. His concern with this dual role of trade stems from an attempt to determine whether there is anything inherent in trade that makes it uniquely susceptible to being used to influence power relationships between two countries. He attributes the relationship between trade and national power to the ability of a sovereign state "to interrupt its own import and export trade which is at the same time the import and export trade of some other country."[11]

For Hirschman the economic gains from trade, together with the ability of a state to regulate trade at its own borders, create the conditions for the use of trade relationships as an instrument of national power. He concludes: "The power to interrupt commercial or financial relations with any country, considered as an attribute of national sovereignty, is the root cause of the influence or power position which a country acquires in other countries, just as it is the root cause of the dependence on trade."[12]

The contention that it is the sovereign right of a state to interrupt trade flows, which politicizes all trade relationships, raises the question of whether the greater political leverage rests with the importing or with the exporting states. The classical mercantile perspective would lead one to expect the exporter to have the upper hand. Hirschman, however, in focusing on power relationships that result from interdependence as opposed to autonomy, contends that the importing state has more political power than the exporter. This is true because "under conditions of incomplete use of resources, . . . it will generally be easier to switch imports than exports, all countries ready to sell, and none ready to buy."[13] Thus Hirschman sees the dependence of a state upon export markets as creating a higher degree of vulnerability than the dependence upon imports. The policy implication is that imports are to be encouraged to enhance the strength of the importer relative to the exporter.

This conclusion is striking because although it is mercantilist in its concern with trade as an expression of state strength, it treats imports as a source of strength and not weakness. In attempting to determine how to increase the ability of state A to coerce state B, he does not look to the economic autonomy of state A. Instead, he argues that state strength is enhanced by the ability of state A, through trade (importing), to enrich state B. Thus for Hirschman, in general, an increase in trade enhances the power of importing states relative to those dependent on exports.

Hirschman's argument that significant political costs attend the economic gains from trade for the exporter raises the issue of whether the economic benefits can be separated from the power relationships that arise among states. These economic benefits become politicized because they are subject to the "negative power of the nation-state to stop trade."[14] Hirschman suggests that the power relationship can be separated from the economic relationship only "by a frontal attack upon the institution which is at the root of the possible use of economic relations for national power aims—the institution of national economic sovereignty."[15] This attack would involve the creation of an international sovereign authority to regulate trade. International economic collaboration would then be achieved through the transfer of the power to organize, regulate, and interfere with trade from member states to this international organization.[16]

Krasner, like Hirschman, assumes economic relations among states to be subordinate to national political goals. Hirschman, however, believes that the subordination of international trade to political concerns is the crucial political problem posed by international trade. His prescription is to free economic relations from this subordination by requiring states to transfer some portion of their economic sovereignty to an international organization. Krasner, in contrast, takes as his point of departure that states will never relinquish any aspect of sovereignty unless forced by a hegemon to do so.

Arguing from a systemic perspective, Krasner contends that the system will be open when openness coincides with the national interest of each state in a position to ensure that others will accept an open trading structure.[17] This is most likely to happen in a hegemonic system in which a single state perceives itself to benefit both politically and economically from trade.

> The hegemonic state will have a preference for an open structure. Such a structure increases its aggregate national income. It also increases its rate of growth during its ascendancy—that is, when its relative size and technological lead are increasing. Further, an open structure increases its political power, since the opportunity costs of closure are least for a large and developed state. The social instability resulting from exposure to the international system is mitigated by the hegemonic power's relatively low level of involvement in the international economy, and the mobility of factors.[18]

Thus, while Hirschman sees openness to be the result of the transfer of economic power from the state to an international organization, Krasner contends that openness results from the concentration of power in one state.

Krasner's analysis of the implications of trade relationships among states differs from Hirschman's in two fundamental respects. First, the theory of comparative advantage, in Krasner's framework, does not unambiguously lead to the "gains from trade." Krasner begins by acknowledging that neoclassical trade theory suggests that free trade will enhance "aggregate economic utility." He goes on to observe that free trade has not been the norm throughout history. He then uses this divergence between theory and practice to suggest that the relationship between the degree of openness of the international economy and the rate of economic growth of a state is "elusive." Krasner argues that "only by maintaining its technological lead and continually developing new industries can even a very large state escape the undesired consequences of an entirely open economic system."[19]

These undesired consequences stem from the possibility that other states will acquire the technology necessary to become potential competitors. Krasner does not specify what form this competitive threat takes. If one introduces the issue of social stability, however, these "undesired consequences" can be reasonably defined as the social instability that results from increased import competition. Specifically, this social instability is caused by the need for adjustment within the importing country of the factors of production (labor and capital) that have been rendered noncompetitive through an increase of lower-priced foreign imports. Thus to enhance social stability, an important component of state strength, a state will be inclined first to restrict exports to prevent the diffusion of technology. Ultimately, states will restrict imports to maintain social stability.

Second, since Krasner sees no necessary relationship between trade and economic benefits, his concern is with how an increase in trade will lead to a reduction in state autonomy. He argues that without a hegemon, states, in attempting to "maximize national goals," will erect trade barriers, thereby reducing the openness of the international economy. The national goals that states attempt to enhance through the manipulation of trade barriers are aggregate national income, social stability, political power, and economic growth.[20] In specifying these goals, Krasner does not indicate which are related to Hirschman's economic notion of *the gains from trade* or to the political aspect of trade, the *dependence on trade*. His argument fails to include these two dimensions because his primary emphasis is on the importance of state autonomy in international economic relations.

This focus on state autonomy essentially precludes a consideration of both the economic benefits from trade to the importer and the exporter and the political benefits to the importer that result from the ability to "enrich" the exporter. In contrast to Hirschman, Krasner looks at the dependence on trade from the perspective of the importing as opposed to the exporting state. As a result, whereas Hirschman concludes with a discussion of the need to create an international organization to sustain a high level of openness in the international economy, Krasner concludes by predicting that closure will best reflect the future political interests of most states, in the absence of a hegemon. Because of this emphasis on national autonomy, his analysis misses the trade-off that states must make between the economic gains from trade and the political costs of a reduction in policy autonomy.

The possibility that states will decide to take advantage of the aggregate economic benefits of trade does not challenge Krasner's primary contention that "it is the power and the policies of states [not transnational actors] that create order where there would otherwise be chaos or at best a Lockian state of nature."[21] States have an interest in the stability of the international trade regime because of the economic benefits. Krasner's definition of the national interest does not, however, include the economic benefits from trade and, because of this, fails to specify the trade-off between the economic costs of forgoing trade and the political benefits of increasing state autonomy.

A concern with the economic costs of forgoing trade raises the question of how states can take advantage of the economic benefits while minimizing the political costs of enmeshment in international trade. These costs are both international and domestic in scope. The international political costs refer to the loss of autonomy to impose unilateral barriers to trade. The domestic political costs stem from the need on the part of the state to resist pressures for protection from domestic industries threatened by foreign competition.

Neither Hirschman nor Krasner explains how to minimize these political costs. Hirschman does suggest that the economic gains from export will lead toward a general increase in trade. A high political price, however, will be attached to this. That price is the increase in dependence, which can only be reduced through an agreement among states to relinquish some portion of their economic sovereignty. In addition to the international political price attached to increased trade for exporting states, Krasner adds that there are domestic political costs for importing states. These costs include social dislocation in industries that cannot compete with imports. Thus both exporting and importing can be interpreted to lead to a reduction in state strength.

Yet, international trade continues to grow in an international economic order that has not required member states to relinquish their economic sovereignty. It continues to grow in part because in the international state system trade policy has been separated from power politics except on relatively rare occasions when the costs of economic sanctions are weighed against the costs of military action. In terms of domestic politics states also recognize the utility of economic adjustment motivated by an increase in imports. In both international and domestic politics, states choose to sustain a relatively open trading system because the opportunity costs of forgoing trade outweigh the political benefits of autonomy. Although the international trading system is based on a political agreement among states, the objectives of this agreement are primarily economic. To pursue these economic goals, states have had to agree to forgo the use of export or import controls to manipulate the foreign policies of their trading partners and to resist domestic political pressures for protection.

Jan Tumlir takes as his point of departure the belief that trade relations among states are inherently economic and not political in nature.[22] In contrast to Hirschman, his analysis focuses on the gains from trade to both the importing and the exporting state apart from the political or "dependency" dimension that can emerge between trading partners. In contrast to Krasner, Tumlir sees an identity between an open trading system and the national interest of a state. On the basis of these two assumptions, Tumlir argues that states face neither economic nor political costs in participating in an open trading system.

Tumlir defines the costs of entrance into the international economic order to be those national objectives that must be sacrificed for the state to comply with the rules of the international trade regime. He does not, however, include in this definition of costs the loss of state autonomy. He further argues that the rules of the international trade regime do not conflict with the national goal of economic growth and concludes that the constraints on a state's autonomy that result from rules designed to sustain the international economic order involve no real costs.

> The international order does not prescribe or proscribe national goals. It only regulates the means by which nations pursue their goals. Whatever

domestic economic objective a nation may set for itself is usually attainable in various ways among which interference with international transactions—various forms of which are indeed proscribed by international rules—is generally a second-best, third-best or even a lower-order policy. There are many ways of going about national objectives which are at the same time efficient and proof against protest from abroad.[23]

These proscribed second-best policies refer specifically to the unilateral imposition of trade controls. The pressure to impose trade barriers comes from industries that have been rendered noncompetitive through changing trade patterns. Tumlir suggests that the imposition of these trade restraints in response to interest group pressure is a second-best policy because it imposes costs on the entire society that exceed the gain to the industry requesting trade restraint. He concludes:

> So . . . the costs of a government's interference with the market, when undertaken in defiance of international rules, always exceed the gain of the group on whose behalf the government intervened. International rules thus can be seen to protect the interests—one would like to say rights—of societies as wholes, as well as the position of governments against organized pressure groups.[24]

Tumlir suggests that the optimal policy upon which the international economic order should be based is one of economic adjustment. He argues that economic adjustment motivated by changes in patterns of demand, sources of supply, and the development of new technologies can never be totally avoided. At best this change can only be postponed. Postponement, however, will only create greater social and political instability in the future when the need to adjust is finally acknowledged. Through economic adjustment, states can achieve economic change while maintaining political stability.

> As the world economy grows, patterns of demand change, new sources of supply emerge, availability of certain materials may decline and substitutes must be developed. It is in the increasing, uncontrollable, and sometimes radical change that human societies seek some overall stability; and such stability as they may hope for can only be attained through prompt adjustment by the economic agents affected by each manifestation of change. Attempts to block, postpone or slow down the

adjustment—in the illusion that it is possible to avoid the social and political strains which it implies—only makes the society and economy more vulnerable to the ongoing changes and sets the stage for more violent instability later on.[25]

To mitigate the political pressure aimed at blocking this industrial change, states choose to enter into international agreements. These agreements are composed of rules designed to constrain the influence of domestic pressure groups to block economic adjustment. These rules then provide the foundation for the trade regime upon which the international economic order is based. Here, some limits on the autonomy of state policy are consistent with the national interest.

Tumlir, because he sees trade as primarily contributing to economic growth and not linked directly to other foreign policy considerations, does not believe that the creation of an international trade regime need involve "an agreement transferring certain aspects of sovereignty to a supranational authority."[26] He goes on to argue that the creation of an international trade regime is in fact costless because the policy instruments that states agree to give up do not help to meet the intended policy objectives especially in the case when they are used by all states simultaneously.[27]

Tumlir's analysis is useful in that he suggests that it may not detract from the national interest when states relinquish some degree of policy autonomy in order to realize the economic benefits from trade. When Tumlir argues, however, that "nothing of practical value is given up by sovereign governments adhering to such an agreement," he obscures the domestic political costs incurred by a government when it agrees not to use an expedient, if not efficient, response to industry complaints.[28] The ability of a state to impose temporary quantitative restrictions or to raise tariffs is of significant practical value in terms of placating domestic interest groups, especially if the costs can be imposed on politically quiescent ones. In addition, in terms of international relations, states give up a practical, although expensive, means to manipulate the foreign policy of a trading partner through threatening to regulate either imports or exports.

THE INTERNATIONAL REGIME AS A REFLECTION OF THE NATIONAL INTEREST

Thus in an analysis of trade policy, political and economic costs and benefits need to be weighed against each other. Since states do not relinquish sovereignty to the international regime that regulates trade, there is nothing to prevent a participant state from deciding that the political benefits of closure outweigh the economic costs. On the other hand, a commitment to a set of rules that govern an open trading system may provide a state with additional leverage with which to resist political pressure for protection. Thus states comply with international rules to the extent that they are defined to be consistent with the national interest.

The congruence of these rules with the national interest of participant states creates the possibility for yet a third basis for an international trade regime. The first was Hirschman's policy recommendation that states transfer some part of their economic sovereignty to an international organization created to govern trade relationships among member states. The second was based on Krasner's analysis, which suggests that a hegemon will sustain an open trading system because it will benefit from both increased aggregate economic growth and increased political power relative to other states. In contrast to both Hirschman and Krasner, Tumlir argues that "it is necessary to contemplate the possibility of leaderless order, or of an order which is the common responsibility of a number of countries.[29]

This description best describes the current basis of the international economic order that is sustained by the GATT. The GATT was created to regulate trade among member states in such a way as to allow the international market to work. It is a political agreement in which the member states agree to collaborate to benefit from trade. States adhere to international rules embedded in the GATT in order to avoid the economic costs of protection. The *national interest*, then, rather than being identified with the interest of a specific sector that may be weakened by trade, is defined as the relatively efficient allocation of factors of production throughout the entire economy.

This international market creates economic pressures for

change within declining sectors. If the cause of the change is indigenous, it is seen as a part of the process of "creative destruction," essential to the process of economic growth. If, however, the cause of industrial decline can be attributed to an increase in foreign imports, imports are portrayed as undermining a state's industrial base. It is this tension between economic efficiency and the resistance to industrial change that lies at the heart of contemporary disputes over trade policy. States that choose to join the international trade regime, specifically the GATT, adhere to the rules in order to capture the aggregate gains from trade. These rules in turn help states to resist political pressures from industry groups that attempt to define *trade policy* as the interest of a specific declining sector rather than in terms of the economy as a whole.

Ultimately, the degree of openness of the international economy is based on choices made among and within nation-states. To the extent that the economic costs that attend closure are recognized by policymakers as significant, the state will resist the demands of protectionist interest groups. But the model of collective choice in Chapter 2 leads to the expectation that the interests of industries threatened by imports will be dominant because of their ability to shift the costs of the policy onto politically quiescent interest groups. This potential power of industry interest groups exists, however, in a political environment that includes an international dimension. In contrast to the domestic literature the author contends that by including the international dimension of the decision-making process it is possible to explain why the ultimate action taken by the United States in each of the three cases appears to be inconsistent with predictions based solely on the analysis of domestic interest groups.

The cases studies focus on how the GATT norms and rules are embodied in the U.S. decision-making process. GATT considerations enter into the United States's policy process through the perceptions of decision makers. The primary governmental actor in both the textile and telecommunications cases is the Office of the Special Trade Representative (STR). The STR's perceptions are colored both by continual negotiations and by interactions with other negotiators in an effort to sustain the GATT norm of progressive trade liberalization. The STR negotiators are, however, also extremely sensitive to the potential reactions of the U.S.

Congress and, because of this, continually attempt to formulate proposals with the intent of gaining congressional approval. In the auto case, the ITC has the responsibility for interpeting the GATT escape clause procedure. While the STR perceives that its role is to ensure that U.S. trade negotiations meet with congressional approval, the task of the ITC is to shield Congress from specific industry pressures.

The United States has not always adhered to a liberal economic policy. The following chapter reviews the development of U.S. trade policy to illustrate the attempts made by the United States to reconcile the domestic political costs of protection with the perceived economic benefits derived from the GATT. Specifically, it traces the development of U.S. trade policy from the unilateral determination of trade barriers (the U.S. tariff policy through the Smoot-Hawley Tariff Act of 1930) to the bilateral trade agreements program, which began in 1934. This provides a background for the creation of the multilateral trade regime in 1947. The three cases then demonstrate how the GATT rules embedded in the U.S. trade policy process reduce the ability of industrial sectors to define the national interest as their own.

NOTES

1. Albert O. Hirschman, *National Power and the Structure of Foreign Trade* (Berkeley: University of California Press, 1945), p. 13.

2. Stephen Krasner, "State Power and the Structure of International Trade," *World Politics* 28 (April 1976):317–47.

3. See Jan Tumlir, "International Economic Order: Rules, Cooperation and Sovereignty," in *Issues in International Economics*, ed. Peter Oppenheimer (London; Oriel Press, 1980), pp. 1–15: idem, "National Sovereignty, Power and Interest," *ORDO* 31(1978):1–26.; and idem, "Evolution of the Concept of International Economic Order: 1913–1980," in *Changing Perceptions of Economic Policy*, ed. Francis Cairncross (New York: Methuen, 1981), pp. 152–94.

4. The need for international collaboration to sustain a liberal international trading order is evident in the following remarks of Gerald Meier. He points out that "while the welfare economist argues the optimality of free trade, national governments are only too prone to embrace protectionist policies. Protection—rather than free trade—is the natural state in the world economy, and nationally competitive trade policies displace the mutual gains from trade. Free trade must, therefore, be enforced by some authoritative policy formation process, with an international mechanism for resolving conflicts over market access and access to

supplies." See Gerald Meier, *International Economics: The Theory of Policy* (New York: Oxford University Press, 1980), p. 122.

5. Ernst B. Haas, "Why Collaborate? Issue Linkage and International Regimes," *World Politics* 32 (April 1980): 357.

6. Ibid., p. 378.

7. Hirschman, *National Power*, p. 13.

8. Harry Johnson contends that the theory of comparative advantage implies not only that states benefit in economic terms from trade but that these economic gains can be translated into gains in political power. He argues: "No matter whether a country is absolutely strong or absolutely weak, it can maximize the power available to it by concentrating on those activities in which it is relatively more powerful and hiring the services of specialists in those activities in which it is relatively weaker." See Harry Johnson, "Technological Change and Comparative Advantage: An Advanced Country's Viewpoint," *Journal of World Trade Law* 9 (January–February 1975):1.

9. Hirschman, *National Power*, p. 14.

10. Ibid., p. 18.

11. Ibid., p. 15.

12. Ibid., p. 16.

13. Ibid., p. 32.

14. Ibid., p. 77.

15. Ibid., p. 79.

16. Hirschman describes the need for and the role of this international organization as follows. He writes: "If we want to turn from these sterile alternatives between autarky and economic penetration to the achievement of international economic collaboration, the exclusive power to organize, regulate, and interfere with trade must be taken away from the hands of single nations. It must be transferred to an international authority able to exercise this power as a sanction against an aggressor nation." Ibid., pp. 79–80.

17. Krasner posits a continuum in international economic structures between complete autarky (if all movement of goods across borders is restricted) and openness (if no restrictions exist).

18. Krasner, "State Power," p. 322.

19. Ibid., p. 320.

20. Ibid., p. 319.

21. Ibid., p. 343.

22. Jan Tumlir, "National Interest and International Order," *International Issues no. 4.* (London: Trade Policy Research Center, 1978), idem, "International Economic Order," pp. 1–15.

23. Tumlir, "National Interest and International Order," pp. 15–16.

24. Tumlir, "International Economic Order," p. 6.

25. Ibid., p. 2.

26. Tumlir, "National Interest and International Order," p. 16.

27. Competitive tariff increases lead to increased unemployment for all states owing to the loss of export markets.

28. Tumlir, "National Interest and International Order," p. 16.

29. Ibid., p. 16.

4

U.S. TRADE POLICY IN RETROSPECT

The following account traces the major changes both in the policy process and in the substantive premises upon which U.S. trade policy is based. These changes have resulted from changing perceptions of the degree to which the U.S. economy should be enmeshed in the international economy. In the 1930s policymakers came to recognize that an autonomous tariff policy was no longer politically feasible if the United States wished to benefit from international trade. This meant that in order to expand export markets through the reduction of foreign tariffs the United States had to establish a policy of negotiating tariff reductions rather than setting them autonomously.

This shift from autonomous to negotiated tariffs required a shift in the authority to set the actual tariff rates from Congress to the executive. Congress, because of its constitutional role in levying taxes, originally had the responsibility for setting the U.S. tariff because it is essentially a tax. Yet, Congress does not have the constitutional authority to enter into negotiations with foreign states. To enable the United States to negotiate tariff reductions, Congress passed the Reciprocal Trade Agreements Act of 1934. This legislation authorized the executive branch of the government to enter into bilateral trade negotiations in which the U.S. tariff could be lowered without congressional ratification. This policy shift was motivated by the belief that increased trade could help the United States pull out of the depression.

During World War II, Great Britain and the United States held negotiations in which the creation of an open international economic order based on multilateral trade negotiations and trade agreements was linked to the economic prosperity of the postwar world. The Atlantic Charter, signed in 1941 between the United States and Britain, stated that these countries would

> endeavor with due respect for their existing obligations, to further the enjoyment by all states, great or small, victors or vanquished, of access, on equal terms, to the trade and raw materials of the world which are needed for their economic prosperity, [and further that they] desired to bring about the fullest collaboration between all nations in the economic field with the object of securing, for all, improved labor standards, economic advancement and social security.[1]

The continuation of negotiations during the war over how to restructure the international economy resulted in the proposed charter for the International Trade Organization (ITO). Although the ITO was never ratified by Congress, the commercial policy chapter provided the framework for the first round of multilateral trade negotiations (MTNs). The agreement that made these negotiations binding came to be known as the General Agreement on Tariffs and Trade (GATT).

The GATT embodied the U.S. commitment to reciprocal tariff reductions formalized in the Reciprocal Trade Agreements Act of 1934. It provided member states with a framework in which to negotiate all trade agreements simultaneously. This eliminated the need to conduct a series of bilateral trade negotiations. In addition to multilateral bargaining, the GATT also provided the institutional framework for the collective monitoring of member countries' trade restraints. It further required from each member a commitment to the progressive liberalization of existing trade barriers. These factors have led to increased trade and thus increased interdependence among GATT members.

This increase in interdependence poses a pervasive tension in the GATT between those norms such as reciprocity derived from the sovereignty of member states and those that lead to increased interdependence.[2] Notwithstanding the concern of states to maintain complete sovereignty over their trade policy, the increase in interdependence that accompanies increased trade has led to the concomitant strengthening of the interdependence norms of the GATT. A GATT official had characterized this interdependence or "principle of multilateralism" upon which the GATT is based to consist of "common responsibilities, joint decisions, and international surveillance—the continuous presence of a concerned forum in which a country can complain and seek mediation for its grievances."[3]

The following discussion places the GATT in the context of the history of American trade policy through an analysis of the principles upon which U.S. trade policy is based, the political institutions in which this policy is made, and the specifics of the trade legislation. This chapter provides a background for later analysis of the impact of the GATT on U.S. business-state relations.

AMERICAN TRADE POLICY: 1922–34

The basic principles that guide contemporary American trade policy were formulated during the period between 1922 and 1934. This period begins with the Fordney-McCumber Tariff and comes to an end with the passage of the Reciprocal Trade Agreements Act of 1934. The principles of trade policy established during this period include nondiscrimination, opposition to quantitative restrictions, and negotiated tariff reductions. The following section defines these principles and demonstrates how they have been integrated into American trade legislation and policy.

The United States maintained a high autonomous tariff from 1922 through the beginning of the trade agreements program in 1934. This was a continuation of the upward trend in the level of the U.S. tariff that had begun after the Civil War. The Underwood-Simmons Act of 1913 stands as the only significant exception to this trend; here the Wilson administration attempted to return to a policy of a tariff for revenue purposes only, the traditional position of the Democratic party. World War I, however, made this legislation inoperative, because the reduction in the importation of many commodities during the war reduced trade more than any previous tariff legislation.[4]

After the end of World War I, the Republicans, the traditional protariff party, captured the presidency and increased their majority in Congress, thereby setting the stage for new tariff legislation. The party platform of 1920 had pledged to carry out "a revision of the tariff as soon as conditions shall make it necessary for the preservation of the home market for American labor, agriculture, and industry."[5] These necessary conditions soon developed in agriculture. The expansion of agriculture to accommodate increased wartime demand in conjunction with the return of European producers to their prewar production levels resulted in a tremendous worldwide overproduction of agricultural commodities. During 1920/21 the average monthly price of wheat fell from a high of $2.58 a bushel to a low of $0.93.[6]

In an attempt to counteract the declining price of agricultural goods, President Warren Harding called for "an instant tariff enactment, emergency in character and understood by our people that it is for the emergency only."[7] Congress did pass this emergency legislation for agricultural goods in the Emergency Tariff Act of 1921. In response to political pressure from industries that had expanded production to replace imports during World War I, the permanent legislation for agricultural tariffs was extended to include manufactured goods. William Kelly notes that, "the outcome was a tariff with rates higher than any in the long series of protective measures. The average rate on free and dutiable products under the Tariff Act of 1922 was more than 50% higher than under the 1913 Underwood-Simmons Tariff."[8]

Both the 1922 and the 1930 tariff acts were based on the principle that the tariff rate should equalize the foreign and domestic costs of production. This was considered to be the "flexible" provision of the legislation, as it allowed the president, in principle, to raise or lower a duty prescribed by the act by 50 percent whenever an investigation of the Tariff Commission determined that this was necessary to equalize the difference in cost of production between the United States and her primary competitors. The cost equalization principle was the only basis upon which the president could lower tariffs. Neither the 1922 nor the 1930 act contained any provision that allowed the president to negotiate treaties for the reduction of tariff rates.

The Tariff Commission came into existence in 1916. Congress created the commission to make the tariff more scientific and to remove the determination of tariff rates from politics. The scientific principle upon which the Tariff Commission was to base its determination of a tariff, the equalization of the foreign and domestic costs of production, however, was in itself biased against imports. In addition, since the cost determination was impressionistic and vague, the commissioners based their recommendations primarily on their predisposition toward trade. Kelly argues that given the impossible scientific task the commission had been given by Congress, it would have been very difficult to have had an objective commission even if its membership had been nonpartisan.[9] He goes on to suggest that after 1922 appointments to the commission were based on the politics of the appointee rather than on "open-mindedness, ability, and training"—in other words, all the appointees had protariff reputations.

Congress considered the height of the U.S. tariff to be strictly a domestic concern. Congress only regarded the tariff as an issue that concerned other countries if it was discriminatory—that is, if for an equivalent good the tariff would vary according to the country of origin. Discrimination loomed as an inevitable result of the conditional most-favored–nation (MFN) treatment in which tariff concessions were generalized to third countries only in return for "equivalent compensation." In conditional MFN treaties, discrimination results from not automatically extending to third countries negotiated bilateral tariff reductions.

The unconditional MFN clause avoids the problems involved in negotiating and determining this equivalent compensation by freely extending negotiated tariff reductions to third parties. The United States officially adopted this policy in 1923 to protect U.S. goods from being discriminated against in foreign markets. The legislative basis for the policy shift to the unconditional MFN treatment was Section 317 of the Fordney-McCumber Tariff Act of 1922, which authorized the president to impose penalty duties of up to 50 percent of the value of the good on any or all products from countries found to be discriminating against U.S. exports whenever "the public interest will be served thereby."[10] At issue in the interpretation of this statute was whether Congress differentiated between discrimination that resulted from conditional MFN agreements and intentional discrimination through the imposition of quotas on U.S. exports.

Vice-chairman of the Tariff Commission, William Culbertson, argued that Section 317 did contain a definite, if implicit, opposition to all discrimination and therefore did include the discrimination resulting from the use of the conditional form of the MFN clause. He concluded that "it would seem to follow logically that in the revision of our commercial treaties we should adopt the unconditional form of the most-favored-nation clause."[11] On the basis of this argument and with the support of Secretary of State Hughes, President Warren Harding approved the adoption of this policy in 1923. Congress did not object to the change, although it never explicitly mentioned any intent to adopt the unconditional MFN clause. When this change was first adopted, Congress had no ground for objections because the United States maintained such a high nonnegotiable tariff that the MFN policy amounted to "universal severity and universal ill treatment."[12]

Notwithstanding the U.S. policy of prohibitive tariffs—which in many cases were as restrictive as quantitative restrictions (quotas)—the United States officially opposed the use of quantitative restrictions as a means of regulating trade. The United States made this opposition formal through the ratification of the League of Nations Convention on the Abolition of Import and Export Prohibitions and Restrictions. The United States opposed quantitative restrictions because they limited the price mechanism and prevented adjustments via changes in trade volumes to take place. In addition, they were used to discriminate against American exports.

The United States continued to argue that tariffs were preferable to quotas because they offered equality of treatment and proceeded to raise them once more in 1930. This legislation, the Smoot-Hawley tariff, was the last tariff schedule compiled by Congress. Like the 1922 legislation, it was the outgrowth of a Republican administration's call for a limited tariff revision on agricultural products. Instead of being "limited," this legislation became a classic example of logrolling in Congress. The process by which the tariffs were determined further indicated the inability of Congress to pass a limited or objective tariff revision. Raymond Vernon argues that "this statute has attracted superlative abuse not alone because it set American tariffs so high, but also because the rates were set with such a single-minded concern for the wishes of specific producer groups as to shock the sense of fitness and propriety of many of those who were exposed to the process. . . . The rates in the act were, in effect, largely an expression of the relative power of lobby groups."[13] E. E. Schattschneider characterized the Smoot-Hawley Tariff as a "revision of a protectionist law by protectionists for people whom they sought to make more and more protectionist."[14] Kelly further observed

> that in many instances the Tariff Act of 1930 had no effect on the domestic market because many of its increased rates were redundant. . . . In those import-competing industries amply protected by the 1922 legislation, little further displacement of imports could result from higher tariffs.[15]

The Smoot-Hawley tariff did, however, substantially reduce U.S. exports owing to foreign retaliation. In response to the U.S. tariff increase the British expanded their system of Imperial preferences in the 1932 Ottawa agreements. Other states also joined the British in their retaliation against U.S. tariff increases. As a result, U.S. exports fell from an average of $5 billion during the 1925–29 period to about one third of that figure in 1933 and 1934.[16] This decline—75.2 percent between 1929 and 1933—was greater than the worldwide decline in trade of 54 percent during the same period.[17]

The Reciprocal Trade Agreements Act of 1934, which provided the legislative basis for U.S. trade policy from 1934 to 1962, was presented to Congress as an emergency remedy for U.S. exports. Secretary of State Cordell Hull told the House Ways and Means Committee in 1934, "The primary objective of this new proposal is both to open the old and seek new outlets for our surplus production, through the gradual moderation of the excessive and more extreme impediments to the admission of American products into foreign markets."[18]

In his message to Congress asking for this authority, Franklin Delano Roosevelt argued that it was necessary as an emergency measure because "of the startling decline of world trade entailing far-reaching unemployment at home, and because of the need for speedy action on the part of the U.S. government in altering trade terms to match quick action by foreign governments."[19] Roosevelt further contended that the executives of most foreign governments already had authority to negotiate reciprocal trade agreements and that if the United States was not to have its trade superseded, it would have to be in a position to act.[20]

The opposition argued that the sacrifice of certain domestic industries through the trade agreements program would add an additional destabilizing element into an already unstable domestic economic situation. Others opposed the legislation because it constituted an unconstitutional delegation of the power to levy taxes to the president. In addition, the opposition contended that trade protection was an integral part of the domestic recovery program.

Roosevelt, however, prevailed over the opposition and, in June 1934, signed the Reciprocal Trade Agreements Act into law. The act authorized the president to negotiate tariff reductions on a reciprocal basis when these reductions would lead to increased export opportunities for U.S. products by as much as 50 percent. As a result of this legislation, not only did the U.S. tariff become negotiable, but the rate was fixed by way of a trade agreement that did not require Senate approval. This act—the Hull program—sought

1. to secure the removal of restrictive foreign barriers to American exports;
2. to check the trend toward discriminatory trade practices of foreign countries and the uneconomic bilateralization of trade; and
3. to restore to the world a commercial system based on equal treatment.[21]

The trade agreements program was based on the principle of reciprocity, because of the protectionist bias of Congress, although unilateral tariff reductions may have led to a more rapid expansion of trade. It was "the practical considerations of political acceptability that argued strongly for reciprocal rather than unilateral action."[22] Proponents of the act argued that reciprocal tariff reductions were the most effective way to compel foreign governments to reduce trade barriers resulting from protectionist pressures and nationalistic political philosophies.

Congress retained a potential veto over the program through a provision that terminated the authority of the president to enter into trade agreements after three years. Congressional satisfaction with past performance thus became the price of continuing the program into the future. This provision applied only to the president's authority to negotiate agreements and not to the agreements themselves.

To ensure that the negotiated tariff reductions did not threaten U.S. industries, the act also stipulated that "the President shall seek information and advice with respect thereto from the United States Tariff Commission, the Departments of State, Agriculture, and Commerce and from such other sources as he may deem appropriate."[23] To implement this provision the president established an interagency committee that was known as the Interdepartmental Committee on Trade Agreements and was made up of representatives from the Departments of Agriculture, Commerce, and Treasury, the National Recovery Administration, and the Office of the Special Advisor of the President. It was given the responsibility for supervising the program and making specific recommendations to the president on the proposed trade agreements. The representative from the State Department chaired the committee.

The other major administrative committee for the trade agreements program was created to comply with the requirement in the legislation that "any interested person must have an opportunity to present his view to the President or any such agency the President must designate."[24] This committee, the Committee for Reciprocity Information, gave notice and held public hearings before the negotiation of a specific trade agreement.

The 1934 act further stipulated that the agreements had to be negotiated on an item-by-item basis, as opposed to a linear reduction of all duties by a uniform percentage. This meant that each tariff rate was negotiated individually. In determining the depth of the cut, consideration had to be given to the height of the rate, the competitive strength of the protected industry concerned, and the probable effect a duty reduction would have on it."[25] This selective approach tended to result in relatively moderate tariff reductions because they were evaluated in terms of the preferences of a particular industry rather than broadly through considerations of the national interest.

In addition to reducing the level of foreign trade restraints, the Reciprocal Trade Agreements Act also attempted to create incentives for other countries to eliminate the discriminatory treatment of American products by offering nondiscriminatory treatment in return. This was done by generalizing all tariff reductions to third countries through the use of the unconditional MFN clause. To ensure that the United States did not "give away" access to the U.S. market through the generalization of these tariff reductions, the United States only negotiated trade agreements with principal suppliers of a particular product. This negotiating strategy permitted the generalization of concessions under the MFN clause without a serious loss of bargaining leverage.

The Reciprocal Trade Agreements Act was significant in that for the first time since the Underwood-Simmons Act of 1913 U.S. tariff rates started moving downward, and the apparently irresistible drive toward increased protection was checked.[26] Most of the agreements entered into by the United States prior to World War II involved the reduction of redundant or ineffective duties, although two agreements with Canada in 1935 and 1938 and an agreement with Great Britain were important in that they made some progress in reducing the Imperial preference.[27]

THE INTERNATIONAL TRADE ORGANIZATION

Although the trade agreements program did not substantially liberalize U.S. trade policy, a comprehensive code of behavior emerged from the bilateral trade negotiations. In discussions between the Americans and the British during the war it was agreed that the multilateral adoption and enforcement of this code was the next logical step beyond bilateral agreement. After extensive negotiations, the British and the Americans drew up proposals for the ITO to be considered by an International Conference on Trade and Employment held under the auspices of the United Nations.

The ITO was designed to administer and enforce the new rules governing international trade.[28] It was to be set up as a UN organ open to all UN membership. The plans for the ITO included a permanent secretariat, which would receive outside assistance from expert advisers and technicians. The plenary power was to reside in a conference of all members, each having one vote, with the day-to-day functions administered by an 18-member executive board.

The ITO was conceived in an attempt to avoid some of the errors made during the interwar period. William Diebold suggested that two lessons from this period had an important influence in shaping the ITO Charter. The first was the belief that trade barriers were not reduced because the interwar international conferences limited themselves to the endorsement of broad principles that did nothing to prevent individual governments from acting in response to specific domestic pressures. The drafters of the ITO tried to apply this lesson by making the document detailed and including within it specific commitments to avoid particular trade practices except under certain circumstances, which they also tried to specify.[29]

The second lesson embodied in the ITO Charter was that commercial policy could not be considered by itself but had to be considered as a part of a more general program for economic and social stability. As a result, the enlarged scope of the charter includes detailed rules for tariffs, quotas, exchange controls, and state trading as well as provisions for international commodity agreements, agreements on restrictive business practices, and international investment. The charter also contains a chapter on full employment, although it did not provide detailed provisions because the participants in the negotiations could not agree on a single policy.

Initially, the United States felt very optimistic about the prospects for congressional ratification of the ITO Charter. This optimism manifests itself in the following statement by Clair Wilcox, chairman of the U.S. delegation at the preliminary negotiations over the ITO Charter in 1946.

> Of the many tasks of economic reconstruction that remain, ours is by all odds the most important. Unless we bring this work to completion, the hopes of those builders who preceded us can never be fulfilled. If the peoples who now depend upon relief are soon to become self-supporting, if those who now must borrow are eventually to re-pay, if currencies are permanently to be stabilized, if workers on farms and in factories are to enjoy the highest possible levels of real income, if standards of nutrition and health are to be raised, if cultural interchange is to bear fruit in

daily life, the world must be freed in large measure, of the barriers that
now obstruct the flow of goods and services. If political and economic
order is to be rebuilt, we must provide, in our world trade charter, the
solid foundation upon which the superstructure of international cooperation is to stand.[30]

The administration did not even send the ITO Charter to
Congress for ratification until 1949. At this point President Harry
Truman asked for a joint resolution authorizing American participation in the ITO. In Congress, however, the ITO encountered
substantial opposition both by protectionists who contended that
the ITO would be a superstate capable of directing American trade
policy and by a coalition of American business who believed that
the charter incorporated too many barriers to free trade. This
group, called the "perfectionists" by Diebold, opposed the continuation of existing preferences and the inclusion of quantitative restrictions for balance-of-payments reasons. They found the ITO
Charter to be

> a dangerous document because it accepts practically all of the politics of
> economic nationalism; because it jeopardizes the free enterprise system
> by giving priority to centralized national governmental planning of
> foreign trade; because it leaves a wide scope to discrimination, accepts
> the principle of economic insulation and in effect commits all members of
> the ITO to state planning and full employment. From the point of view of
> the U.S., it has the further grave defect of placing this country in a
> position where it must accept discrimination against itself while extend-
> ing the MFN treatment to all members of the organization. It places the
> U.S. in a permanent minority position owing to its one-vote-one-country
> procedure. Because of that, membership in the ITO based on this Char-
> ter would make it impossible for the U.S. to engage in an independent
> course of policy in favor of multilateral trade.[31]

The opposition of this group to the ITO was significant because
previously they had supported the trade agreements program.
This coalition of perfectionists and protectionists made the opposition to the ITO on the part of the business community seem more
unified than it actually was.

Richard Gardner argued that the attempt of Great Britian to
incorporate into the charter a detailed statement of its favorite
economic doctrine was the primary cause for business criticism in
the United States.

> The United States pressed formal undertakings for the elimination of the Imperial Preference, quantitative restrictions, and discrimination of all kinds. The United Kingdom pressed equally detailed undertakings to protect domestic policies of full employment. The result was an elaborate set of rules and counter-rules that offered imperfect standards for national policy. These rules and counter-rules satisfied nobody and alienated nearly everybody.[32]

When Congress finally began to consider the ITO after the final negotiations on the charter were completed in Havana during 1949, it had already begun to become disillusioned with the United Nations. In January 1950 President Truman tried to persuade Congress in his State of the Union message that the ITO Charter "is an integral part of the larger program of international reconstruction and development . . . and an essential step forward in our foreign policy."[33]

However, Congress never put the ITO Charter to a vote. In December 1950 the *State Department Bulletin* announced, "The interested agencies have recommended, and the President has agreed, that, while the proposed Charter for the International Trade Organization should not be resubmitted to the Congress, Congress be asked to consider legislation which will make American participation in the General Agreement on Tariffs and Trade more effective."[34]

THE GENERAL AGREEMENT ON TARIFFS AND TRADE

The GATT initially bound states to the tariff reductions made at the first round of the postwar MTNs. The agreement was based on the commercial policy chapter of the ITO Charter and was created to be a specific trade agreement within the broader institutional context of the ITO Charter. Some 22 countries signed the Final Act of a General Agreement on Tariffs and Trade on October 30, 1947. The first signatories intended that it would be absorbed into the ITO once the charter had been ratified by member states.

The GATT's major accomplishment centers around the organization of seven tariff conferences since 1947. These conferences, known as *rounds*, involve any contracting party willing to negotiate. The decision to conduct another round of tariff negotiations is made during an annual meeting of the member states. These tariff negotiations have been initiated typically by the United States. The first six rounds corresponded to the renewals of the Reciprocal Trade Agreements Act. The Kennedy Round was the international counterpart of the Trade Expansion Act of 1962, whereas the Tokyo Round corresponded to the Trade Reform Act of 1974.

The 1945 extension of the Reciprocal Trade Agreements Act provided the basis for the American authority to participate in the initial round of tariff reductions. This legislation, which marked a high point in congressional support for the program, authorized the president to reduce tariffs by 50 percent of the rates in effect on January 1, 1945. This negotiating authority allowed for the reduction of tariffs that had already been cut in previous bilateral trade negotiations. Congress, however, has never fully endorsed American participation in the GATT. In the 1951 extension of the trade agreements legislation, Congress included the provision that "the enactment of the Act shall not be construed to determine or indicate the approval or disapproval by the Congress of the Executive Agreement known as the General Agreement on Tariffs and Trade."[35]

To avoid the necessity for congressional ratification, the GATT was framed as a trade agreement within the meaning of the trade agreements legislation. As a result none of the member states were required to modify existing legislation that came into conflict with GATT obligations. This limitation allowed governments to accept the legal obligations of the GATT "provisionally." Except for the tariff concessions and the MFN guarantee, participating governments agreed to bind themselves only to "the fullest extent not inconsistent with existing legislation."[36] In other words, government action required by existing law would not be considered to be in violation of GATT obligations.

The participants in the initial GATT negotiations further decided not to make it a more formal international organization. This decision was initially required to help the United States claim that the GATT was merely a trade agreement, but "these legal reasons were eventually overtaken by a much more serious political concern to avoid the appearance of sneaking the ITO into effect by the back door."[37] Hence the GATT Charter did not provide for an executive body nor for a secretariat.

As the agreement made no provision for secretariat services, the GATT used the secretariat of the Interim Commission for the ITO. The secretariat was created in 1948 to prepare for the implementation of the ITO and was asked to supply the GATT with secretariat services until the ITO came into existence. After the ITO was not ratified, the secretariat continued to be affiliated with the GATT and remains the GATT's only formal link to the United Nations. The GATT secretariat publishes tariff rates, details of restrictive practices, quota arrangements, and other regulations of international trade as well as provides staff support for the tariff negotiations.

Membership in the GATT is open to any country. New members automatically benefit from the MFN tariff rates set in the previous negotiating rounds. Because of this, the GATT expects a prospective member to enter into tariff negotiations with existing contracting parties prior to receiving formal membership. Once these negotiations are completed, a country officially becomes a member upon receiving the approval of two thirds of the contracting parties. To avoid conflict between members, the GATT provides that an existing member is not required to extend MFN treatment to a new member. The Charter states that "the Agreement would not apply as between any two contracting parties which had not entered into tariff negotiations with each other, either of which, at the time either became a Contracting Party, did not consent to such application."[38] In addition, the GATT possesses no powers of expulsion.

Until the Kennedy Round the tariff negotiations were conducted on an item-by-item basis. To begin the negotiations, the principal suppliers of a product would submit lists of requests for tariff reductions to their trading partners.[39] After the request lists had been received, each participant made a list of offers that it was willing to make. These offer lists were sent simultaneously by the secretariat to only those other countries that submitted offer lists.

Members negotiated two at a time until the final agreement was reached. The final tariff rates that resulted from these bilateral negotiations were then automatically generalized to all members of the GATT through the MFN clause. Subsidiary suppliers—not directly involved in the tariff negotiations—were expected to provide a small concession in exchange for their windfall gains resulting from the MFN clause.[40]

Participants, however, are not obligated to make a concession. Yet, countries seem more likely to make concessions in a multilateral context because before the negotiations begin each country knows what the others are willing to offer. If the offer of an individual country is not enough in itself, the knowledge that a second or third country is willing to pay something too for a given concession allows the negotiations to open under more propitious auspices than might have been the case in a classical bilateral situation.[41]

Although the MFN clause and the resulting nondiscrimination is considered to be the cornerstone of the GATT, the agreement does allow for some exceptions. The GATT allows quantitative restrictions (quotas) for the purpose of resolving a balance-of-payments shortage. The agreement included this provision because when it was first formulated, several members had a severe shortage of foreign exchange and were concerned about having insufficient dollar reserves to pay for imports. To reduce the political tension that could result from this foreign exchange constraint, the GATT stipulated that "a contracting party may impose quantitative restrictions either to forestall the imminent threat of, or to stop, a serious decline in its monetary reserves, or in the case of a contracting party with very low monetary reserves, to achieve a reasonable state of increase of its reserves."[42] The General Agreement does, however, obligate those contracting parties who do invoke quantitative restrictions to relax import restrictions as the balance-of-payments improves, to consult with other members upon request, and to apply the restrictions on any given product in a nondiscriminatory manner, to the extent this is possible.

The fact that the agreement does allow quantitative restrictions in exceptional circumstances indicates the pragmatic character of the organization. Gerard Curzon and Victoria Curzon argue that the "GATT was never intended to be more than a flexible and pragmatic document representing the maximum that countries were prepared to agree upon when it was signed."[43]

This pragmatism is also reflected in the absence of any explicit provisions for violations in the agreement. A contracting party can, however, claim that it is not deriving full benefit from adherence to the agreement as a result of another contracting party failing to carry out its obligations or by the application of any measure, whether or not it conflicts with the provisions of the GATT.[44] Thus the nullification and impairment of benefits derived from the GATT need not be the result of an explicit infringement of the agreement. This clause was originally included to deal with governmental measures not covered by the agreement that reduce the anticipated commercial benefits of tariff concessions.

In the case of nullification and impairment the GATT requires the countries involved in the dispute to engage in bilateral consultations outside of a formal framework. If they do not work out a satisfactory resolution on a bilateral basis, a panel of conciliation chosen from among the delegates is appointed. This panel examines the complaint and makes recommendations for the resolution of the dispute. If the countries involved do not accept the recommendations, the member that filed the complaint can ask for the authority to retaliate by way of withdrawing concessions. The Contracting Parties can authorize this action by a majority vote. Typically, these measures are not necessary, and panels of conciliation resolve the majority of disputes at the GATT.

THE TRADE AGREEMENTS PROGRAM: 1947–58

The renewal of the trade agreements legislation gave the president the authority to engage in multilateral tariff reductions at the GATT. Vernon, in his analysis of the influence of the GATT on American foreign policy, argues that this multilateral context for tariff reductions did in fact result in greater tariff reductions than would have been the case under bilateral negotiations. He contends that the reduction in American tariff levels between 1948 and 1953 "which perforce bit into more sensitive segments of the American tariff structure than the earlier reductions had done, could have only been achieved in the exceptionally favorable circumstances which a multilateral negotiation provides for such reductions. . . . Some of the more important reductions, such as in the wool tariff, required courageous political decisions, taken in the interest of the nation as a whole and in the face of strong antagonistic domestic interests."[45]

At the same time the United States was negotiating multilateral reductions in tariff levels, Congress changed the trade agreements program to ensure that these tariff reductions did not pose a competitive threat to sectors of the U.S. economy. The most important of these changes involved the escape clause and peril point provisions.

The Escape Clause

The first modification of American trade policy prior to the first GATT negotiations was implemented by way of an executive order in 1947 that established procedures for dealing with escape clause applications. During the 1945 renewal debate, the administration agreed to incorporate the escape clause into all future bilateral and multilateral trade agreements without formal congressional action, although formal procedures by which applications would be filed and considered were never established. The executive order required that the United States must permit the withdrawal or modification of tariff reductions "if, as the result of unforeseen developments, the concession granted by the U.S. on any article in the trade agreement is imported in increased quantities and under conditions which cause or threaten injury to domestic producers of the same or similar articles."[46] It further authorized the Tariff Commission to conduct investigations of applications for escape clause action and to make a recommendation to the president, who would ultimately decide whether to grant the industry relief "in light of the public interest."[47]

The 1953 and 1954 trade agreements legislation did not introduce any significant changes into the escape clause. In 1955, however, Congress amended the escape clause to make it easier for the Tariff Commission to find injury. Instead of having to demonstrate that the entire industry was injured, under the new provision the industry could request trade protection for a specific product if it could show injury, even though the industry as a whole was holding its own against imports.

The 1955 act also added a new escape clause provision related to considerations of national security. This required the director of Defense Mobilization to advise the president whenever he believed that a product was being imported into the United States in such quantities as to threaten national security. If the president concurred, an investigation would be held to determine whether a threat to national security did exist. If, on the basis of such an investigation, the president found that the article was being imported in such quantities as to impair the national security, he could take action to adjust the import of the article to a level that would reduce the threat.[48]

The 1958 Trade Renewal Act included even more stringent protectionist provisions to the escape clause. In this legislation the law was changed to allow an industry to request a tariff increase of up to 50 percent of the 1934 rates. This would allow for substantially higher rate increases, as the previous base had been the 1945 tariff schedule. In addition, the legislation also required that if the president decided against a recommendation, his order could be overruled by Congress within 60 days by a concurrent resolution of two thirds of each house.

During the 1947–61 period, 131 applications were filed for escape clause relief. In 40 of these cases the majority of the Tariff Commission's six members found injury. The president increased tariffs in 13 cases and rejected the findings of the commission in the others. Congress did not overrule these objections. In part this was due to the ambiguity of the rationale for the commissioners' determination of the relationship among imports, the tariff concession, and the condition of the domestic injury. The interpretation of the escape clause also varied among commissioners. Those commissioners who believed that the escape clause should function to protect existing patterns of production interpreted "a shift from the production of one article to the manufacture of another to be positive evidence of serious injury even if the article was already produced by the firms concerned."[49] The absence of any consensus upon which to evaluate these cases did not leave Congress with any definitive principle upon which to oppose the president's decision.

The Peril Point

During the 1951 renewal debate, protectionists in Congress concerned by the tariff reductions negotiated at the GATT and by the lack of criteria with which to determine relief in escape clause cases succeeded in including the peril point provision in the trade agreements legislation. The peril point had been a part of the 1948 legislation and repealed in 1949. Tariff levels under the peril point indicated that the industry would probably be injured by imports. These peril points were determined by the Tariff Commission in advance of the negotiations and were in principle the best offer U.S. negotiators could make without having to explain the reductions to Congress.

To determine the peril point, the president was required to furnish the Tariff Commission with a list of all products on which the United States was considering negotiating concessions.[50] The Tariff Commission was then required to hold public hearings and to report to the president the limit to which a tariff could be reduced without causing injury to a domestic industry. If the president chose not to go along with the recommendations of the Tariff Commission, he was required to report his reasons to the House Ways and Means Committee and the Senate Finance Committee.

Although protectionists argued that under the peril point procedures the Tariff Commission would set appropriate rates based on economic criteria, opponents of the provision questioned the belief that tariffs could be determined scientifically. The administration also believed that no precise tariff rate could be determined in advance of any negotiations because tariff reductions were considered in terms of the benefits to be gained from concessions received as well as in terms of general foreign policy considerations.[51]

The escape clause added an element of uncertainty to the trade agreements negotiated by the United States because importers were afraid that an increase in imports would trigger an escape clause action. It was, however, the peril point provision that brought the Reciprocal Trade Agreements program to an end because in the hearings to determine the peril points U.S. offers were always made public before the negotiations ever began. This put U.S. negotiators at too great a disadvantage in the MTNs. Even though the president did not always adhere to the recommendations of the Tariff Commission, the use of peril points severely restricted the ability of the American negotiators to offer equal concessions. This became a serious problem at the Dillon Round of the GATT (1960–62) when the European Economic Community (EEC) was compelled to settle for "adequate reciprocity" pending the outcome of a further round of negotiations in which they expected the United States to be in a position to negotiate on a reciprocal basis.[52]

THE TRADE EXPANSION ACT OF 1962

The Trade Expansion Act of 1962 replaced the Reciprocal Trade Agreements Act of 1934. In support of this change John Kennedy argued that the Trade Agreements Program had become obsolete as a result of the restrictions that had been added during the renewals of the legislation. In addition, he believed that new negotiating methods were necessary to deal with the EEC because the EEC could not negotiate as a single entity except on the basis of linear tariff cuts.

The new legislation allowed the executive to change from the item-by-item to the linear (across-the-board) method of tariff negotiations. The legislation further granted the executive the authority to reduce duties up to 50 percent of their July 1962 level and to eliminate tariffs on products dutiable at 5 percent or less. Anticipating British accession to the EEC before the Kennedy Round, the act also included a provision that allowed for the elimination of tariffs on industrial products within categories in which the United States and the EEC together accounted for 80 percent of the value of free world exports during a representative period.[53] If Britain did not become a member of the Common Market, the only item that would still meet this 80 percent test was aircraft. When France vetoed Britain's membership in January 1963, this dominant supplier provision became irrelevant.

In addition to the introduction of linear tariff cuts, the 1962 act included two other innovations in American trade policy. For the first time the trade program offered adjustment assistance to firms and workers injured by imports. Under this provision individual firms and workers could petition the Tariff Commission for an investigation to determine whether they were eligible for adjustment assistance. If the Tariff Commission found serious injury or the threat of serious injury, to obtain assistance the firm was required to present an adjustment proposal to the secretary of commerce. Once approved, the firm became eligible to receive technical assistance, financial assistance in the form of loans or loan guarantees, and tax assistance that would include special carry-backs and carryovers of operating losses.[54] Groups of workers, designated by the secretary of labor to be entitled to adjustment assistance, could receive retraining and relocation allowances as well as unemployment compensation of up to 65 percent of a worker's average weekly wage for one year.[55]

The second major innovation was that the coordination of all U.S. trade negotiations was centralized in the new Office of the Special Trade Representative (STR). The STR received the designation of the chief representative of the United States in the negotiation of any trade agreement (both bilateral and multilateral) and served as chairman of the Cabinet-level interagency trade committee, the Trade Policy Committee. This committee was created to recommend basic policies in trade agreement matters, including escape clause and relief actions, as well as to suggest possible U.S. responses to foreign import restrictions.[56] Previously, the United States had been represented at negotiations by teams headed by the State Department. Congress established the position of the STR in response to industry and congressional complaints that the State Department had not been sufficiently responsive to the interests of industries injured by imports.

Prior to U.S. participation in trade negotiations, the STR was required to compile a public list of commodities that were being considered for tariff negotiations. The president sent this list to the Tariff Commission, which had to determine and then inform the president within six months of the probable economic effects of the proposed tariff cuts. This broader economic assessment of the proposed tariff reductions replaced the peril point provisions.

After presidential approval of this list, public hearings were to be held by the Trade Information Committee on the impact of the tariff cuts on U.S. industries.[57] Only after these hearings could the STR recommend to the president those tariff cuts that the United States was willing to negotiate. Upon approval of the final list by the president, U.S. negotiators could enter into MTNs.

Notwithstanding the care with which the U.S. list was to be

drawn up, the trade act included an elaborate escape clause provision in case a concession resulted in an unanticipated influx of imports. This act eliminated the segmentation clause, which allowed the industry to request protection for a specific product and made it relatively easy for firms to claim injury. The removal of this allowed, although did not ensure, a broader definition of *the industry* than had previously existed.[58] In addition, *injury* was redefined so that imports injuring or threatening to injure an industry had to be "in major part" the result of trade agreement concessions. The previous definition of *injury* allowed for the use of tariff increases to offset disadvantageous factors other than imports, such as technological changes.[59] Under the new law increased imports had to be the major cause of injury to an industry.

Once the Tariff Commission presented its report to the president, he could evoke the escape clause and impose a quota or increase duties of up to 50 percent of the 1934 rate, negotiate an orderly marketing agreement with exporting countries in which they "voluntarily" agree to limit exports, or authorize the firms and workers in the injured industry to request adjustment assistance.[60] The president could also reject the determination of injury made by the Tariff Commission. If he chose to elect this option, he had to report his reasons to Congress. This decision could be overruled by a majority vote of the total membership of both houses within 60 days of receiving the report. Previously, the law allowed this kind of resolution to be brought to the floor of Congress by any member without going through committee—that is, the resolution was given privileged status. This, however, needed a two-thirds majority to override the decision of the president and was never used.

The Trade Expansion Act provided the authority for the United States to enter into the Kennedy Round of the GATT negotiations. The decision to hold another round of tariff negotiations was made at a meeting of the Contracting Parties where they resolved that "a significant liberalization of world trade is desirable, and . . . for this purpose, comprehensive trade negotiations, to be conducted . . . on the principle of reciprocity, shall begin at Geneva on 4 May 1964, with the widest possible participation."[61]

THE KENNEDY ROUND

The actual negotiations at the Kennedy Round began with each participant presenting a list of exceptions to the 50 percent linear cut that had been agreed upon in the preliminary negotiations. A period followed in which these exceptions were justified. John Evans, in his discussion of the Kennedy Round, notes that "after the linear participants had expended a decent quota of time and energy on the justification procedures, the negotiation of industrial tariffs moved to the bilateral stage."[62] Most of the negotiations remained bilateral until the participants reached the final agreement.

The weighted average of the Kennedy Round reductions on nonagricultural items came out about 35 percent of the prenegotiation rates for the linear countries. The reductions were less in those countries that chose not to engage in linear tariff reductions and for those products that had been negotiated by sector.[63] The United States reduced tariffs on about 65 percent of its total dutiable imports. This reduction proved greater than 1947 negotiations in which tariffs were reduced on about 54 percent of total dutiable imports.[64]

THE TRADE ACT OF 1974

The proliferation of nontariff barriers mitigated the success of the Kennedy Round tariff reductions. Although the use of nontariff barriers (NTBs) may not have increased after the Kennedy Round, the reduction of tariffs made them more important than they had been in the past. Thomas Curtis, the House delegate to the Kennedy Round, stated in a speech before the National Foreign Trade Council:

> Many of us like to think that the decades since the war have been marked by a continuing movement toward freer world trade and payments. The Kennedy Round in this vision is seen by shortsighted persons as the crowning achievement of the drive forward for freer trade, but they have ignored the fact that as tariffs have been dismantled . . . quotas, licenses, embargoes, and other rigid and restrictive trade barriers have been created.[65]

Other members of the GATT shared this concern about NTBs to trade, and within five months after the conclusion of the Kennedy Round the Contracting Parties set out a "Programme of Work" to begin preparations for the next round of negotiations. This program specifically called for comprehensive studies of tariff barriers as well as NTBs affecting industrial trade. A 1976 staff report prepared by the Senate Finance Committee defined NTBs to be

> those policies of national governments which are intended to protect domestic markets from imports through nontariff means, for example, quotas, and onerous customs procedures. In addition, nontariff measures include domestic policies which, intentionally or unintentionally, result in the cost of national programs being imposed on foreign nations or foreign persons rather than on the citizens or governments of the country which established the program. Examples of the latter kind of nontariff measure are export subsidies, regional incentive programs, government procurement restrictions, product standards, environmental standards, and packaging and labeling requirements.[66]

The intent of the Contracting Parties in the following trade negotiations was to establish rules to reduce the extent to which these NTBs restricted international trade.

In 1974 Congress passed the Trade Reform Act, which provided the legislative basis for the United States to participate in the Tokyo Round of the GATT. This act allowed for a 50 percent reduction of the post−Kennedy Round tariffs and for the elimination of tariffs less than 5 percent. The act also granted the president the authority to enter into agreements on NTBs. These agreements, however, had to be submitted to Congress, which could only approve them without amendment.

Like the 1962 act, the Trade Act of 1974 designated the Tariff Commission to investigate the probable economic effect of tariff concessions on a list of products drawn up by the president. The legislation also made it easier for firms to claim injury in escape clause hearings by making it unnecessary to link injury to tariff concessions. The demonstration of injury as the result of import competition was sufficient. In addition, imports only had to comprise a *substantial* cause of injury, which in this context was defined to be greater than any single other cause. The previous act required that imports account for at least 51 percent of injury—that is, be greater than all other causes combined. The act also reintroduced the segmentation rule so that in the determination of injury the industry could be very narrowly defined.

Once presented with the decision of the Tariff Commission on injury and its recommendations for relief, the president was required to decide within 60 days (120 in the case of a tie vote) whether to evoke the escape clause and grant import relief through tariff increases, the negotiation of orderly marketing agreements, the imposition of quotas, or any combination of these measures. The president could also direct the secretary of labor to give favorable consideration to workers' petitions for adjustment assistance. If he decided not to follow the recommendations of the Tariff Commission, he was required to report his reasons to Congress, which retained oversight authority.

The 1974 act also included provisions for the creation of an elaborate system of industry, labor, and agriculture advisory committees. Business groups suggested—in support of the need for these committees—that in the past the multilateral negotiations had been characterized by the absence of a two-way dialogue between industry and government beyond the exchange of data requested by the government. Arguments were also made in the Senate that to remain competitive with other participants in the MTNs the United States needed the assistance of industry representatives. During the Senate Finance Committee hearings, Senator Herman Talmadge spoke for the need to remedy the situation: "The American business people who had some knowledge of international trade were excluded totally from our negotiations, while the Japanese, the Germans, and the French, and the European Economic Community had the best industrial team that was available at the hands of the negotiators day and night to give expert advice."[67]

In response to these remarks, Secretary of Commerce Frederick Dent reported that the Commerce Department had already canvassed 600 industry representatives in an attempt to determine how to set up effective consultation procedures and who would serve on the committees. The legislation ultimately designated the president to appoint a general policy advisory committee for industry, labor, and agriculture to provide policy advice on the trade

negotiations. In addition, the president could appoint sector committees at the request of a specific product sector if he found it to be
necessary to facilitate the progress of the multilateral negotiations.

THE TOKYO ROUND

Although the Tokyo Round concentrated primarily on NTBs, some
tariff reduction by way of a linear tariff cut did result from the
negotiations. The majority of the debate over these reductions
concerned the formula to be used to determine the depth of the
tariff cut. The result constituted a compromise between the EEC's
preference for harmonization, which required that higher tariffs be
reduced by a higher percentage than lower tariffs, and the American proposal, which would have reduced all tariffs by an equal
percentage, that is, a straight linear cut. The outcome of these
negotiations was an average reduction of tariffs on manufactured
goods by the industrialized countries of 26.4 percent.[68]

The codes, unlike the tariff reductions, only bound those
countries that signed the agreements. The government procurement code and the subsidy countervailing duties code stand out as
the most important codes negotiated at the Tokyo Round. The
government procurement code—unlike most of the codes on NTBs,
which were negotiated to avoid protectionist measures—was an
attempt to liberalize international trade.[69] This agreement established a framework for the equality of treatment for foreign and
domestic suppliers in government procurement contracts through:

1. Making information available through foreign sources on the rules of
   bidding;
2. Providing adequate time for foreign suppliers to prepare bids; and
3. Publishing both the winning bids and the winners of the bids.

These requirements were designed to ensure that all prospective
suppliers, not only domestic ones, had the same information and
the same chances of winning the contract.[70]

The code did not include all areas of state purchasing. The
United States excluded defense procurement as well as procurement by the Departments of Energy and Transportation, the Postal

Service, the Tennessee Valley Authority, and Amtrak. Moreover, the code only covered purchases over $190,000. The specific areas of coverage were negotiated on a bilateral basis, and its provisions would not apply either to nonsignatories or to signatories that had not arrived at a mutual bilateral arrangement.[71]

The subsidy countervailing duty code qualifies as perhaps the most important agreement negotiated at the Tokyo Round. It also generated the most controversy. This code permits the imposition of countervailing duties equal to the amount of the subsidy when it can be demonstrated that the imports in question did benefit from a subsidy and that these imports caused "material injury" to the domestic industry. The EEC considered this injury clause to be an improvement over the previous U.S. legislation, which did not require an injury test. In compensation for this concession the United States requested that the code include a more precise definition of *export subsidies* as well as the agreement that signatories would not use domestic subsidies, which could distort trading patterns.

Owing to the need to include the injury test, the subsidy countervailing duty code required the most changes to make U.S. law consistent with the obligations contained in the agreement. The new U.S. law stipulated that the Department of Treasury (this has since been changed to the Department of Commerce) would first determine whether an import was directly or indirectly subsidized upon receipt of a complaint from the industry affected. Once the department makes this determination, the ITC (formerly the Tariff Commission), by designation, conducts an investigation to determine whether the industry had incurred or had been threatened with material injury.[72] This determination relies on evidence that suggests that there has been a fall in output of a product and that this decline was brought about by the subsidized imports. This legislation constitutes a new provision of U.S. law separate from the current U.S. countervailing duty statute to apply only to other signatories of the code. This change, as well as the others necessary to bring American law into conformity with the GATT codes, was included in the Trade Agreements Act of 1979, passed by Congress on July 26, 1979.

To facilitate the implementation of the GATT codes, the United States also reorganized the trade bureaucracy. A White House fact sheet announced that the intent of this trade reorganization was to "expand exports, improve enforcement of the U.S. trade law and otherwise upgrade the government's trade activities in response to the MTN agreements."[73] President Jimmy Carter explained in this trade reorganization message to Congress that changes were necessary both to implement the MTN codes in the United States and to monitor the implementation efforts abroad "reporting back to American business important developments about foreign implementation."[74]

The reorganization plan involved centralizing policy development, coordination, and negotiating functions in the Office of the Special Trade Representative and making the Commerce Department the focus of nonagricultural trade policy implementation. While the STR would retain the lead policy role with respect to the escape clause and market disruption cases, the Commerce Department would investigate antidumping and countervailing duty petitions, administer the export licensing program, and conduct national security investigations. Previously, these responsibilities had been under the jurisdiction of the Treasury Department. The reorganization also involved the expansion of the functions of the Trade Policy Committee to include coordinating policy on import remedies, energy trade issues, East-West trade policy, international investment policy, and international commodity negotiations. A Trade Negotiation Committee was created to coordinate the implementation of the negotiating objectives set by the Trade Policy Committee.

This reorganization reflected a movement in the United States toward a more conservative trade policy stance. The dissatisfaction of Congress with the lack of interest that the Treasury had shown in determining whether imported goods were subsidized prompted the shift from the Treasury to the Commerce Department of the subsidy countervailing duty determinations. While the Treasury Department has the reputation of supporting liberal trade policies because they are antiinflationary, the Commerce Department has the reputation of supporting the interests of industry in bids for protection. The Council of Economic Advisors (CEA) tends to agree with the Treasury, again because of its concern with the cost of protection. The State Department also supports open trading policies—but for reasons different from the Treasury and the CEA.

It identifies the national interest with international stability in the economic relations of the United States. Thus it opposes most potential import restraints because they would disrupt the trade flows of other nations. The Department of Labor, given its concern with American jobs, tends to side with the Commerce Department in discussions over whether the United States should impose trade restraints. The Office of the Special Trade Representative sees Congress as its main constituency. Its overall orientation is toward the maintenance of an open trade regime, although the STR negotiators remain sensitive to congressional reaction to a particular trade agreement.

The most prominent conflict over questions of U.S. trade policy within the executive branch appears to be between the Office of the Special Trade Representative, acting as the proponent of a liberal trade policy, and the Department of Commerce, which has been advocating a more nationalist trade orientation for the United States. This conflict manifested itself in the debate over the 1982 reciprocity trade bill. This bill sought to ensure that U.S. goods enjoy access to foreign markets equivalent to that the U.S. market offers to foreign goods. To accomplish this, the legislation threatened to restrict the U.S. market to Japanese goods as a way to put pressure on Japan to liberalize its trade policy. Initially, the Commerce Department openly supported the bill.[75] The STR did not endorse the bill because of its protectionist bias.[76] In objecting to the bill, William Brock, chief STR, noted that "it would violate the GATT and could spark retaliation by other countries."[77]

Although Congress did not pass this bill, there remains in the United States an increasing tension between the political forces for trade protection and for trade liberalization. To date, however, the GATT appears to have helped to sustain an open trade policy within the United States. In turn, the United States has supported the GATT. The following three case studies provide evidence of U.S. adherence to the GATT trading regime.

NOTES

1. William Brown, *The United States and the Restoration of World Trade* (Washington D.C.: Brookings Institution, 1950), p. 47.

2. This distinction between "sovereignty norms" and "interdependence norms" is made by Jock A. Finlayson and Mark W. Zacher in "The GATT and Regulation of Trade Barriers: Regime Dynamics and Functions," *International Organization* 35 (Autumn 1981): 561–602. Here they state that regime norms "can be distinguished according to whether they are derived from the traditional structure of international politics (sovereignty norms), or from international interdependencies in particular issue areas that incline states to maximize welfare through collaboration (interdependence norms)" (p. 564).

3. Ibid., p. 597.

4. William B. Kelly, Jr., "Antecedents of Present Commercial Policy, 1922–1934," in *Studies in United States Commercial Policy*, ed. William B. Kelly, Jr. (Chapel Hill: University of North Carolina Press, 1963), p. 3.

5. Ibid., p. 7.

6. Ibid., p. 7.

7. Ibid., p. 7.

8. Ibid., p. 7.

9. Ibid., p. 21.

10. Ibid., p. 38.

11. Ibid., p. 39.

12. Ibid., p. 52.

13. Ray Vernon, "America's Foreign Trade Policy and the GATT," *Essays in International Finance*, no. 21 (Princeton: Princeton University Press, October 1954), p. 2.

14. E. E. Schattschneider, *Politics, Pressures, and the Tariff* (Hamden, Conn.: Archon Books, 1963), p. 99.

15. Kelly, "Antecedents," p. 12.

16. William Diebold, *New Directions in Our Trade Policy* (New York: Council on Foreign Relations, 1941), p. 6.

17. Grace Beckett, *The Reciprocal Trade Agreements Program* (New York: Columbia University Press, 1941), p. 2.

18. Diebold, *New Directions*, p. 7.

19. Beckett, *Reciprocal Trade Agreements Program*, p. 9.

20. Roosevelt's message to Congress included the following statement: "Other governments are to an ever increasing extent winning their share of international trade by negotiated, reciprocal trade agreements. If American agricultural and industrial interests are to retain their deserved place in this trade, the American Government must be in a position to bargain for that place with other governments by rapid and decisive negotiation based upon a carefully considered program, and to grant with discernment corresponding opportunities in the American market for foreign products supplementary to our own. If the American Government is not in a position to make fair offers at a given moment rapidly to alter the terms on which it is willing to deal with other countries, it cannot adequately protect its trade against discrimination and against bargains injurious to its interests. U.S., Congress, Senate, *Reciprocal Trade Agreements*, 73d Cong., 2d Sess., April 26, 1934, S. Rept. 871, p. 8.

21. Diebold, *New Directions*, p. 6.

22. Harry Hawkins and Janet Norwood, "The Legislative Basis of United States Commercial Policy," in *Studies in United States Commercial Policy*, ed. William B. Kelly, Jr. (Chapel Hill: University of North Carolina Press, 1963), p. 73.

23. Ibid., p. 110.

24. Steven Robert Brenner, "Economic Interests and the Trade Agreements Program, 1937–1940: A Study in Institutions and Political Influence" (Ph.D. diss., Stanford University, 1977), p. 100.

25. Hawkins and Norwood, "Legislative Basis," p. 73

26. Diebold, *New Directions*, p. 23.

27. Charles Kindleberger, *The World in Depression: 1929–1939* (Berkeley: University of California Press, 1973), p. 238.

28. The ITO was one of three UN special agencies that were created to deal directly with international economic relations. The other two were the International Monetary Fund, which was established to manage the system of fixed exchange rates, and the International Bank for Reconstruction and Development. The bank, known now as the World Bank, was set up to "promote the long-range balanced growth of international trade . . . by encouraging international investment for the development of the productive resources of members." This description is taken from Harold Jacobson, *Networks of Interdependence: International Organization and the Global Political System* (New York: Alfred A. Knopf, 1979), p. 236.

29. William Diebold, "The End of the ITO," *Essays in International Finance*, no. 16 (Princeton: Princeton University, 1952), pp. 11–12.

30. Ibid., p. 4.

31. Ibid., p. 20–21.

32. Richard Gardner, *Sterling Dollar Diplomacy: The Origins and Prospects of Our International Economic Order* (New York: Columbia University Press, 1980), p. 379.

33. Diebold, "The End of the ITO," p. 2.

34. Gardner, *Sterling Dollar Diplomacy*, p. 348. This passage is taken from the *State Department Bulletin* 23 (1950): 977.

35. Robert Hudec, *The GATT Legal System and World Trade Diplomacy* (New York: Praeger, 1975), p. 356.

36. Ibid., pp. 45–46.

37. Ibid., p. 46.

38. Gerard Curzon, *Multilateral Commercial Diplomacy* (London: Michael Joseph, 1965), p. 39.

39. Ibid., p. 72.

40. Gerard Curzon and Victoria Curzon, "GATT: A Trader's Club," in *The Anatomy of Influence: Decision Making in International Organizations*, ed. Robert Cox and Harold Jacobson (New Haven: Yale University Press, 1974), p. 73.

41. Curzon, *Multilateral Commercial Diplomacy*, p. 73.

42. Kenneth Dam, *The GATT: Law and International Economic Organization* (Chicago: University of Chicago Press, 1970), p. 151.

43. Curzon and Curzon, "GATT," p. 299.

44. Curzon, *Multilateral Commercial Diplomacy*, p. 42.

45. Vernon "America's Foreign Trade Policy," p. 8.

46. Hawkins and Norwood, "Legislative Basis," p. 78.

47. The American escape clause was incorporated into Article 19 of the GATT.

48. John M. Ledy and Janet L. Norwood, "The Escape Clause and Peril Points under the Trade Agreements Program," in *Studies in United States Commercial Policy*, ed. William B. Kelly, Jr. (Chapel Hill: University of North Carolina Press, 1963), p. 141.

49. Ibid., p. 153.

50. Ibid., p. 129.

51. Ibid., p. 131.

52. Gerard Curzon and Victoria Curzon, "The Management of Trade Relations in the GATT," in *International Economic Relations of the Western World: 1959–1971*, ed. Andrew Shonfield (London: Royal Institute of International Affairs, 1976), p. 174.

53. Ledy and Norwood, "Escape Clause and Peril Points," p. 115.

54. Hawkins and Norwood, "Legislative Basis," p. 121.

55. Ledy and Norwood, "Escape Clause and Peril Points," p. 115.

56. *Congressional Quarterly Weekly Report*, June 1, 1962, p. 930.

57. Thomas Curtis and John Vastine, *The Kennedy Round and the Future of American Trade* (New York: Praeger, 1971), p. 11.

58. Hawkins and Norwood, "Legislative Basis," p. 120.

59. Ledy and Norwood, "Escape Clause and Peril Points," p. 160.

60. Hawkins and Norwood, "Legislative Basis," p. 129.

61. Dam, *The GATT*, p. 72.

62. John W. Evans, *The Kennedy Round in American Trade Policy: The Twilight of the GATT?* (Cambridge, Mass: Harvard University Press, 1971), p. 72.

63. Ibid., pp. 282–84.

64. Ibid., p. 281.

65. Ibid., p. 305.

66. U.S. Congress. Senate. Finance Committee. Subcommittee on International Trade, *Multilateral Trade Negotiation Studies #6 Part 1*. 96th Cong., 1st Sess., August 1979, p. 12.

67. U.S. Congress. Senate. Finance Committee. *Hearings on the 1974 Trade Act*, 93d Cong., 1st Sess., March-April 1974, p. 224.

68. Stephen Krasner, "The Tokyo Round: Particularistic Interests and Prospects in the Global Trading System," *International Studies Quarterly* 23 (December 1979):510.

69. *World Business Weekly*, March 3, 1980, p. 14.

70. Ibid.

71. For a discussion of the U.S.-Japan bilateral negotiations over the government procurement code, see Chapter 7.

72. *World Business Weekly*, February 11, 1980, p. 14.

73. U.S. Office of the White House Press Secretary, *White House Fact Sheet*, July 19, 1979, p. 1. (mimeo)

74. *Congressional Quarterly Weekly Report*, September 29, 1979, p. 2165.

75. Art Pine, "Trade Representative Brock Battles Threat of Protectionism in U.S., Other Countries," *Wall Street Journal*, March 23, 1982, p. 56.

76. The Commerce Department ultimately backed off when the Reagan administration decided not to support the bill.

77. Art Pine, "Compromise Bill on Trade 'Reciprocity' Developed by Administration, Senators," *Wall Street Journal*, May 20, 1982, p. 10.

5

TEXTILES
The Politics of Protection

INTRODUCTION

The textile and apparel industry in the United States has been one of the most effective in persuading the government of the need for import restraints. One out of eight industrial jobs in the United States is in the textile and apparel industry, which employs over 2.25 million workers. In defense of the need for import restraints, the industry argues that the increase in foreign textile and apparel imports threatens these jobs.

When lobbying for trade restraints, the industry primarily emphasizes the impact of trade upon U.S. employment. Rodney Grey, a Canadian textile negotiator, suggests that this concern with employment obscures the possibility that trade protection is primarily a response to the political strength of the industry. He contends, "This is a policy where, for the time being at any rate, economics can only be understood as politics."[1] A Treasury Department memo on trade and adjustment also reflects this view: "Perhaps the most convincing argument put forward by the textile industry has been that they have the political power to obtain import protection."[2]

Interest group politics plays a prominent role in this case. U.S. trade negotiators were convinced that the coalition of the textile and apparel industries had the political strength to block the ratification of the Tokyo Round trade agreements. The political strength of the industry in Congress stems in part from its dispersion throughout most congressional districts in the United States. The industry draws its ability to take advantage of this geographic dispersion from a well-organized coalition of trade associations and labor groups. The American Textile Manufacturers' Institute ranks as the industry's preeminent trade association. It works together with the American Apparel Association and 15 other unions and trade associations, which together make up the textile and apparel steering group. Through the steering group, these organizations coordinate their political activities directed at import restraint.

This case offers the least support for the Raymond Bauer, Ithiel de Sola Pool, and Lewis Dexter's contention that congressional autonomy provides the basis for the politics of U.S. trade policy. The findings here differ dramatically from the description of the latent sentiment in favor of textile protection in "Textiletown," which had been dependent upon textile mills for employment. They characterized Textiletown as still committed to protectionism but at the same time more interested in pursuing a strategy of diversifying its industrial base. Bauer, Pool, and Dexter argued that business attitudes toward the decline of the textile and apparel industry could be characterized by one of the following:

1. Hope that the industry would survive in Textiletown as a part of a more diversified economy;
2. No hope for survival with some regrets; and
3. No hope for survival with no regrets.[3]

The domestic political power of the textile and apparel industry has led to the creation of a series of international agreements regulating the trade in textile and apparel products. These agreements, which include the Short-Term Arrangement, the Long-Term Arrangement, and the Multifiber Arrangement, sanction bilateral restrictive agreements between importers and exporters of textile and apparel products. They manifest themselves as the products of extensive negotiations between both industry and government within the United States as well as between the importing and exporting countries. As these agreements do not lie formally within the GATT framework and are negotiated primarily with developing countries, the United States has had a considerable amount of political leverage in determining the terms upon which these agreements are based. In this respect the case offers some support for the importance of national autonomy in U.S. trade policy. However, once these terms have been established, this analysis suggests that the agreements do limit the ability of the United States to restrict textile imports on a unilateral basis.

A policy decision to support an open trading system underlies the U.S. commitment to the international textile agreements. The United States accepts some degree of restraint on its discretion over trade restraints in order to help prevent the disintegration of the GATT trading system. In the textile and apparel sector, some system of controlled restraints became necessary to avoid the proliferation of anarchistic restrictions that had the potential of undermining the entire GATT framework. A GATT paper on textile trade reveals this danger.

> By the early 1960s it had become obvious that a special effort of international cooperation would be needed to avert a real danger of uncontrolled proliferation of [these] restrictions. The situation was becoming more and more unsatisfactory both to the importing industrial countries and to the exporting developing countries. For the importing countries, it was getting extremely difficult to find means of sharing equitably the burden of imports and of adjusting their textile industries. On the other hand, the developing countries were faced with varied and increasing obstacles to their exports. Finally, it constituted a danger to the structure and effectiveness of the GATT itself, when it could one day be seen as inoperative in such an important sector of world trade.[4]

Although the textile program stands as an exception to the U.S. policy of liberal trade, and the regulation of textile trade stands as an exception to GATT principles, the underlying justification for the regulation of textile trade is the maintenance of the liberal trading system.

The international regime in textile trade requires some adjustment on the part of importing countries through the yearly growth in quotas. Yet the bilateral agreements that limit textile and apparel trade do offer some protection to U.S. producers. To the extent that

U.S. firms do not become more capital-intensive, these restrictions create additional jobs. They also improve the profitability of U.S. producers by reducing the competitive pressures from low-cost producers. Thus the major components of pragmatic liberalism are inherent in U.S. textile and apparel policy. While the trade restrictions do appear to be more pragmatic than liberal, they are embedded in an international framework that stipulates that these trade restraints be continually liberalized.

In this case, the policy decision made by the United States to adhere to the international agreements that provide for the regulated liberalization of textile and apparel trade acts as a constraint on the ability of the industry to influence trade policy. This chapter analyzes the attempt by the textile and apparel complex to block the ratification of the Tokyo Round negotiations in Congress. The analysis focuses specifically on the intragovernmental debate in the executive branch over the Carter administration's "Textile Program." The agreement between the industry and the government, which this policy statement represents, helped to consolidate the industry's support for ratification of the Tokyo Round agreements.

This white paper did include concessions tightening some import restraints, which made it more difficult for exporters to respond to changes in fashion. This increase in protection was the price that the Carter administration believed it had to pay to obtain the support of the textile and apparel industry for the ratification of the Tokyo Round trade agreements. However, the white paper offered these restrictions in the context of a textile and apparel program that included yearly increases in textile and apparel quotas as well as significant tariff reductions on textile and apparel products negotiated at the Tokyo Round.

The changes were implemented in a way that did not violate the international agreement regulating textile trade. Thus, in spite of the intense pressure for increased protection, the Multifiber Arrangement as embedded in the U.S. policy process limited the ability of the industry to insulate itself from foreign competition. An assessment of these changes by the Council of Economic Advisers points out this lack of success: "This agreement combined with the textile tariff cuts in the MTN [multilateral trade negotiations— the Tokyo Round] will make U.S. textile consumers slightly worse off and textile producers slightly better off."[5] The textile and apparel white paper illustrates the U.S. policy of pragmatic liberalism in that it both reduced the possibility of rapid increases in imports, which could cause serious social dislocation among workers within the industry, and facilitated a wealth transfer from consumers to producers by making it difficult for exporters to respond to changes in demand.

In order to provide a political and institutional context in which to analyze the white paper, the chapter initially discusses the industry's arguments in support of import protection. The second section of this chapter reviews the evolution of U.S. textile policy and the international framework in which it is implemented. The international framework in which textile trade is regulated provides the context within which the white paper was negotiated. The discussion then turns to an analysis of the executive branch debate over the white paper.

WHY IMPORT RESTRAINT?

The following discussion of the U.S. textile and apparel industry provides an economic perspective with which to evaluate the industry's arguments for import protection.[6] The industry's arguments for protection emphasize the need to protect U.S. employment. These arguments rarely include an evaluation of the impact that changes in technology have on employment levels in the industry. Although productivity increases resulting from technological innovations account for some of the decline in employment, government policy has emphasized primarily what appears to be the impact of imports on employment. The U.S. government made this point explicitly in a GATT study of the textile and apparel industry made prior to the negotiation of the Multifiber Arrangement. The report submitted by the U.S. government states:

> Between 1969 and 1971 the combined textile and apparel employment dropped by almost 90,000 workers. This declining employment in a basic consumer product industry in the face of rising demand resulted in large measure not because of improved productivity, but rather because of low-cost imports which forced an increasing number of United States plants to shut down.[7]

In contrast to this position, an Organization for Economic Cooperation and Development (OECD) study of the industry suggests that although textiles and apparel are among the few branches of the manufacturing industry where import growth generally appears to have a significant impact on employment changes, the effect of the increase in labor productivity on employment levels has been a more significant factor than increased imports.[8] The industry has been able to obscure the impact of technological change on employment in its argument for import restraints by emphasizing the unique adjustment problems it faces owing to the magnitude and composition of the work force. Industry representatives make the argument that the low skill and education requirements in textile and apparel jobs allow it to employ a high proportion of women and minorities. They further stress that 81 percent of apparel workers and 48 percent of textile workers are women, whereas 28 percent of the employees in both industries are minorities and that the social importance of this employment is crucial because of the lack of alternative employment in many regions where the industry is located.[9]

The industry's position on trade holds that these jobs are threatened when the American industry is forced to compete with producers from low-wage countries. Foreign imports gain competitive importance in the United States owing to the worldwide diffusion of the standard technologies within the sector that do not have high skill requirements. Because of this diffusion of technology, countries with low labor costs do have a comparative advantage in the production of textile and apparel products. The U.S. industry argues that imports from these low-wage countries will force the majority of U.S. textile and apparel firms out of business. It goes on to make the case that the United States cannot afford to let this happen because of the devastating social and political impact of plant closures due to the inability of the labor force to adjust.

This view is echoed within the government. Arthur Geral, a U.S. textile official argued, "Textiles are a unique case because they employ two to three million workers." He explains that the basis for the government policy vis-à-vis textile imports is a domestic social policy aimed at retaining employment opportunities in underdeveloped regions in the United States. Geral justifies these import restraints to protect the industry on the grounds that it often provides the first job for entrants into the industrial economy in the United States.[10]

The OECD study of the textile and apparel industry, however, was not so pessimistic with respect to the impact of imports on employment in the textile and apparel industries of advanced industrial countries. It suggests that although wage costs rank as an important determinant of international competitiveness, wages only make up 38 to 47 percent of manufacturing costs. Whereas developing countries may have had a competitive edge in wages, the report argues that the advanced industrial countries have a permanent competitive edge in the development of new labor-saving technologies as well as in innovations that save energy and raw materials. Thus the report concludes that it is unlikely that—even under conditions of free trade—the textile and apparel industries in the advanced industrial countries would disappear. Instead, the OECD report indicates that the industry would specialize in specific products in which productivity increases would compensate for relatively high labor costs.

In making a political argument for import protection, the industry excludes any consideration of the impact of technological innovation on either employment or the ability of the industry to compete in the international market. Their policy prescriptions also fail to mention the cost of the imposition of quotas on low-cost goods. By excluding these factors, the industry can make a logically coherent case for protection that eliminates the need for adjustment to foreign competition. The political debate between the industry and the government involves the degree to which U.S. trade policy will subject the industry to import competition, thereby forcing it to adjust. While the industry has made a convincing case to the government in support of its need to be protected from sudden and very large increases in imports from low-cost producers, the government has successfully resisted adopting a policy that would remove all incentives for adjustment that are motivated by international competition.

The following section describes the evolution of U.S. trade policy in textiles and apparel and of the international framework that regulates trade in this sector. Here, the commitment of the U.S. government to this international framework limits the ability of the U.S. industry to obtain an increasingly restrictive import policy, which would obviate the need for any adjustment. The OECD report indicates that the U.S. industry would survive in spite of increased international competition. Thus the attempt on the part of the industry to eliminate any need for adjustment indicates its political power to effect a wealth transfer from consumers to itself. On the other hand, the extent to which the government manages to maintain a policy that, though restrictive, allows for some growth in imports indicates the presence of a source of limits on the political effectiveness of the industry. The government's ability to resist the political pressure of the industry is bolstered by the international regulation of textile and apparel trade.

TRADE POLICY IN THE TEXTILE AND APPAREL INDUSTRY

Throughout the postwar period, the primary policy instrument that the U.S. government used to aid the textile and apparel industry was import restraints. Import restraints became an expedient solution to the problems that the industry was facing because, in contrast to subsidy programs, tariffs and quotas were relatively easy to administer and brought short-run results quickly. In addition, since the textile and apparel industry had produced primarily for the U.S. market, both the industry and government believed rising levels of imports to be the source of the industry's problems.

As indicated in the previous discussion, the textile and apparel industry faces numerous problems, and they do not stem entirely from low-priced foreign imports. Although the decline in employment in these two industries can in part be attributed to increased imports, it also results from technological changes in the production process and increases in capital intensity in the industry. Furthermore, both supply and demand in the textile and apparel industry remain unpredictable due to constantly evolving technologies, changes in the price and availability of raw materials, the volatile structure of that part of the demand that is concerned with fashion, and the unpredictable response of consumers to attempts to fabricate taste.[11] Thus while imports were not always the cause of the problems faced by the industry, both the government and industry believed the restriction of imports to be the solution.

The 1930s witnessed the setting of a precedent for trade restraint in the textile and apparel industry. Textile trade emerged as an issue during the New Deal because the National Industrial Recovery Act required the industry to improve labor conditions. The act set standards for wages, limited the maximum hours of work per week, and abolished child labor. In effect, this policy substantially increased the production costs for U.S. firms. The industry was able to persuade the government that because the increase in production costs had been due to changes in government policy, the government had the responsibility to protect the industry from foreign competition. In response to this pressure, both the governments of the United States and Japan condoned a private industry-to-industry restraint agreement that set quotas on Japanese imports to the United States during 1937 and 1938.

The industry again used market distortions introduced by government policy as a part of their rationale for import protection from Japanese products in the mid-1950s. American cotton textile producers then argued that they were at a disadvantage in trying to compete against imports because surplus U.S. cotton was being sold abroad by the government at world market prices that were substantially lower than the domestic price, owing to the agricultural price support program. In 1957 Buford Brandis, then chief economist for the American Cotton Manufacturers' Institute, calculated that the world market price of U.S.-grown raw cotton stood at about 20 percent below the price in the United States as a result of the government's cotton export program.[12]

In addition to the U.S. price support program, the U.S. industry argued that it was particularly vulnerable to Japanese imports because after Japan's accession to the GATT the United States and Canada remained the only countries to offer MFN treatment to Japanese goods. GATT members could continue to discriminate against Japanese goods because—under Article 35 of the GATT—member countries retained the right to refuse to apply the provisions of the General Agreement to a new member country. When Japan acceded to the GATT in 1955, 14 countries—representing about 40 percent of the trade of the GATT contracting parties—invoked Article 35 against Japan.[13] As a result these restrictions diverted Japanese textile shipments to the U.S. market. In spite of protests from the industry the United States continued to lower duties on textile products. During the 1955 GATT negotiations for tariff reductions the State Department argued that it was necessary for the United States to reduce duties on Japanese goods in order to rebuild Japan's democracy. This position prevailed, and during these negotiations the United States reduced tariffs on 30 cotton items.

In the aftermath of these negotiations, Japanese exports of cotton textile products increased substantially. This increase put the American Textile Manufacturers' Association in a strong position to argue that only quantitative restrictions (quotas) on Japanese imports would protect the industry from complete devastation. This industry pressure led to negotiations between the United States and Japan in December 1955 in which the government of Japan agreed "voluntarily" to restrict exports of cotton goods to the United States for two years.

In 1957 the Japanese government, under increased pressure from the United States, implemented a five-year program of controls on the export of cotton textile and apparel products to the United States. The United States requested this extension of the initial restraint agreement to avoid the possibility that Congress might legislate unilateral quotas on Japanese goods. Legislated quotas would have been less flexible and could have been more restrictive than those imposed voluntarily by Japan. This agreement set a precedent in the regulation of textile trade because it combined an aggregate quantitative limit on Japanese textiles with limits on narrower groups of products and categories within groups.[14] U.S. producers preferred this type of agreement because it limited the quantity of imports of specific items that could seriously threaten small highly specialized manufacturers. In contrast, Japanese producers would have preferred aggregate limits, which would have given them more control over product mix.

While this agreement did reduce Japanese exports to the United States, aggregate U.S. textile imports rose from $154.3 million in 1956 to $248 million in 1960. A large part of this increase came from Hong Kong. In 1958 U.S. imports of cotton textiles from Hong Kong reached 67.9 million square yards; in 1959 they rose to 206.3 million; and by 1960 they had climbed to 289.7 million square yards.[15] This increase in imports from Hong Kong more than compensated for the reduction in shipments from Japan. Hong Kong, however, refused to implement a program of voluntary export restraints in spite of pressure from the U.S. government.

In the United States the authority of the president to enter into bilateral restraint agreements in textiles was embedded in the Agricultural Act of 1956. This legislation granted the president "the authority to negotiate agreements limiting exports from foreign countries or imports into the United States of textiles or textile products."[16] This legislation, however, did not authorize the president to impose quotas unilaterally without congressional approval.

In order to counter renewed industry pressure for legislated quotas, the United States sought the creation of a multilateral framework at the GATT that would regulate bilateral agreements between importing and exporting countries. To create a context within which to consider multilateral trade restraints in textile and apparel, the United States asked the Contracting Parties in 1959 to consider the question of market disruption. Market disruption consisted of the following elements:

1. A sharp and substantial increase or potential increase of imports of particular products from particular sources;
2. These products are offered at prices that are substantially below those prevailing for similar goods of comparable quality in the market of the importing country;
3. There is serious damage to domestic producers, or the threat thereof; and
4. The price differentials referred to above do not arise from governmental intervention in the fixing or formation of prices or from dumping practices.[17]

The Contracting Parties acknowledged that the phenomenon of market disruption has led governments to take a variety of exceptional measures "including discriminatory actions both inside and outside the GATT framework by importing countries and export control systems by exporting countries."[18] They ultimately agreed that "it was the aim of all countries involved in situations of market disruption to find constructive solutions consistent with the basic aim of the GATT and that consultation on such problems should be facilitated if necessary on a multilateral basis."[19] Although these "constructive solutions" were likely to involve violations of the GATT principles and rules, GATT officials were more interested in avoiding the uncontrolled proliferation of quantitative restriction than in preventing any institutionalized exceptions to the GATT rules that discourage the use of quantitative restrictions (quotas) and require that restraints not be applied selectively to a specific country or group of countries.

In June 1961 the United States requested the GATT council to reach an agreement on the orderly development of textile trade that would allow for the progressive increase in export markets of developing countries as well as for orderly adjustment in import markets. In response to this request the negotiations between importing and exporting countries created the framework for the Short-Term Arrangement (STA) for cotton textiles. The aims of the STA were:

1. to significantly increase access to markets where imports are at present subject to restriction;
2. to maintain orderly access to markets where imports are at present subject to restriction; and
3. to secure from exporting countries where necessary, a measure of restraint in their export policy so as to avoid disruptive effects in import markets.[20]

The STA was set up to be a preliminary agreement to cover the period between October 1, 1961, and September 30, 1962. The Long-Term Arrangement (LTA) followed—signed October 1, 1962—and stayed in effect through 1973. The STA included two substantial departures from the GATT framework. It allowed importing countries to discriminate among suppliers through the negotiation of bilateral agreements restricting imports. It further sanctioned the use of quotas. These quotas, however, could not be less than the actual exports between July 1960 and June 1961.

In return for these concessions, the importing countries agreed to increase the quota by 5 percent a year. This was increased to 6 percent in the LTA. The agreement also provided that in the event of market disruption bilateral negotiations would be conducted to determine quotas. If the exporting country would not agree to negotiate, importing countries could then impose unilateral import restraints.

The successful implementation of the agreement hinged on the ability of both importing and exporting countries to reach an agreement on the definition of *market disruption*. In an attempt to provide an institutional basis for discussion over the meaning of *market disruption*, the STA mandated the creation of a provisional Cotton Textile Committee within the GATT to oversee the implementation of the agreement. The LTA made this committee a permanent part of the agreement.

The Cotton Textile Committee, composed of representatives of both importing and exporting countries, was initially designated to collect statistics on trade in cotton textiles and undertake studies requested by member countries. More important, the STA gave the committee the authority to consider divergences of opinion with respect to the interpretation and application of the agreement.[21] In this role the committee had the responsibility for mediating any conflict between importing and exporting countries that was not resolved on a bilateral basis. The committee, although given a mandate to resolve conflict, failed to receive any enforcement powers. Its only source of leverage was, and continues to be, the reluctance on the part of nation-states to break an international commitment.[22]

The Cotton Textile Committee renewed the LTA in 1967 and 1970. During this period the entrance of new suppliers and the rapid increase of U.S. imports of man-made fiber products not regulated by the LTA led to renewed pressures from the U.S. industry for an extension of the LTA to cover wool and man-made textile and apparel products. This pressure led first to the negotiation of bilateral agreements with Japan and four other Asian countries between 1969 and 1971. These bilaterals were followed by negotiations between 50 importing and exporting countries held at the GATT in 1973 to reach "a mutually satisfactory arrangement on trade in textiles."[23]

The Multifiber Arrangement (MFA) resulted. The MFA sought to increase worldwide textile and apparel trade at a rate that did not disrupt the markets in importing states. To achieve this end, the MFA extended the notion of market disruption to cover man-made fiber and wool textile and apparel products.

The MFA provides for two types of restrictive measures. In Article 3, if an importing country believes that its market is being disrupted by a specific textile and apparel product, it can request the exporting country to limit its shipments. If the exporting country refuses, importing countries can then impose unilateral quotas on specific products. The annual quota cannot, however, be less than the level of trade in the previous 12 months and must be increased by 6 percent a year.

Under Article 4, importing and exporting countries can enter into bilateral negotiations to restrict textile exports on a comprehensive basis where there exists a real risk of market disruption. The risk of market disruption is less strict than the Article 3 condition of market disruption. Article 4 agreements tend to be attractive to exporting countries because in principle they are to be less restrictive than those negotiated under Article 3. Typically, however, they cover more categories of products.

To oversee the implementation of the arrangement, those states that participated in the negotiations delegated to the Textile Committee of the GATT the authority to create the Textile Surveillance Board (TSB). Although—like the Textile Committee of the GATT—the TSB received no enforcement powers, "participating countries bound themselves in advance to follow, to the best of their ability, the recommendations of the TSB."[24] The TSB consists of eight members representative of both importing and exporting countries and a chairman elected by the countries participating in the agreement. The TSB determines whether the importing countries have complied with the provisions of the MFA in determining the extent and size of quotas.

Importing countries invoking Article 3 restrictions must notify the TSB. When the TSB receives this notification, or when there is a complaint from either party, the TSB requires each party to present its case. In dispute settlement proceedings the TSB is able to maintain some degree of impartiality because its members act as independent experts rather than as national delegates. They do not present the case for their country if one arises and have been known on occasion to disagree with their country's position. Thus for a country to invoke market disruption as a cause for import restraint, it must reach an agreement with the exporting country as well as demonstrate to the TSB the validity of its claim. The TSB makes decisions on the basis of reaching a consensus. Quotas negotiated under Article 4 are also reported to the TSB, which reserves the right to comment.

GATT textile officials contend that in general the TSB is successful in keeping members from violating the terms of the agreement. They report that the TSB has discretely persuaded countries to change the terms of their textile agreements to conform to the MFA. However, no consensus exists between the importing and exporting countries with respect to how well the TSB functions. While a U.S. respresentative stated that the TSB is what makes the agreement work, a representative from Hong Kong argued that the MFA is in itself a compromise and to further compromise the terms of the MFA in a specific dispute was equivalent to undermining the agreement. But most members believe that the transparency provided by the TSB acts as a source of discipline on actions taken by the participating members.

Given the volatile nature of the textile and apparel industry, GATT textile officials argue that a restrictive agreement such as the MFA was probably necessary to allow for the orderly expansion of textile trade. The discipline provided by the TSB in conjunction with the growth and flexibility provisions in the MFA, they argue, is sufficient to allow for the "natural, dynamic evolution of the textile industry and textile trade while at the same time protecting importing countries from damage caused by a rapid increase of low cost imports."[25]

The white paper did not come up for discussion in the TSB, although the members of the committee did discuss it among themselves.[26] The policy changes made by the United States were not brought up in the TSB because, although the U.S. government was under tremendous pressure to negotiate more restrictive textile quotas than were in place, the compromise ultimately adopted by the government did not require the United States to violate the terms of the MFA. The willingness of the U.S. government to resist the industry's demands was based in part on the U.S. commitment to the MFA as well as on a reluctance to have to justify its actions before the TSB. Thus the TSB acted as a constraint on the U.S. policy even though no overt interaction between the committee and U.S. negotiators took place.

THE TEXTILE WHITE PAPER

The attempt on the part of the textile and apparel industries to prevent negotiators from reducing the U.S. tariff on their products during the Tokyo Round began obscurely with President Carter's veto of the Carson City Silver Dollar Bill (H.R. 9937), November 11, 1978. Carter vetoed this legislation because of an amendment added by Senator Ernest Hollings (D–S.C.) that would have exempted all textile and apparel products from tariff reductions at the Tokyo Round negotiations of the GATT. In the *Memorandum of Disapproval*, Carter argued:

> This bill could not address the real causes of the industry's difficulties. In return for any transient benefits, the bill would prompt our trading partners to retaliate by withdrawing offers in areas where our need for export markets is the greatest—products such as tobacco, grains, citrus, raw cotton, paper, machinery, poultry, and textile–related areas such as mill products and fashion clothing. The loss of these exports is too high a price for our nation to pay. If the two and a quarter million workers in the textile and apparel industry are to survive in their jobs, we must work to keep the world economy strong and international trade free.[27]

In the same statement Carter also designated the Office of the Special Trade Representative to "begin a new policy review and report quarterly on the textile and apparel industry, with special emphasis on imports and exports so that appropriate actions can be taken more promptly."[28]

In spite of Carter's veto, many in the administration (especially in the Office of the Special Trade Representative) considered the success of this bill in Congresss to be indicative of the ability of the textile apparel coalition to block the ratification of the Tokyo Round agreements. Prior to the actual ratification of the multilateral trade agreements, the European request that the United States extend the waiver on duties imposed on subsidized goods provided the textile and apparel industry another opportunity to flex its political muscle. This extension of the subsidy-countervailing duty waiver required congressional approval. The Trade Act of 1974 initially included the waiver to allow the administration to negotiate "in an atmosphere conducive to reaching agreement on an international regime to regulate the use of subsidies."[29]

The extension of the subsidy-countervailing duty waiver became an issue near the end of the GATT negotiations because the EEC feared that its subsidized exports to the United States would be subject to these duties. The extension was critical because the Europeans threatened to pull out of the negotiations without it. Once it became clear that Congress would not pass the subsidy-countervailing duty extension before it expired January 3, 1979, the EEC issued a statement warning the United States that "unless the threat of countervailing duties was removed . . . the common assumption of shared responsibility on which we have based the Tokyo Round would no longer exist."[30]

Without the countervailing duty waiver the Treasury would be required automatically to impose countervailing duties on approximately $130 million of dairy products (primarily cheese and butter cookies) and $13 million of canned ham. U.S. law did not yet require that the industry demonstrate injury before countervailing duties were levied. (The United States did later agree to this during the Tokyo Round negotiations.)

From the outset of this dispute, it proved difficult to determine the seriousness of both EEC and U.S. textile industry threats to stall the negotiations. As the total duties that would be collected were minimal in the context of the entire amount of trade at stake in the Tokyo Round, the basis for the EEC position cannot be considered to be primarily economic. If collected for an entire year on imports at 1977 levels, the duties would be $50 million.[31] This figure becomes insignificant in light of the amount of trade covered by the Tokyo Round. It may be impossible to determine whether the EEC would have been willing to forgo the successful conclusion of the MTNs because of the failure to extend the waiver, just as it was difficult to determine whether the textile industry actually had the political strength to block the ratification of the MTN. In both cases substantial room existed for bluff.

The EEC did, however, appear serious in its insistence on the countervailing duty waiver extension. Mr. Dell, the secretary of state for trade for the EEC, characterized the possible failure of Congress to pass the waiver extension as "a weight hanging over the entire negotiations and a totally unnecessary impediment to progress."[32] Some member states even urged immediate withdrawal from the Tokyo Round.

The STR negotiators took this call for the waiver extension seriously. They perceived the EEC to be a fragile coalition of member states and believed that any one member could not afford to lose face over this issue. The French, who were especially nervous about trade liberalization given the depressed state of the French economy at the time, also may have wanted to use this issue to undermine the Tokyo Round negotiations.[33] Thus the STR was convinced that the extension of the waiver was critical to the successful conclusion to the Tokyo Round. This waiver, however, relied upon the administration's ability to negotiate with the textile and apparel industries a trade program that would mitigate their political opposition to the MTN in Congress.

The following discussion analyzes the interagency debate over how the government could address the textile industry's requests for policy changes. It is based on interviews with officials in the Office of the Special Trade Representative and memos issued by the CEA and the Department of the Treasury. This discussion demonstrates that notwithstanding the tremendous political power of the textile industry it proved unable to use its influence to persuade the government to implement a textile policy that would freeze the level of imports coming into the U.S. market, thereby violating the terms of the MFA.

During the course of the interagency debate both the CEA and the Treasury argued against including provisions that would violate the MFA. In contrast, the STR expressed more concern with reaching a political settlement with the industry than with keeping within the parameters of the MFA. While the original draft of the white paper never explicitly violated the terms of the MFA, its composers worded it in a way that left the government more vulnerable to fundamental policy changes than the final draft. Ultimately, the final statement of the administration's textile program was ambiguous enough so that the United States did not have to abrogate its international commitments. The textile industry felt compelled to go along with the final package because it risked both the possibility of not getting any kind of commitment from the administration to restrict imports further and the possibility, although slight, of losing congressional support.

The STR's Rationale for the Industry Negotiations

By January 1979 Robert Strauss, the head of the STR, finally believed there was enough momentum to conclude the Tokyo Round negotiations. To sustain this momentum he announced willingness to accommodate some of the textile and apparel industry's demands in exchange for their support for the MTN agreements. The industry had strongly opposed the Tokyo Round trade negotiations because the United States offered tariff cuts in textile and apparel products.

Geza Feketekuty, an assistant to Strauss, characterized the white paper as a part of a coherent strategy on the part of the administration to build a coalition in support of the MTN tariff cuts. The purpose of deals, like the one struck with the textile industry, he suggested, was to secure the political support of those industries that would be faced with increased competitive pressures. He further contended that the problem with the economic theory of free trade was that it did not address the political problems that result from the distribution of income away from noncompetitive sectors of the U.S. economy. He concluded that to liberalize trade without compensating the losers was not politically viable.[34] Alan Wolff, the STR negotiator responsible for the negotiations with the textile industry, also argued for the need of the white paper. He suggested that its intent was to include the interests of the textile industry in the administration's trade policy, a goal consistent with the principles of representative government.[35]

This strategy is probably more consistent with the political sensitivity of the STR rather than a part of a coherent economic policy. Strauss knew he had to have the support of Congress to implement the Tokyo Round agreements, and he was not willing to alienate the textile industry, thereby running the risk that Congress would not ratify the agreements. Strauss received criticism for giving away too much using this strategy. W. Michael Blumenthal, then secretary of the Treasury, argued that Strauss had converted national trade policy into sectoral appeasement after the white paper had been negotiated. [36] To this Strauss responded, "There was no other way to clear the bill."[37] Congress, on the other hand, praised Strauss for his political skills and willingness to listen to grievances and respond.[38]

Evolution of the Administration's Textile Program

At 8:00 A.M. on January 17, 1979, Strauss convened a meeting of major agencies to announce that he had devised a "Proposed

Presidential Textile Program." This program represented the out-come of 45 days of negotiations between representatives of the textile industry and Alan Wolff of the STR. At this point Strauss indicated he wanted to go ahead with the program but would allow the other agencies 12 hours to respond.[39] The following section discusses the response of the CEA and the Treasury to the major points in the draft of the program. These two agencies played a significant role in reducing the strength of the trade restrictions that were ultimately implemented. Some indication that there was a substantial amount of interagency debate over the draft version of the white paper is that the final statement was issued a month after Strauss initially announced the program to the government. The final draft did not emerge from the inter-agency process until it was clear that to implement the policy changes the STR would not need to abrogate the international textile agreements.

The first point of the initial draft gave the STR the personal responsibility to carry out a global import evaluation program that would involve analyzing the rate of growth of textile and apparel imports from all countries in terms of the rate of growth in demand for these goods in the United States. On the basis of this informa-tion the United States would then eliminate "import surges" from countries in the MFA as well as from new suppliers not covered by the agreement, principally the People's Republic of China.

In this introductory statement, the industry attempted to ef-fect two significant policy changes. First, the industry tried to persuade the government to an annual global quota. This would involve setting an aggregate limit on the amount of textiles and apparel products that could come into the United States and then dividing this overall quota into subquotas for individual suppliers. A global quota would result in a significantly more restrictive textile policy than was then in place because to allow for imports from new suppliers existing quotas would have to be reduced. U.S. policy then set limits for individual suppliers on a case-by-case basis. This policy did not require the reduction of existing quotas to accommodate new suppliers because it did not take into account the total level of imports coming into the United States in the determination of individual quotas.

The second major change in U.S. policy implied in this statement was that the growth in quotas be tied to the rate of growth of the U.S. market. This provision could result in a violation of the terms of the MFA because the growth in the U.S. market for textile and apparel products has been about 2 percent per year since the mid–1970s. The MFA, in contrast, requires quotas to be increased by 6 percent per year. In support of this change the industry argues that it is necessary to ensure "the orderly sharing of market growth." In noting the change that this would entail from existing policy, a CEA memo stated, "We have not previously negotiated adjustments on quotas based on an annual analysis of the market for specific textile categories. To do so would destroy the exporters' guaranteed access to the U.S. textile market."[40]

The second major point in the draft program involved a commitment on the part of the administration to eliminate harmful fluctuations in shipments from countries where quotas were undershipped in the previous year. This attempt "to promote the MFA concept of the orderly growth of trade" would be accomplished by limiting shipments to the previous year's shipments plus one half of the unfilled portion of the previous year's quota as a matter of principle for all countries and all categories of goods.[41]

This change would involve a departure from existing U.S. textile policy because it would significantly reduce the flexibility provisions granted to exporters. These flexibility provisions allow suppliers to ship at above-quota levels in products in which they have a strong market. The flexibility provisions mandated by the MFA include swing, which allows exporters to move yardage from one category to another; carryover, which allows shortfalls in one year to be transferred to the next year; and carryforward, which permits yardage to be borrowed from the next year. Since the cause of unfilled quotas is often the rapidly changing conditions of the textile market, this downward reduction of quotas would not allow suppliers to be able to regain their original position in the U.S. market. In response to this provision, the CEA argued that it would have the largest welfare impact through raising prices to domestic consumers. A CEA memo further stated that it was bad economics and a horrible precedent. The Treasury Department argued that this would reverse 18 years of U.S. textile agreements that have allowed for the orderly, but positive, growth in U.S. textile imports.

In addition to these limits on unused quotas from all textile exporters, the preliminary version of the white paper also provided that imports from Hong Kong, Korea, and Taiwan be held at 1978 trade levels or 1979 base levels, whichever were lower. It further stipulated that the growth in quotas of shipments from these countries was to be "reviewed annually and if necessary adjustments made to assure that such growth is commensurate with the estimated rate of growth in the United States market."[42] In response to this both the Treasury and the CEA noted that this would be a clear abrogation of our bilateral agreements, which permit a 6 percent increase in quotas per year.

To ensure that the above restrictions in textile and apparel imports would protect sensitive products, the white paper also promised to improve the quality and timing of monitoring efforts and to strengthen the present system to allow for faster feedback and response among industry, labor, and the government. To this suggestion the CEA responded that it was difficult to imagine a procedure that would allow faster feedback, as the textile industry and the STR worked out this new policy before it was shown to the rest of the the U.S. government. The Treasury commented that as industry teams follow U.S. negotiators to foreign countries and consult daily with U.S. negotiators, it was difficult to imagine what more the government could give them, short of inviting them into the negotiating room.

The initial version of the white paper also provided for a "snapback clause," which would restore the tariffs on textile and apparel products to their pre-MTN (Tokyo Round) levels in the event that the MFA would not be successfully renewed prior to its expiration on January 1, 1982. The white paper also stated that if the MFA were not renegotiated, legislative remedies would be proposed that would give the president the authority to impose unilateral quotas on textile and apparel products. The CEA opposed this snapback provision because it would require the United States to break negotiated tariff bindings automatically.

The increase in tariffs required by this snapback clause would have a direct impact on U.S. trade with the EEC. The United States does not impose quotas on textile trade with the EEC. While the majority of the white paper was directed at the low-cost exports of developing countries to the United States, this provision had the potential of affecting U.S. textile trade with Europe. Because the EEC ranks as one of the major trading partners of the United States, this provision posed more serious potential political implications for the future stability of the international trading system.

A strict interpretation of the first draft would have almost completely insulated the U.S. textile and apparel industry from import competition, thereby undermining U.S. commitments to the orderly growth of textile trade made under the MFA. The original draft of the white paper did not provide the government with much leverage to resist industry attempts to eliminate the possibility of market disruption. This policy diverged from the original intent of the MFA, which was to restrict imports only once there is evidence of market disruption. To avoid the increased probability of stringent textile and apparel restraints, the interagency committee discussion of the white paper raised three options, although all three were not politically viable.

The first option proposed to quiet the textile and apparel industry by withdrawing our proposed tariff cuts on these products from the MTN. Support existed within the Treasury for this position because it was strongly opposed to Strauss's deal with the industry. The MTN negotiators believed, however, that the United States could not keep the Tokyo Round negotiations alive if the United States was not willing to offer cuts in sensitive areas. The EEC continued to push the United States for even more than the 25 percent cut in textile tariffs, which the U.S. had originally proposed. The United States was vulnerable to this request because before the Tokyo Round the average tariff on textiles and apparel was 23.4 percent as opposed to an overall average of 8.2 percent.

Two further criticisms to this suggestion came from the CEA and from within the Treasury. A CEA memo argued that dropping textiles from the MTN, although preferable to Strauss's program, could jeopardize the chances for a successful conclusion of the Tokyo Round. The Treasury suggested that another problem with dropping textiles and apparel from the MTN was that although the elimination of these offers would only reduce the average depth of the U.S. cut from 40.5 percent to 33.7 percent, which alone was not too bad, it might create a precedent for other industries. The result could be the beginning of a withdrawal/unraveling process with other industries such as steel and autos waiting for a similar exemption.

The second option, supported by the Treasury, proposed that Strauss meet the textile industry head-on—that is, do nothing and risk that they did not have the political strength in Congresss to block the MTNs ratification. Given the prior indications of the industry's political strength, the STR negotiators believed this strategy to be too risky.

The third option suggested using less restrictive language in the agreement to allow for a high degree of flexibility in the implementation of the program. This strategy was consistent with the initial aim of the STR in its decision to strike a deal with the textile and apparel industry and was ultimately adopted. Alan Wolff, who did most of the negotiating with the industry, argued that the administration could not give the industry the complete protection it wanted. He further contended that the U.S. government was not in the business of preventing adjustment to international competition.[43] From his perspective the white paper fulfilled what the industry needed to support the MTNs but at the same time fell far short of the industry's initial demands.

After a series of interagency meetings, most of the objections of the CEA and the Treasury were incorporated into the language of the final statement. During the interagency debate over the text of the white paper, the STR maintained that the key to the success of the program was the ambiguity of the language. The Treasury Department expressed a concern that the industry would try to press the administration for a strict interpretation if the text was ambiguous. In contrast to the Treasury, the CEA decided shortly before the final draft that the STR had been convincing in its contention that some ambiguity was necessary to give U.S. negotiators more flexibility to be less protectionist in the long run. Prior to the approval of the white paper, the CEA indicated that Strauss had probably given away too much but that the final document had eliminated the most restrictive elements of the program.

In the negotiations between Wolff and the industry, the crucial compromise hinged over the question of global quotas. While the industry asked for global quotas as a means to preserve U.S. textile and apparel production, Wolff would only offer "to conduct a global import evaluation." The final version stated that this global import evaluation would be analyzed in the context of U.S. market growth and conditions in the industry. He argued that to look at imports from a global perspective could be helpful to the industry and at the same time not equivalent to the imposition of a global quota.[44] He refused, however, to delete mention of a global import evaluation from the final draft.

Increasing the ambiguity of the language resolved the debate over the limitations of unused quotas. The final draft stated, "Year-to-year increases in such cases should *not normally exceed* [emphasis added] the previous year's shipment's plus one-half of the unfilled portion of the previous year's quota."[45] This is a much weaker version of an earlier draft that stated that these guidelines for granting year-to-year growth should be set as a matter of principle. The final version also stated that after this was done, the growth and flexibility provisions would again apply.

Although the final draft did not mention Korea, Hong Kong, or Taiwan specifically, as had been done earlier, it did retain the restrictions on the flexibility provisions from "major exporting countries." The renegotiation of these bilaterals to reduce the probability of surges stands as one of the major policy changes that did result from the white paper. The final draft remained ambiguous with respect to tying the growth of imports from these countries (including the flexibility provisions) to the rate of growth of the U.S. market.

In addition, the final version also indicated that the U.S. government would make an effort to improve the quality and timing of monitoring imports. It gave no indication, though, as to how industry representatives could become more closely involved in negotiating textile agreements. Instead, it emphasized the administration's commitment to current policy.

The final agreement also retained the snapback clause—which would restore textile and apparel tariffs to pre-MTN levels in the event that the MFA was not renewed. This could potentially pose a problem with respect to the EEC. However, since at the time the United States was committed to renegotiating the MFA, it was not clear that this would create substantial problems. Furthermore, if the MFA did collapse, textile policy would be in such chaos, with or without the snapback clause, that textile trade would probably end up more restrictive than it is now.

In this agreement the government offered the industry a commitment to tighten the flexibility provisions in bilaterals, which cover imports from Korea, Hong Kong, and Taiwan. The industry further received from the government a relatively weak commitment to reduce quota growth in the event that filling unused quotas combined with the quota increase and the flexibility provisions provided by the MFA could create a surge of imports and thereby cause market disruption. The U.S. government also made a veiled commitment to negotiate trade restraints with the People's Republic of China. The industry, however, did not get a firm commitment from the government that a global quota would be imposed or that the rate of increase in quotas would be limited to the rate of growth of the U.S. market.

EPILOGUE

The publication of the administration's textile program appeared to be what Strauss needed to dislodge the subsidy-countervailing duty waiver legislation from the House Ways and Means Committee. Vanik, chairman of the Subcommittee on Trade of the Ways and Means Committee, had refused to move on the bill until the White House had negotiated an agreement with the textile and apparel industry because he was afraid the industry would try to attach an exemption from the MTN tariff cuts to the waiver extension again.[46] Once the textile program was made public, most of the supporters of the textile and apparel industry withdrew their opposition to the bill extending the countervailing duty waiver.

In the committee the opposition that remained to the waiver consisted of representatives of the producers who would have to compete with subsidized goods. Congressman Hughes from New Jersey testified that the livelihood of 200 employees of the Deer Park Baking Company would be threatened by the waiver. To this Strauss responded, "I am not running a butter cookie program. I am trying to conduct national policy."[47] This statement seems to reveal that the butter cookie industry does not have the political clout necessary to compete with the textile and apparel industries.

Once the opposition from the textile and apparel industry was removed, the House Ways and Means Committee approved the waiver extension 29 to 1 after receiving an unanimous endorsement from the Trade Subcommittee.[48] Vanik got the bill to the floor of the House without amendments. The House finally approved it on March 1, 1979. Shortly thereafter the Senate also passed it.

This decision by the U.S. Congress to pass the waiver elated GATT officials.[49] They saw it as removing the primary obstacle blocking the EEC foreign ministers from giving final approval to the GATT Tokyo Round package.[50] Strauss had accomplished his primary goal. By removing congressional opposition to the counter-vailing duty waiver, he took away the main excuse the EEC had for delaying the conclusion of the Tokyo Round negotiations.

IMPLEMENTATION

A telegram sent to U.S. embassies describing the administration's textile program provides the main source of evidence for the following analysis of the implementation of the white paper. This telegram was issued prior to the official announcement but after the interagency negotiations were concluded. The cable stated that the policy embodied in the white paper did not indicate a drastic change in the current U.S. textile policy nor in the U.S. support for the MFA. It stressed that the program did not require the United States to seek changes in existing agreements other than those with major suppliers but that the improved monitoring efforts promised to the industry might lead to a more prompt use of consultation rights in existing agreements. Any changes, however, that would result from these discussions would be carried out in terms of the U.S. rights and obligations in the MFA. The cable further stated that bilateral discussions had begun with Korea, Taiwan, and Hong Kong that were aimed at reducing surges in imports. The concluding statement of the cable emphasized that the entire program, including the changes in these bilaterals, was consistent with U.S. obligations under the MFA.

The U.S. textile delegation negotiated an agreement with Taiwan during August 1979 that tightened the flexibility provisions for textile products with specific quota limits. These negotiations reduced swing from 6 percent to 2.5 percent, and carryover/carryforward from an average of 11 percent to 3 percent. A Treasury

Department memo reported that this was relatively easy for Taiwan to accept because their exports were declining owing to a slowdown in the U.S. economy. In addition, those products not covered by specific quantitative restrictions would be subject to a consultation arrangement. This appeared to be a more flexible system than that proposed by the white paper.

Hong Kong proved less forthcoming in agreeing to negotiate stricter controls. It ultimately accepted a balanced package in which the U.S. negotiators made concessions in some categories in return for tightening up the flexibility provisions to avoid surges in sensitive categories. However, a representative from the Hong Kong delegation argued that if given the choice Hong Kong would not have accepted the modifications.[51] He believed these negotiations were the result of a one-sided insistence on the part of the United States to modify the existing agreement and felt bitter because Hong Kong was being made to pay the price for the resolution of a U.S. domestic political dispute. Negotiators reached a similar agreement with Korea.

These negotiations stand as the primary tangible changes in U.S. textile and apparel policy that were carried out to implement the white paper. These actions alone did not meet the industry's expectations for the increase in trade protection it believed the administration had promised. Stanley Nehmer, a consultant for the industry, argued that Carter was not making good on his promises.[52] He believed that in the white paper the administration had made a commitment to implement a global quota and limit quota growth to the growth of the U.S. market. The disappointment within the industry due to the absence of a substantial policy change was also evident in the testimony by a representative of the U.S. Apparel Council before the House Trade Subcommittee. This testimony made the point that although the president's white paper called for a global import evaluation, only tentative efforts have been made in this regard.[53] In general, the industry did not believe that it received the protection that it was promised in the white paper and continued to argue for globalization and tying the quota growth to that of the domestic market in the 1981 renegotiation of the MFA.

In response to the industry's complaints, an official in the Commerce Department's textile office commented that the industry always pushes for more than it needs and that the administration basically did follow through with the promises it made in the white paper. He believed that limiting the possibility of surges within the existing bilaterals was essentially what the administration promised in the agreement.[54] When asked if the concern over surges was legitimate, a senior GATT textile official responded that existing agreements made surges possible but that the industry exaggerated the frequency with which they had occurred.[55] He explained that the case the industry cited most frequently was the result of a dock strike in New York in 1977 that resulted in large quantities of cotton and man-made fiber imports entering the United States during a short period of time because shipments had been piling up on the docks. He emphasized that this could not be considered to be representative of normal trade flows in textiles.

A consensus did not emerge within the U.S. government over the protectionist implications of tightening the flexibility provisions. The Treasury remained critical of the actions taken by the United States. A Treasury Department draft of a memo on positive adjustment argued that these flexibility provisions were a crucial factor responsible for positive adjustment in the industry. The memo further stated that the rigidities in the bilateral agreements that were introduced by the reduction in flexibility provisions would result in a significant reduction in the rate of adjustment to imports in the textile and apparel industry. The memo concludes: "If the U.S. textile and apparel policy continues along lines set forth in the white paper, positive adjustment in the domestic industry could be significantly reduced."[56] In this memo the Treasury Department reiterated its concern that the industry would try to press the administration for a stricter interpretation of the "global import evaluation," which could become equivalent to a global quota.

CONCLUSION

The Treasury Department memo does suggest that the industry did obtain some increase in trade protection—although less than expected. The textile and apparel industry was not reticent in

articulating its expectations and acknowledging its ability to influence legislation. Prior to the publication of the white paper, Arthur
Gundersheim, a representative of the textile and apparel industry,
stated that if "U.S. officials want the influential industry's support,
or at least its acquiescence, they will have to produce something
that will help our industry."[57]

In part, the industry's political effectiveness stems from its
ability to make a compelling argument that links any increase in
imports to a loss of American jobs. Repeatedly in Congress, industry representatives argue successfully that the U.S. textile and
apparel industries will inevitably perish because U.S. trade policy
currently permits the rate of increase in imports to exceed the
domestic growth rate. In contrast, both the GATT and the OECD
argue that owing to changing patterns of demand and changing
production technologies in the textile and apparel industries, there
exist significant opportunities for intraindustry specialization in
the advanced industrial countries. Thus even under relatively
liberal trade conditions, there is reason to believe that the textile
and apparel industry in the United States would not disappear.

The pragmatic component of U.S. textile and apparel policy is
devised to respond to the political strength of the industry and to
the difficulty textile workers have in finding new jobs. In this case
the industry representatives managed to obscure the redistributive
effects of import quotas by emphasizing the social dislocation
caused by imports. This case suggests, however, that U.S. adherence to the MFA did provide the government with some leverage
to resist the demands of the industry to insulate itself completely
from international competition.

NOTES

1. Rodney Grey, "The Context for the Multifiber Arrangement" (Paper prepared for the Conference on International Trade in Textiles and Clothing, Brus-
sels, Belgium May 1980, p. 1.

2. U.S., Department of Treasury, "Positive Adjustment: A Case Study of
Textiles," (Washington, D.C. Mimeographed, 1980).

3. Raymond Bauer, Ithiel de Sola Pool, and Lewis Dexter, *American Business
and Public Policy: The Politics of Foreign Trade* (Chicago: Aldine, 1972), p. 307.

4. Paul Wurth, "The Arrangement Regarding International Trade in Tex-

tiles," (Geneva, General Agreement on Tariffs and Trade) September 1980, pp. 5—6. Mimeo.

5. Council of Economic Advisors, memo, January 26, 1979. (Mimeographed.)

6. Much of the criticism of the industry's arguments for protection will be taken from an unpublished study of the textile and clothing industries undertaken by the OECD (Paris) in 1980.

7. GATT Study on the Textile and Apparel Industry done in preparation for the negotiations on the Multifiber Arrangement, Geneva, General Agreement on Tariffs and Trade 1973, 1/3797 P.V-54.

8. This is taken from the unpublished OECD textile study, Paris, 1980.

9. "A Stitch in Time: The Multifiber Arrangement and American Jobs," a pamphlet published by a coalition of textile and apparel trade associations and unions, March 1981.

10. Interview with Arthur Geral in the Commerce Department Office of Textiles, July 1980.

11. Grey, "Context," p. 4.

12. U.S., Congress, Subcommittee on Trade of the House Committee on Ways and Means, *Compendium of Papers on US Foreign Trade Policy* (Washington, D.C.: Government Printing Office, 1957), p. 831.

13. Kenneth Dam, *The Law and International Economic Organization* (Chicago: University of Chicago Press, 1970), p. 348.

14. I. M. Destler, Harushiro Fukui, and Hideo Sato, *The Textile Wrangle* (Ithaca, N.Y.: Cornell University Press, 1979), p. 30.

15. International Trade Commission, *The History and Current Status of the Multifiber Arrangement* (Washington, D.C.: International Trade Commission January 1979), p. 3.

16. Ibid., p. 5.

17. International Trade Commission, *History*, p. 6.

18. Dam, *The Law*, p. 299.

19. Ibid., p. 299.

20. International Trade Commission, *History*, p. 9.

21. Ibid., p. 11.

22. The legitimacy of this agreement is enhanced by the fact that the chairman of this committee is the director general of the GATT.

23. International Trade Commission, *History*, p. 12.

24. Paul Wurth, "The Arrangement," p. 12.

25. Ibid., p. 8.

26. Interview with a GATT textile official, April 1981 (not for attribution).

27. This is found in U.S. Congress, Subcommittee on Trade of the House Committee on Ways and Means, *Background Material on the Multifiber Arrangement (1979 Edition)*. 96th Cong. 1st Sess. (Washington, D.C.: Government Printing Office, 1979), p. 65.

28. *Memorandum of Disapproval*, White House (Office of the White House Press Secretary), November 11, 1978.

29. U.S., Congress, Senate, 96th Cong. Sess. *Hearing before the Subcommittee on International trade of the Committee on Finance*, statement of Robert Munheim, counsel of the Treasury, March 19, 1979, p. 16.

30. Michael Hornsby, "EEC and America set for a Confrontation over Duties," *Times* (London), October 17, 1978.

31. Greg Conderacci, "Can Trade Talks Survive Inaction on Duty Waiver?," *Wall Street Journal*, October 20, 1978, p. 22.

32. *Times* (London), September 25, 1978.

33. Interview with a STR staff (not for attribution).

34. Interview in Washington, D.C., with Geze Feketekuty, January 1981.

35. Interview in Washington, D.C., with Alan Wolff, February 1981.

36. Clyde Farnsworth, "Pressure Mounting on Trade Packages: Lobbyists Pursue Special Waivers," New York *Times*, March 25, 1979, p. 1F and 4F.

37. Ibid.

38. *Congressional Quarterly Weekly Report*, July 7, 1979, p. 1370.

39. These agencies were: State, Treasury, Labor, the Council of Economic Advisors, and Commerce.

40. "Council of Economic Advisors Memo," (draft) January 17, 1979. (Mimeographed.)

41. "Proposed Presidential Textile Program," January 18, 1979, p. 3. (Mimeographed.)

42. Ibid.

43. Interview with Alan Wolff.

44. Ibid.

45. "Administration Textile Program," (draft, mimeographed) February 15, 1979, par. 3 under import controls.

46. Washington *Post*, February 2, 1979, p. 1.

47. Clyde Farnsworth, "Strauss Opposed on Trade Pact: House Unit Sees Injury to the US," New York *Times*, February 8, 1979, p. 11.

48. "Textile Import Accord Clears Way for Duty Waiver Bill," *Congressional Quarterly Weekly Reports*, February 24, 1979, p. 338.

49. Jan Guest, "GATT Officials Elated at US Waiver," *Guardian*, March 30, 1979, p. 18.

50. Ibid.

51. Interview in Geneva, April 1981 (not for attribution).

52. Interview with Stanley Nehmer in Washington, D.C., July 1980.

53. U.S., Congress, House, 96th Cong., 2nd Sess., Statement of George Varish on behalf of the United States Apparel Council before the Oversight Hearings of the Trade Subcommittee of the House Committee on Ways and Means, July 21, 1980.

54. Interview in Washington, D.C., February 1981 (not for attribution).

55. Interview in Geneva, March 1981 (not for attribution).

56. U.S., Department of the Treasury, Office of International Trade, "Positive Adjustment: A Case Study of Textiles," mimeographed (Washington, D.C.: Department of the Treasury, January 1980), p. 13.

57. Greg Conderacci, "Is the Trade Pact in Trouble?" *Wall Street Journal*, January 30, 1979, p. 16.

6

AUTOS
The Politics of Escape

INTRODUCTION

Between January and May of 1980, imports constituted 26.7 percent of all cars sold in the United States, the highest import penetration in U.S. history.[1] Japanese imports accounted for the majority (77 percent).[2] During the same period, production of American-built cars declined by 25.8 percent.[3] In response to these two trends both the UAW and Ford lobbied Congress for protection from Japanese imports. When Congress was not sufficiently forthcoming, they both filed a petition with the ITC for relief from import competition.

Ford, in defense of its petition before the ITC, argued that this action did not constitute a break with the past support of the U.S. auto industry for an open U.S. trade policy. Ford representatives argued that a vote by the commission for import relief would provide only temporary protection for the industry, which would allow the automobile industry to adjust to increased import competition and once again be competitive in the international market. In its petition Ford further states:

> It is Ford's belief—all too well substantiated by its declining sales, employment and profits—that relief is now in order. Congress had provided an avenue for such relief: Section 201 of the Trade Act. Indeed the

125

position in which Ford and other members of this industry find themselves is precisely that which Section 201 was designed to remedy by
providing temporary relief from competition to domestic producers so
that they can take steps to enable them to meet unrestricted import
competition in the future.[4]

The UAW and Ford, in support of their petitions, contended
that in the absence of this temporary relief the current increase in
imports would permanently impair the ability of American producers to compete in either U.S. or foreign markets. Fred Secrest, a
Ford official, in his response to the question "What if the amount of
protection you get isn't sufficient to get U.S. cars selling, and at a
higher price?"[5] stated:

> What have we lost? Has the country been severely injured? There
> wouldn't be any more people out of work than there were before. You
> would have a few people who would be driving new Datsuns but instead
> are driving old Plymouths. Inflation and oil consumption would rise a
> little. But if it was a mistake, it would be a critical mistake. The alternative
> of doing nothing risks the kind of scenario in which in ten years or so
> there would be no basis for a continuing domestic automobile industry.[6]

By casting the probable outcomes in terms of either relatively
small and known short-run costs of import protection or the unknown but possibly devastating long-run effects of no protection,
the petitioners convinced themselves from the outset that the ITC
would decide in favor of import relief. Notwithstanding their
expectations, the commission by a 3–2 vote rejected the petition.
Ultimately, the industry did receive some import relief in the form
of a voluntary restraint agreement (VRA) implemented by the
government of Japan. This VRA, however, proved to be significantly less restrictive than the remedies proposed by the UAW and
Ford in their ITC petitions.

In this case the interest group politics framework helps to
explain why Japan was willing to implement a VRA on auto exports to the United States. The Reagan administration used the
threat of legislated quotas as leverage to persuade Japan to restrict
exports to the United States. This posed a viable threat because
legislated quotas would probably be more restrictive and less flexi-

ble than those "voluntarily" agreed to by Japan. In addition, it was a credible threat because of the intense pressure on Congress to help the industry out of its financial crisis.

This case can also be explained partially by the congressional autonomy framework in that Congress was able to shield itself from direct industry pressure by diverting the UAW and Ford to the ITC. Once at the ITC, they had to demonstrate that increased imports constituted the major cause of the industry's financial problems. In this forum, interest group political pressure alone lacked sufficient influence to obtain the desired changes in U.S. trade policy. Yet, once the ITC rejected the case, the UAW and Ford went back to Congress to obtain import relief. At this point Congress did not appear to be able to ignore or to act autonomously from industry pressures.

The willingness of Japan to implement a VRA also lends some support to the view that states attempt to maximize national autonomy in trade policy. Here, the goal of national autonomy was to ensure the future financial viability of the American automobile industry. This definition of national autonomy is based on the assumption that a viable automobile industry forms an important component of the U.S. national interest. From this perspective the national interest dictated that the United States use its political power to restrict Japanese imports.

At the time of the VRA's negotiation, the 1980 recession had reduced aggregate demand for autos in the United States; so it was not clear how much the reduction in Japanese imports would increase U.S. car sales. To the extent that the VRA would increase the sales of U.S. cars, it would help to maintain social stability by creating jobs for unemployed autoworkers. Increased automation, however, permanently eliminated many of the jobs in the auto industry. To the extent that the VRA would permit U.S. auto producers to raise their prices, it would redistribute wealth from consumers to producers of autos. The VRA also helped to diffuse the political momentum in Congress for legislated import restraints. These legislated import restraints would have been an explicit violation of the GATT agreement. In these terms the VRA can be considered a pragmatic resolution to the trade conflict with Japan over auto exports. The cost of this agreement to American consumers reflected the price the United States had to pay to sustain its commitment to a liberal trading system.

This chapter demonstrates that the commitment on the part of the United States to adhere to the GATT escape clause provisions constrained the ability of the auto industry to influence trade policy and reduced the price the United States had to pay to diffuse the political pressure for protection. In order to comply with the GATT escape clause provisions the industry had to demonstrate to the commission exactly how imports had been a cause of injury. Their political strength in itself proved insufficient to influence the decision of the commission.

This chapter begins with a brief discussion of the growth of the U.S. auto industry to suggest why the auto industry found itself at such a competitive disadvantage. A discussion follows concerning the debate over auto imports in both Congress and the executive branch prior to the ITC hearings. The following section provides the legal context for the UAW and Ford petitions. The fourth section focuses on the ITC proceedings and covers the arguments linking injury to imports made by the UAW and Ford; the counter-arguments made by representatives of the importers; the ITC staff report on the auto industry; and finally, the rationale underlying the questioning and the decisions of the commissioners. The final policy decision on auto imports considered in this chapter is the action taken by the Reagan administration that led to the Japanese VRA.

THE DEVELOPMENT OF THE U.S. AUTO INDUSTRY

The U.S. automobile industry traditionally supported the progressive liberalization of international trade in the United States to induce other countries to remove barriers that limited exports of U.S. automobiles. By the early 1930s the United States had become the world's largest exporter of automobiles.[7] During this period, American firms exported mass production methods to their European subsidiaries that had been perfected in the United States during World War I. Although the use of mass production posed a competitive threat to European producers, U.S. firms eventually found themselves at a competitive disadvantage because the autos assembled abroad were designed for the U.S. market. By the mid-1930s European producers began to adopt the American assembly line methods of production to make autos more suited to conditions in the European market. These automobiles were small, low-priced, and relatively low-powered units with low costs of operation. Retaliatory tariff increases on U.S. products in response to the Smoot-Hawley Tariff Act further reduced the demand for U.S.-produced automobiles in Europe.

After World War II, conditions in the American and European markets continued to diverge. While American consumers reestablished their preference for roomy powerful automobiles, European manufacturers concentrated on building small, low-priced units with low costs of operation and maintenance.[8] During the 1950s, U.S. exports became progressively less competitive in world markets because they cost more to operate than European cars. As the relative importance of U.S. exports declined, U.S. manufacturers supplied world markets primarily through direct foreign investment.

During the 1950s and 1960s when U.S. exports declined, European exports to the United States increased. By 1959 U.S. automobile imports—which in 1957 represented only 3.5 percent of the American market—surged to 10.2 percent.[9] U.S. producers responded to this increase in popularity of small imports with the introduction of compacts that were shorter and narrower than the standard American models. Initially, however, these models lacked price competitiveness with the European imports. In 1968 U.S. producers did not make a car that sold for under $1,800, whereas 17 models of imports were selling for less than this amount.[10] In 1968 when both Ford and GM decided to produce a small car that was price competitive with European imports, both firms emphasized the price over considerations of quality.

American auto manufacturers had resisted producing small fuel-efficient cars because they made high profit margins on accessories, for example, power steering and brakes, which were best suited to the larger models. At hearings on the auto industry held by the committee in spring 1980, Charles Vanik, the chairman, stated: "Detroit wanted big cars because big cars meant big bucks."[11] The staff report goes on to suggest: "Detroit didn't mind losing 15 percent of the total U.S. auto market because this segment represented mostly small cars which had low profit margins.[12] William Tucker explained:

> Industry executives discovered that they could build a much bigger car with a lot more frills for very little more money, yet still command a much higher price in the market place. The manufacturing costs of a Cadillac from 1950 to 1975 rarely exceeded the manufacturing costs of a Chevrolet by more than $300. Yet a fancy Cadillac could often sell for three to four thousand dollars more in the marketplace. Therefore Detroit tended toward bigger cars because they could produce bigger profits.[13]

Although U.S. firms reluctantly entered the small-car market, in its first year the Pinto outsold Volkswagen and became the best-selling small car in the United States.[14]

The demand for small cars increased suddenly in 1973 after the Arab oil boycott, which followed the Yom Kippur War. The oil boycott resulted in gasoline shortages as well as a sudden rise in U.S. gasoline prices. This increase in demand for small cars caught both U.S. and foreign producers totally by surprise. Tucker indicates that "none of the manufacturers were prepared to meet this sudden upsurge in demand. Volkswagen and Toyota ran short of cars just as much as did the American companies."[15] Once the price of gasoline stabilized, however, consumers returned to their previous preference for larger cars. Evidence of this shift in demand can be seen in the growing inventories of small cars within six months after the end of the Arab oil embargo. Tucker describes that at this point "Ford suddenly found itself with a ninety-six-day supply of Pintos on its hands (a sixty-day supply is regarded as normal) and General Motors found itself stuck with a 110-day supply of Vegas. But Cadillac inventories were down to 26 days and Cadillac plants were put on double shifts."[16]

Price controls on oil, which kept the domestic price below the world market price, sustained the demand for large cars. Gasoline prices in real terms declined after reaching a peak during the Arab oil embargo until 1979 when again they began to rise sharply after the Iranian revolution. In order to encourage auto manufacturers to increase fuel efficiency without raising the price of gasoline, in 1975 Congress passed the Energy Policy and Conservation Act, which set the minimum standards for gasoline mileage for U.S. autos between 1978 and 1985.[17] The law required passenger cars to have a fleet average of 27.5 miles per gallon of fuel consumption by 1985. Although initially firms could use captive imports (cars produced by foreign subsidiaries) in calculating their fleet average; the UAW pushed through Congress a provision that required that every automobile included in the average had to be at least 75 percent U.S. origin.

Initially, the auto companies opposed the corporate average fuel economy (CAFE) standards because they feared that consumers were not interested in fuel-efficient cars. The U.S. auto manufacturers claimed: "First, . . . the technology was not available to achieve these standards; but, more importantly, the U.S. auto consumer would not buy the small auto that would be required to meet the standards. In short, the U.S. auto industry would collapse because of lack of consumer acceptance."[18] A Department of Transportation (DOT) study supported the auto industry in its findings.

> Even at the end of 1978, the greatest demand in the U.S. market was still for V-8 powered vehicles, import penetration of smaller cars was still under 16 percent, and there was great concern over the unsold inventory of Japanese models. Consumers were acting in an economically rational manner, given that the real price of gasoline was less than it was in 1960 and gas was in plentiful supply.[19]

Even with the CAFE standards, in 1979 U.S. automakers were still producing 60 percent intermediate and large cars and only 40 percent compacts and subcompacts.[20]

After the Arab oil embargo GM did institute a program to downsize its model line. *Downsizing,* a term invented by GM, involves redesigning existing models during the annual model changeover with a shorter wheelbase to reduce weight, without a dramatic change in design concept. Weight reduction and aerodynamic improvements—rather than fundamental changes in technology—improve fuel economy. Downsizing typically requires design changes primarily to the body of the car, with relatively minor changes to the basic powertrain, steering, and suspension systems.[21]

Ford, lacking the resources of GM, perceived GM's downsizing program as an opportunity to increase its own share of the large-car market. As a result Ford only began its downsizing program in 1978 with its compacts, followed by the standard models in 1979 and intermediate cars in 1980. Because downsizing proved too expensive for Chrysler in conjunction with developing a front-wheel drive auto, Chrysler's strategy was to come out with a front-wheel drive car and "stretch" it. Front-wheel drive requires more demanding technology changes than downsizing.[22] Chrysler also planned to sell all the larger models that it could.

Although the strategies of these firms to develop smaller cars varied, they all revealed an underlying belief that the auto firms had sufficient control over the market to "walk it down" at their own pace. The Iranian revolution shattered this belief in the fall of 1978; it resulted in yet another sudden increase in U.S. gasoline prices. These price increases translated into a sudden rise in the demand for small cars. The DOT report suggests that despite the efforts of the auto industry to downsize and come up with plans to produce front-wheel drive automobiles again the U.S. industry was not prepared for this sudden shift in demand.

> Although U.S. manufacturers had been increasing their production of smaller cars during the period between 1974 and 1979, they still relied heavily on the consumer's desire for large cars and were not ready for the unexpected and rapid change in consumer tastes that followed the Iranian shortfall of 1979.[23]

The U.S. automobile industry proved especially vulnerable to the decline in demand for large cars because when the Iranian oil crisis hit, it had begun a massive conversion process to prepare for the production of front-wheel drive cars. Industry analysts estimated that the cost of this conversion process would be more than $70 billion (in 1980 dollars) between 1979 and 1985. The decline in sales in conjunction with this massive investment program resulted in net losses on operations for the industry as a whole. The ITC reported that between "January and June 1980, the industry incurred a loss of $2.9 billion, compared with a net operating profit of $2.7 billion in the corresponding period of 1979."[24]

In response to this decline in sales, the industry began to lay off workers. At the peak of auto production in 1978/79 the industry employed about 1 million workers directly involved in the manufacture of automobiles and another 1.4 million workers in supplier industries. In 1980, when motor vehicle production dropped from a peak of 14.7 million units to 9 million units, the industry laid off 300,000 autoworkers, and another 350,000 to 650,000 people in auto-related industries lost their jobs.[25] Capacity utilization of the full-size and luxury models fell from 98.5 percent between January and June 1979 to 42.8 percent during the same period in 1980.[26] Most of the workers, however, who lost their jobs were working at factories that made primarily large cars or large V-6 or V-8 engines. A the same time, factories producing small cars operated at capacity and still did not match demand.

Whereas U.S. manufacturers could not produce enough small cars to meet American demand, foreign producers had surplus capacity. The Japanese importers to the United States stood particularly well positioned to take advantage of this increase in demand for small cars because they had been building up large inventories of small cars prior to the Iranian revolution. Japanese manufacturers had also been expanding dealer networks in the United States in order to increase their marketing capacity. This Japanese export drive to the United States was based on the expectation that the political instability in the Middle East and the depletion of oil reserves would eventually lead to a rise in the price of gasoline, thereby increasing the desirability of fuel-efficient cars.

The 1979 oil price rise signified an end to the isolation of the North American auto market. The average price per gallon of gasoline in January 1979, in current dollars, was 69 cents; by December 1979 the price of gasoline had increased to 105.2 cents.[27] This price rise marked the end of the period in which low energy prices acted as a NTB to protect the U.S. automobile industry. A DOT study suggested that "until the Arab oil embargo of 1973–74, the U.S. producers enjoyed what amounted to a protected market in large cars—protected in the sense that U.S. carmakers catered to the U.S. consumer's traditionally strong demand for vehicles of large size and horsepower."[28]

Fred Secrest of the Ford Motor Company also made this point. He explained:

> The American auto industry and its customers lived behind a kind of tariff wall for years and didn't know it. That was cheap gasoline. For decades it was cheap in this country though it was always expensive in

> the rest of the world. All of a sudden that went away. The industry was faced overnight with removal of protection that had caused it to make cars averaging 12 to 15 miles per gallon.[29]

The House Subcommittee on Trade staff report posed the dilemma faced by the U.S. auto industry in 1980 as a result of this loss of import protection.

> The major problem facing the domestic auto industry is: How can it satisfy the U.S. auto consumers' demand for small, fuel-efficient autos when over half of its production facilities are geared to produce large, less fuel-efficient autos? Cash flow is needed to retool, but imports are eating into the profits needed for $80 billion in new investment.[30]

So U.S. producers found themselves caught in the middle of a transition to increased capacity for small-car production that could not be accelerated. In addition, they were incurring losses due to the decline in sales of large cars. In response to this situation the UAW and Ford attempted to persuade Congress of the need to impose trade restrictions in order to improve both employment levels and industry profitability. The following section discusses the initial efforts of the UAW and Ford to persuade the government to impose some kind of import restraints on foreign automobiles. Ultimately, both the administration and Congress indicated that the industry would have to go to the ITC before any decision to restrict imports would be made.

PRE-ITC: THE EXECUTIVE BRANCH AND CONGRESS

In late 1979 Ambassador Rubin Askew (head of the Office of the Special Trade Representative) told the Japanese that to diffuse potential political pressures for auto import restraints they would have to invest in the United States. The STR again raised the issue of Japanese investment in the United States at an interagency meeting in December 1979. At this meeting other agencies raised questions about pursuing this idea further in light of the obvious ambivalence on the part of the Japanese.[31] In response to this opposition, the representative from the STR argued that Japanese investment in the United States was necessary to help mitigate the possibility of a strong protectionist drive on the part of the U.S. auto industry. He suggested this was a serious danger, given rising levels of unemployment and imports. The STR representative believed that Japanese investment would solve the potential political problems that the industry could create. None of the other agencies present at the meeting, however, supported the STR on this action.

In opposition to the STR's position on Japanese investment, a Treasury Department memo suggested that forcing Japanese auto producers to invest in the United States would set an "unfortunate precedent." If the United States took this action with Japanese autos, it could easily begin to use this as a policy response in other sectors and for other countries. The Treasury further opposed this policy because implicitly it would promote a concern with bilateral trade balances by sector. This would involve a major departure from U.S. policy, which has been to consider multilateral payment balances across products. The Treasury's suggestion was just to let the issue of Japanese investment "fade away."

The issue of Japanese investment emerged again in January 1980 in a meeting at the Department of Labor between a representative of the UAW and government officials from the Departments of Labor, Treasury, State and the Office of the Special Trade Representative. At this meeting the STR's expectation that the auto industry would request the government for import restraint proved to be correct. The UAW representative suggested that the problem of Japanese imports could be handled either through voluntary export restraints imposed by the Japanese or by Japanese investment in the United States. When questioned by the STR representative as to whether the union would be satisfied with meaningful commitments from Japanese producers to invest within the next six months, he responded that the UAW would still want a voluntary reduction of Japanese exports until 1985.[32] Nothing conclusive came out of this meeting aside from a suggestion that the Department of Labor look into the possibility of holding a seminar with the Japanese on U.S. labor relations. This suggestion was intended to address the major reasons given by the Japanese for not investing in the United States, which all hinged on the Japanese belief that labor management relations would not be as smooth in the United States as they are in Japan.[33]

Toyota and Nissan gave the following reasons for not esta-
blishing U.S. facilities:

1. U.S. labor rates are much higher in the United States than in Japan.
2. Quality would suffer because U.S. autoworkers are not as conscien-
   tious as Japanese workers.
3. There are more work stoppages in the United States.
4. Most of their suppliers reside in Japan.
5. The yen/dollar relationship is unpredictable.
6. General Motors, Ford, and Chrysler would soon be building autos
   that directly compete with fuel-efficient Japanese models; thus there
   would be a glut of small cars on the U.S. market by the time the
   U.S. plant would be operative.[34]

In February 1980 Douglas Fraser, president of the UAW, vis-
ited Japan to urge the Japanese automakers to set up manufacturing facilities in the United States. Fraser told the Japanese that
"they ought to build cars where they sell them" and pointed out
that American firms have set up plants in Europe to make cars for
the Europeans.[35] In addition, Fraser asked for an orderly marketing agreement to restrain exports until 1982 in order to give American manufacturers breathing room during the transition to the
production of smaller, more fuel-efficient cars.[36] Fraser further
stated that if the Japanese auto producers did nothing within the
next three months to restrain exports, they would face the serious
possibility of congressional legislation mandating import restraints.
To emphasize the seriousness of this possibility, he reminded the
Japanese that hearings before the House Subcommittee on Trade
had been set for March to deal with this issue. Fraser commented,
"After that, it [protectionist legislation] could snowball very, very
rapidly. It could happen in six or eight weeks."[37] When asked
whether he would have the votes to push this legislation through
Congress, he said, "We will have."[38]

Prior to Fraser's arrival in Japan, the Japanese government had
also met with the representatives of Toyota and Nissan Motor
companies to urge them to consider both American investment
and export curbs.[39] An official at the Ministry of International
Trade and Industry (MITI) said the government was trying to
promote orderly exports of automobiles to the United States to
lessen tensions between the countries. The MITI spokesman said,

"We are urging automobile industry representatives to take the US-Japan relations into account."[40] MITI also stated, however, that it was up to the Japanese industry to decide how they were going to respond.[41] By the end of February the representatives of both Nissan and Toyota met with Foreign Minister Saburo Okita to inform him that their executives had agreed that to start up production of autos in the United States at this time would prove highly risky.[42] In spite of this rejection, MITI sustained some hope that it might still be possible to work out solutions to the problems the automakers felt they faced with U.S. investment. But in response to MITI's continued encouragement, a Nissan spokesman commented: "Even if we decide to build a plant now, actual production would not start for two years, and then it might be commercially unfeasible because of the resurgence of the U.S. auto makers."[43]

Fraser raised the issue of Japanese investment once again in the mid-March 1980 hearings of the House Subcommittee on Trade. In these hearings he justified local content requirements, which would force foreign automakers to produce in the United States on the grounds that "each company has an obligation to generate employment in those countries in which it has a substantial volume of sales."[44] He further suggested that in addition to creating North American investment and jobs, foreign investment would not, like import restraints, eliminate competition between foreign and U.S. manufacturers. He did not, however, consider Japanese investment as a substitute for import protection and called for an unambiguous message from the U.S. Congress telling the Japanese that a reduction in exports to the U.S. was imperative. To back up this action, he requested the administration to negotiate a VRA with Japan. At the time, though, he did not consider it necessary for the United States to pass legislation imposing quotas on Japanese auto imports.

The Ford Motor Company also testified at these hearings on the need for "fairness" in auto trade. Secrest suggested that a fair U.S. policy would subject both foreign and domestic producers to the same domestic content requirements to comply with the CAFE standards. In effect, this would force them to manufacture in the United States, because to qualify under the CAFE requirements 75 percent of each auto sold would have to be made in the United States. Secrest also asked the committee that either the United

States request a VRA with Japan or legislate a quota on Japanese cars. In his concluding remarks Secrest contended:

> These approaches are not mutually exclusive—and in fact we may need a combination of them. A voluntary agreement would minimize GATT difficulties and perhaps be much faster. It certainly would be more consistent with the historic position of the Ford Motor Company that legislated barriers against open trade can create inefficiencies and inequities. But it's not clear today whether voluntary approaches will work. Frankly, we had hoped that the voluntary route would have begun to solve the problem by now—yet so far the U.S. has a commitment on only a single assembly plant from one of the smaller Japanese producers; and recent press reports indicate Toyota and Nissan still plan no such investments.[45]

George Eads, a member of the CEA, took the same position as the Treasury in objecting to investment motivated by political coercion as opposed to economic considerations. In testimony before the House Subcommittee on Trade, Eads argued that Japanese automakers should invest in the United States only if these investments appear to be economically viable.

He also testified against imposing import restraints on Japanese automobiles. This testimony stemmed from an analysis prepared by the CEA staff of the economic effects of limiting Japanese imports to 1979 levels—a reduction of about 250,000 units. This analysis assumed that a reduction in the number of small cars in the U.S. market would not necessarily compel consumers to purchase an equal number of large autos. Instead, it assumed that one additional large American car would be sold for every two imports not allowed into the U.S. market. The analysis demonstrated that if imports were reduced by 250,000 units:

1. Consumer expenditures would increase by $1 to 2 billion;
2. U.S. oil consumption would increase for several years due to the artificially imposed shortage of fuel–efficient automobiles; and
3. Employment would increase by 20,000 workers—only 5,000 of whom would be in the motor vehicle and parts industries (the remainder would be in ancillary industries: steel, aluminum, etc).[46]

After assessing these costs, Eads concluded:

> The solution does not lie in import restrictions, either formal or informal. They will generate little in the way of additional employment now and will ensure that when our auto companies do have sufficient

capacity to produce small cars, foreign markets will be closed to them. Such restrictions represent a short-sighted response to a genuine short-term problem.[47]

After the conclusion of these hearings, the staff of the House Subcommittee on Trade published a study in which they also argued against import restrictions. They based this opposition in part on the prediction that by the mid-1980s the United States would have adequate production capacity in small cars to be able to compete successfully with foreign auto producers. In the interim the study called for Japan's cooperation in reducing the bilateral deficit in autos with the United States through:

1. The purchase of auto parts, including replacement parts, in the United States;
2. The reduction of trade barriers against U.S. autos and U.S. auto parts in Japan; and
3. The investment in auto assembly plants in the United States.[48]

In response to the reluctance of the trade subcommittee to recommend legislation for import restraint, both Ford and the UAW turned to the ITC in their attempt to have the government restrict Japanese imports. At one point during the House hearings, Vanik, the chairman of the subcommittee, even suggested to Secrest that Ford try to get an injury ruling from the ITC since the industry was in such bad shape. Fraser agreed because he believed the ITC process would take less time than either trying to get anything done in Congress or trying to convince the administration to act. He commented: "We can't wait for the President or the Congress to act. That's too slow. . . . This [the ITC proceedings] will take a relatively short time compared to legislative or presidential action. At least you have a definite time schedule."[49]

THE UAW AND FORD PETITIONS

On June 12, 1980, the UAW filed a petition before the ITC under Section 201 of the Trade Act of 1974 for relief from import competition. The petition argued that the increase in imports into the United States was "a substantial cause of serious injury, or threat thereof, to the domestic industry."[50] The Ford Motor Company filed a petition in support of the UAW on August 4, 1980. Ford cited Japan's continuing efforts to maximize short-term car and light truck exports to the United States and the unwillingness of the U.S. government to negotiate a voluntary restraint agreement with Japan as the factors that led the firm to file the petition.

The principle task of the commission in an escape clause decision is to determine the connection between an increase in imports and the injury to the industry. In making this determination each of the commissioners goes through three steps: first, they define the industry; second, they determine whether the industry is in fact injured; and third, they determine—if injury is found to exist—whether it is primarily a direct result of an increase in imports.[51] If the commission determines by way of a majority vote that the industry is injured by imports, it will recommend to the president specific remedies, which include tariff increases, the imposition of quotas on foreign imports, or a combination of both.

The ITC's injury determination legitimates any actions the United States may take under Article 19 (the escape clause) of the GATT. Article 19 allows member states to withdraw tariff concessions on a temporary basis "that as a result of changed circumstances are causing or threatening serious injury of like or competitive products as a result of unforeseen developments."[52] The rationale for including this clause in the GATT was that if countries had the assurance that they could temporarily suspend a tariff concession under certain conditions, they would be more likely to take risks in negotiating tariff reductions.

Although GATT members can legitimately withdraw tariff concessions under Article 19, they must also be willing to offer compensation to those states whose exports would be reduced. This compensation can take the form of either equivalent tariff reductions on other products or equivalent tariff increases implemented by the country whose products are restricted. In addition, restrictions that result from an escape clause action must be imposed on an MFN basis and cannot be set up in such a way that discriminates against a specific supplier even though the imports from one country may be causing the majority of damage. The underlying intent of Article 19 is that the suspension of tariff concessions should be in place only for as long as it takes for the industry to adjust to increased import competition.

Both the UAW and Ford stressed in their petitions that the industry needed import relief in order to generate the massive capital expenditures necessary to survive the transition to the production of small cars. The union also made the point that this protection would allow the industry to rehire some of the unemployed autoworkers. The UAW specifically requested five years of quotas and tariffs. This protection would consist of:

1. An increase in the tariff on autos from 2.9 to 20 percent;
2. The imposition of a quota based on either 1975 or 1976 import levels; and
3. The exemption of imports from these restrictions if they contained 50 percent local content the first year, 60 percent the second year, and 75 percent the third year.[53]

Ford, in its petition, stressed the need to encourage the American consumer to buy U.S. automobiles in order to increase the profitability of U.S. firms. Ford argued:

> All the requested relief is required for the full five years, because the conversion process cannot be accomplished in less time, and because a shorter period might induce would-be import customers to wait out the period. . . . The length of the restriction period will discourage many consumers from riding out the remedy period. These consumers will purchase domestic vehicles, and they may remain domestic vehicles consumers after the relief period.[54]

Ford further maintained that the increased sales volume that would result from the restriction of imports would aid the industry in maintaining the confidence of the investment community and thereby allow the successful completion of the conversion process.

In contrast to the UAW, Ford did not recommend a tariff increase. Ford did, however, request that a quota be established, based on 1976 imports. This quota would set total imports to the United States at 1.7 million cars and 260,000 small trucks. Because Japanese imports to the United States increased more rapidly than European imports after 1976, this remedy would primarily restrict Japanese imports. European imports would only be marginally affected. Ford supported this remedy "in the expectation that the President will promptly negotiate an Orderly Marketing Agreement (OMA) with Japan."[55]

The 1974 Trade Act mandated that the following conditions were to be met for the commission to recommend import restraints:

1. There must be increased imports—either actual or relative to domestic production—of an article into the United States.
2. The domestic industry producing an article like or directly competitive with the imported one must be seriously injured or threatened with serious injury.
3. The increased imports must be a substantial cause of serious injury, or the threat thereof, to the domestic industry making the article.[56]

The House and Senate report on the escape clause further specified that for an import to be a substantial cause of injury two criteria must be met in all cases:

1. Imports must be an important cause of serious injury; and
2. Imports must be at least as important as any other single cause.

Congress left to the discretion of the ITC commissioners the specification and weight of the factors that are determined to be a source of injury to the industry. Because no established objective criteria exist to use to infer whether imports constitute the main cause of injury, to some extent the injury determination remains left to the subjective judgment of the individual commissioners.

At issue in the auto case was precisely this question of causality. Imports had increased dramatically in 1979 and early 1980. By most indicators of injury—the significant idling of productive facilities, the inability of a significant number of firms to operate at a reasonable level of profit, and the significant degree of unemployment in the industry—the auto industry in 1980 appeared to be injured. The Ford petition indicated:

> The American automotive industry is suffering serious injury. U.S. car and truck production is down by more than 4 million units annually since 1978. More than 300,000 workers have been laid off since 1978, and the number is increasing daily. Profits have collapsed. In the last half of 1979, U.S. producers lost approximately $700 million. Dealer profits have evaporated. Factory sales are down 40.8% from 1979 levels; and a growing number of plants are closing, causing incalculable harm to the economies of the regions in which they are located.[57]

The petitioners expected that the ITC would have little trouble in attributing a causal link between the two factors. Ford's president, Phillip Caldwell, said in a news conference prior to the ITC hearings that "it seemed inconceivable to him that the ITC might conclude that imports aren't injuring the domestic industry." He further commented "that the ITC doesn't even have to look into the reasons why U.S. imports of cars and light trucks are approaching three million units this year."[58]

Ford, in its prehearing brief, also contended that causality was not an issue. The brief argues: "The significant question is whether there has been an increase in imports and a decline in the proportion of the domestic market supplied by domestic producers."[59] Ford believed that the primary task of the commission would be to provide the causal link between the increase in imports and the injury to the industry. This would then allow the United States to meet its international legal obligations, thus mitigating any damaging effects auto import restraint may have on the international trading system.

THE ITC PROCEEDINGS

> The President wants to assure all parties—the auto industry, its workers, consumers, and foreign auto companies—a prompt, expeditious and unbiased review of the impact of imports on the domestic auto industry. He feels that the USITC is the appropriate forum for making this review; and this formal investigation must be completed before any decisions on import relief can be made. The President will decide what actions to take once he has received the USITC report.[60]

The following discussion focuses on the ITC investigation and hearings on the auto industry. The ITC consideration of import relief consists of several stages. Prior to the hearings, briefs are filed both in support of and in opposition to import relief. In addition, the ITC staff conducts an independent investigation of the industry. During the course of the hearings the commission receives testimony from representatives of those organizations in support of the petition, followed by those who are opposed. This structure allows both the commissioners and the other participants to question anyone who presents a statement. After the hearings end, the commission accepts posthearing briefs in which the major arguments are restated and critiqued by opponents. The final stage of the process consists of the commission's vote on whether the industry is found to be injured by foreign imports. If it finds injury, the commission goes on to hold another set of hearings on potential remedies.

In the auto case the commission's decision hinged upon whether the petitioners (the UAW and Ford) could demonstrate causal relationship between the increase in imports and injury to the industry. In analyzing the ITC hearings this discussion concentrates on the arguments made by Ford and the UAW in which they attempt to demonstrate this causal link, the counterargument of the importers, and the ultimate decision taken by the commission.

The United Automobile Workers

The UAW petition argued that the increase in imports from Japan and Western Europe contributed to the concurrent decline in U.S. production, thereby injuring the industry. The UAW petition first established:

> Imports of passenger cars from Western Europe have trended strongly upward since the 1975 recession and were 16.6% ahead of the prior year through the first quarter of 1980. Imports of both passenger cars and trucks from Japan more than doubled between 1973 and 1979 with first quarter 1980 imports running about 50 % ahead of the comparable period in 1979.[61]

The petition went on to describe the extent to which U.S. production had declined.

> US production of passenger cars by 1979 had dropped more than 12 % in units from the profitable levels achieved in 1973 and more than 8% in units from the levels achieved in 1977 and 1979. Production for the first four months of 1980 as compared with the same period in 1979 has dropped a staggering 26.6% in units.[62]

Having established both that imports had increased and that domestic production had gone down, the petition then documents the indicators of serious injury to the industry.

> The plummeting production and sales figures, the major losses suffered by the US operations of Ford and Chrysler in 1979 (Chrysler also in 1978), the losses for US operations now projected for Chrysler, AMC, Ford and even GM in 1980, the fall closing of the Scout facility, the permanent closing of a number of automotive assembly and manufacturing facilities, the current temporary and indefinite layoff of more than three hundred thousand UAW members—all indicate that the domestic industry is indeed seriously injured and is threatened with serious injury within the meaning of the statute as interpreted by the International Trade Commission.[63]

To establish the causal relationship between the increase in imports and the decline in U.S. production, the UAW argued that fuel efficiency was not a relevant dimension upon which to differentiate between imported and U.S. automobiles. Instead, the UAW contended that the distinctive conditions of the U.S. automobile market in conjunction with U.S. government policy toward the auto industry should be used to determine the attributes consumers could expect from U.S. autos. The UAW suggested specifically that these distinctive conditions of the U.S. market included low taxes on gasoline, low taxes and fees on automobiles, and the development of a magnificent system of generally toll-free superhighways.[64] These factors that comprised the postwar U.S. auto policy resulted in the lack of consumer demand for fuel efficiency. This argument emphasizes the factors that influence the decision regarding what kind of automobile to produce rather than those factors that the consumer confronts in deciding upon what kind of automobile to purchase.

Once the petition established that it is reasonable to expect the American consumer to buy U.S.-built cars because the U.S. market and public policy provided incentives for the production of autos that were not fuel efficient, it went on to argue that imports are a close, if not direct, substitute for American automobiles. This substitutability of U.S. for foreign cars in the U.S. market then creates a problem for American producers because the United States is a mature market and future sales will consist of replacing the existing fleet instead of rapidly expanding the number of vehicles in the United States. The UAW concluded, "Thus, the dramatic sales increase achieved by the foreign manufacturers in the United States market place has directly affected the level of sales that could be achieved by the domestic manufacturers."[65]

The Ford Motor Company

Ford shares with the UAW the implicit assumption that the U.S. automobile industry has a right to the U.S. market. This belief manifests itself in their contention that "the U.S. market is largely mature and large increases in demand to provide room for increased imports are not anticipated, once total U.S. demand recovers from the present recession"[66] In its petition Ford essentially made the same argument as the UAW to support its claim that Japanese imports have injured the U.S. auto industry. The Ford petition also attempted to strengthen the case for import restraints by demonstrating that imports constituted the most important cause of injury to the industry. (In order to qualify for import relief the ITC has to establish that imports are the most important cause of injury if other causes are determined to exist.)

The Ford petition anticipated the arguments that the 1980 recession and the shift in consumer demand to small, fuel-efficient vehicles are greater causes of injury to the industry than imports. Ford pointed out two factors to explain why imports were a greater cause of injury to the industry than the recession. First, imports had begun to injure the industry in 1977, two years before the recession began. The indicator they use to substantiate this claim is the decline in after-tax profits of all domestic auto producers on their U.S. operations. This declined 9.6 percent from 1977 to 1978, and 69.9 percent from 1978 to 1979.[67] Second, Ford argued that the recession could not be the most serious cause of injury to the industry because even during the recession sales of imports increased in both absolute and relative terms. Whereas new car sales decreased 15.4 percent in the first quarter of 1980 from the same period in 1979, new car sales of imports rose 20.8 percent.[68] Since consumers continued to buy new imported cars during the recession, Ford argued that the recession could not be a major factor that was injuring the industry. Instead, Ford attributed the financial difficulties of the industry directly to this growing proportion of import sales. The petition claimed:

> Were it not for sharply higher import sales, then the rate of domestic sales in the 1980 trough would have been higher by 1.3 million or more than 18 %. On an annual basis, the loss of 1.3 million domestic sales to

imports cost domestic producers in excess of $2 billion in profits desperately needed to finance their conversion to the new, more fuel efficient cars and trucks the market desires.[69]

Ford concluded that although the recession may have hurt the industry, it did not cause as much damage as imports.

The Ford petition also offered a counterargument to the contention that sales of U.S.-produced cars have declined because the industry does not have the capacity to produce enough fuel-efficient automobiles to meet consumer demand.

> Of course, when the Commission determines that increased imports are a cause of serious injury not less important than any other, its inquiry on the subject of causation is at an end. Nevertheless, there is a further factor requiring brief mention that has been inappropriately suggested as a "cause" of the industry's injury: the alleged inability of US producers to satisfy consumer demand for small, fuel efficient vehicles. This contention is unfounded.[70]

Ford contends that it is unfounded because the shift in demand was to small imports and not to small cars in general and that the "alleged consumer preference for imports is not a cause of injury separate from increased imports."[71]

Ford further considered the shift in demand away from large cars irrelevant. Instead, their brief suggested that the commission should focus on the shift away from American cars.

> In any event, the relevant measurement is not the ratio of the loss of large cars' share to the growth of import share, but rather the sales of domestic producers compared with those of import producers. The significant question is whether there has been an increase in imports . . . and a decline in the proportion of the domestic market supplied by domestic producers.[72]

On the basis of this line of reasoning, Ford, like the UAW, attempted to convince the commission that all cars are essentially similar and that the underlying factors that may have had an effect on consumer demand were irrelevant as causes of injury. Ford concluded that "consumer preference for imports is precisely the problem."[73]

The Importers

In response to the ITC petitions the American subsidiaries of the foreign auto producers attempted to demonstrate that:

1. The recession had a greater effect on depressing demand for American cars than imports; and
2. The shift in consumer demand for small, fuel-efficient cars, both American and foreign, injured the industry more than imports because it resulted in the rapid decline of large-car sales.

The prehearing brief of the Nissan Motor Company provides the basis for the following discussion of the importers' arguments before the ITC. It is representative of the position taken by the majority of the importers.

Nissan argued that the recession that began in 1980 produced the major cause of injury to the domestic industry. To explain why the recession did not equally depress the demand for American cars and imports, Nissan suggested that the demand for imports, unlike American cars, is countercyclical because buyers of imported cars tend to have a higher income and be better educated relative to the general population. Since these attributes indicate that buyers of imported cars are less likely to feel the economic effects of the recession, the Nissan brief concluded that it was not unreasonable to expect the market share of imports to increase during a recession. The brief further pointed out that this increase in market share was found primarily in those states (California and Colorado) that suffered least by the recession and that because states with the lowest import share were hardest hit by the recession, the economic upturn would help the sales of U.S. cars proportionately more than imports.

Nissan also argued that "there can be no question that the shift in demand was a more important cause of the decline in domestic car sales than the increase in imports."[74] Sales of small cars went from 48.5 percent of the market in 1978 to almost 63 percent in 1980. The brief contended that this shift in demand resulted in the increase in sales of both small American and imported cars. Nissan concluded, "The increase in imports was almost entirely a consequence, not a cause of this shift in demand."[75]

The Staff Report

The ITC staff report was based on an independent analysis of the industry. The ITC staff argued that the U.S. auto industry's problems stemmed primarily from a significant decline in the sales of large cars. The report stated: "As demand declined in 1979 and 1980 it also shifted: sales of large cars—the mainstay of the U.S. auto industry—fell in disproportion to overall sales. Having remained relatively stable at about 50% of apparent consumption from 1975 to 1978, large cars declined to 29.9% of apparent consumption by January–June 1980."[76] The shift from large to small cars led to a decline in profitability in the industry because large cars generated a higher profit than small cars. The ITC report found that "as sales shifted to smaller models after 1977, total profit declined accordingly."[77] A lower unit sales volume exacerbated the financial problems caused by this shift. This posed particularly difficult problems for the industry as firms could not postpone planned capital investments because of the shift in consumer demand.

The ITC Staff Report also made the argument that the recession was an important cause of decline in the sales of American cars. It stated:

> The period between January 1979 and June 1980 was marked by rapid increases in the cost of credit, increasing unemployment, declines in real spendable earnings, large cutbacks in consumer spending, and deteriorating consumer confidence in the economy and in future earning power. The decline in automobile consumption is generally accepted to be worldwide, although it has been most severe in the United States.[78]

The commission had the task of deciding whether imports constituted the primary cause of injury. During the hearings, neither Ford nor the UAW managed to explain persuasively to the commission the role that imports played in causing the current state of the industry's problems. In addition, neither Ford nor GM could show how cutting back imports would have a noticeable effect on their investment plans. Ultimately, the commission's attempts to understand the effect of the remedy in the industry's investment strategy proved to be a major determinant of the final decision.

The Hearings

ITC Commissioner Paula Stern began her questioning of UAW President Fraser by asking what the UAW believed the role of fuel economy to be in consumer demand. Fraser replied:

> Number one I think the American consumer is extremely conscious of fuel efficiency. And, secondly, so far the American industry hasn't got the story across to the American consumer that we too build fuel efficient cars. The difficulty, Commissioner, and I suppose time will correct this, is the public perception, which views the American car as a gas guzzler.[79]

Here, the UAW attempted to make the point that consumers overreacted to the gasoline price rise and made "irrational" decisions in purchasing cars in 1980. Restricting imports would help to reduce the damage this irrationality had caused the industry.

Howard Young, director of research for the UAW, went on to argue that the gasoline price rise had an effect on the purchases of domestic cars as well as imports. He stated:

> A lot of people who had owned larger domestic cars went for smaller or more fuel efficient domestic cars. So that it was not simply a shift to imported cars, or it was not just that they [consumers] only perceived the imported cars as being the most—as being the fuel efficient ones they wanted.[80]

Although Stern did not pursue the issue at this point, Young's statement seems to point to an underlying shift to small as opposed to imported cars, an argument that both the UAW and Ford had been attempting to refute.

Young also argued that the interest in fuel efficiency would not lead a consumer to forgo an automobile purchase even if the most fuel-efficient automobiles were not available. This point strikes a similar note to Ford's claim that if imports were reduced, the demand for new automobiles would remain constant and the reduction in the market share of imports would allow U.S. firms to increase their sales. Phillip Caldwell, the president of Ford, testified at the hearings that the quota they proposed, which would reduce imports by 750,000 units, "would provide 750,000 opportunities for us to compete as a single company, and that would be significant."[81]

In response to this remark, Stern questioned Caldwell as to whether the purpose of the quota would be to push U.S. buyers to substitute midsized cars for Japanese subcompacts. Caldwell replied, "NO. NO. The sense of our recommendation is to keep 750,000 units a year in the U.S. plants and then the market will have to kind of decide where it will go."[82] He persisted in claiming that the quota would not divert sales to larger U.S. cars and thereby enable American firms to open plants that produce intermediate and large cars. This argument, however, seems to contradict his prior statement that even without quotas "we feel quite sure we will sell all the Escort-Lynx [Ford's new small car] we can build."[83] Because there would be a lag between the imposition of a quota and the ability of American producers to meet the demand for fuel-efficient cars, his testimony implied that some consumers would be pushed into large and midsized autos.

Caldwell further testified that Ford was expanding its small-car capacity as fast as possible. This raised the question about the utility of remedy. Stern questioned Caldwell as to whether the proposed import relief would result in any acceleration in the introduction of new product lines.[84] Here Stern specifically tried to ask Caldwell whether the remedy would help U.S. manufacturers speed up the conversion process to allow U.S. producers to meet the domestic demand for small cars instead of forcing consumers into larger cars. An affirmative answer from Caldwell would have provided some concrete basis for the remedy. But Caldwell answered:

> Well, actually, we are making an all-out effort right now. What we need, more than anything else, is to not have our market get away from us. This isn't a question of working harder or putting more people on the job. We are flat out right now. And we are flat out because we are market driven, and import market and everything else.[85]

Stern replied that given this response it did not appear that the remedy would help Ford accelerate the program they already had under way. Caldwell's support for the remedy thus appears to be based on the expectation that it would allow the sale of larger cars in the U.S. market immediately after it was imposed and, in the longer run, ensure U.S. producers of a market for their smaller cars.

Stern also followed the same line of questioning with GM. GM's position during the hearings was that it supported Ford and the UAW in their statement of the problem and in their ultimate goal, the health of the U.S. auto industry. GM, however, differed from the petitioners with respect to the means necessary to achieve this goal. The representative from GM suggested that instead of imposing import restraints the United States should negotiate a VRA with the Japanese as well as eliminate some of the "excessive and counterproductive" regulation of the auto industry.[86] GM argued that a VRA was necessary because the rapid increase in Japanese imports to the United States had generated domestic political pressures that could lead to a serious reduction in world trade. In order to diffuse this political pressure GM suggested that Japan take the initiative to avoid the possibility of legislated trade restrictions.

Stern questioned GM, as she did Ford, as to whether import relief would help General Motors speed up the production of fuel-efficient models. The representative from GM, David Potter, responded:

> It might have this effect, and let me conjecture: at this point we have accelerated to the limitations of engineering and machine tool capacity. At this point we are very close to our cash-flow requirements. If there is a further distress to the economy, it might then prove that some import restriction would then generate enough more cash-flow to make sure that we stayed on schedule. It would have that additional assurance. And that's all I can say.[87]

Stern replied: "It would not accelerate it; it would be an extra assurance;" Potter responded, "It cannot accelerate at this point."[88]

When pressed as to the effect of import relief on GM's financing, Potter replied that GM was not in any financial difficulty and that the increased cash flow from import restraints was not crucial to their long-range plans. GM was prepared, however, to argue that if restraints were imposed, this would improve the cash flow situation of the other auto manufacturers and thereby facilitate the success of the conversion process.[89]

The Commission's Decision

All five commissioners found that the auto industry had been seriously injured by Japanese imports. Their ultimate recommendation, however, depended upon whether the increase in imports was a "substantial" cause of injury, that is, a cause greater than any other cause. By a 3-2 vote, the commission decided that imports did not constitute the most significant cause of injury to the U.S. automobile industry. In their discussion of the case the commissioners disagreed over the impact that the recession had on the auto industry, the extent to which consumers switched to small cars and not only to small imported cars, and the degree to which import protection would actually help to solve the industry's problems. This section briefly describes the rationale offered by each of the commissioners for their vote.

William Alberger specifically took issue with the UAW's argument that the decline in demand for U.S. cars was the result of an increase in imports and not the recession. In his analysis he treated the recession as one cause, not a combination of potentially separable causes. He argued that while any one of the components of the recession alone may have been less important than imports, they "worked in unison to bring about what is commonly termed a recession."[90] Thus none of the factors that caused the recession—inflation, unemployment, rising interest rates, and higher energy costs—could be considered as individual causes of injury. He continued, "To say they [recessions] are comprised of a multitude of causes is not to say that reduced demand in a recession cannot be cited as a single cause of the purposes of 201."[91] In defense of this position Alberger further suggested that economic factors could not be disaggregated because as the economy recovers from the recession, the health of the industry would be restored.

In contrast to Alberger, George Moore and Catherine Bedell, the two Republican commissioners, isolated each of the relevant economic components of the recession and found that none of them individually were as great a cause of injury to the industry as imports.

> We reject the notion that the statute permits the Commission to aggregate a number of economic factors which in combination are to be

weighed against increased imports to find substantial cause of serious injury. Further, we believe the economic downturns represent the concurrence of a number of adverse factors.[92]

Moore and Bedell concluded, "No single adverse economic factor has plagued our domestic economy during the past several years which even approaches the disastrous effect caused by imports of passenger automobiles on this domestic industry."[93]

Michael Calhoun's statement responded to Ford's argument that the increase in imports alone was sufficient to warrant an injury determination and that the underlying factors that could be used to explain the increase in imports were irrelevant to the commission's determination of injury. While Calhoun agreed with Ford that a 201 case provided the appropriate remedy when imports were displacing domestic sales, he rejected Ford's repeated statements that the shift in consumer preference to small cars was only an explanation of the increase in imports and not an independent cause.

Instead, he contended that the shift from large to small cars in the United States introduced an independent source of injury to the industry greater than imports. He supported this position by showing that between 1978 and 1979 a shift occurred from large American-made cars to small cars in general. Because the majority of imports are small cars, this shift led to an increase in U.S. consumption of imports. In 1980 the sales of imports increased at a proportionately higher rate than sales of domestic small cars because of U.S. capacity constraints and negative consumer perceptions of American small cars due to product recalls and the reputation of U.S. cars for safety problems. Calhoun claimed, "Ford's low production and capacity utilization rate is due to the adverse publicity resulting from the product and safety problems associated with the Pinto."[94]

Paula Stern concurred with Alberger and Calhoun that both the shift in demand and the recession provided greater sources of injury to the auto industry than imports. Her analysis differed from the others in that it took into account the potential effectiveness of the remedy. Given the cyclical nature of the industry, Stern argued: "If import relief would significantly ameliorate the problem, then imports must be an important cause. If, on the other hand, the domestic industry's injury would not be remedied by import relief, some other factor must be more important than imports."[95] She indicated that "the record shows that all investment plans for domestic production are independent of import relief."[96] Working backward from the conclusion that import relief would lead neither to increased investment nor to more jobs (due to the productivity increases in the new plants), she concluded that imports did not qualify as the major cause of the industry's problems.

Stern's analysis of the industry also indicated that the proposed remedies could trigger retaliatory tariff or other trade barriers, thereby hindering the industry's long-term plans to develop the "world car." This retaliation would reduce the cost advantage of international sourcing of components, the key to the financial success of the world car. Stern pointed out that GM, which accounts for 63 percent of U.S. domestic production, had recently begun a program of international sourcing, which could be threatened by trade barriers, and went on to conclude:

> It is not unequivocally clear that even Ford stands to benefit a great deal from the relief it requested of the Commission. Ford is already a diversified world producer. In the short run, it stands to lose less than GM from any growth of barriers to auto trade around the world, but in the longer run the success of the world car will depend on the world market.[97]

Upon hearing the ruling, Caldwell said he was "very disappointed and shocked." He found the decision to be based on a narrow legal technicality—that is, that although all the commissioners found imports had injured the industry, three could not find imports to be the cause of injury greater than any other cause. Caldwell further remarked: "The country cannot afford the continuing exploitation of its automobile market by the Japanese, which will now be made worse by the effective steps being taken by the Europeans and other countries to limit the importation of Japanese cars and trucks."[98] Stephen Schlossberg—the head of government and public affairs for the UAW—said that the union would not let the matter drop: "If the Commission won't face up to the problem, some other Americans will have to."[99]

After the ITC vote, both the UAW and Ford indicated that they had plans to take the issue back to the president and Congress.

Caldwell announced immediately that the president and Congress should intervene on behalf of U.S. carmakers in spite of the ITC decision.[100] Yet, it was precisely the lack of response they had received from Congress and the president that brought the UAW and Ford to the ITC. When questioned by Commissioner Moore as to why the UAW did not file petition with the ITC closer to the time when they determined imports had begun to injure the industry (the second quarter of 1979), Fraser responded:

> Frankly, Mr. Commissioner, we thought we could get relief elsewhere. Our Ambassador to Japan had contacted me, wrote me he had given a speech in Tokyo in which he was protesting the attitude of the automobile companies of Japan. I went there. I talked to all of the auto companies . . . We were talking to the President, we were talking with certain people in Congress where there was some indication that they might take some steps to get us relief.
>
> COMMISSIONER MOORE: In other words, you tried to exhaust all your other avenues of remedy?
>
> MR. EUGENE STUART: Yes, sir.
>
> COMMISSIONER MOORE: Or help to the industry before you finally came to the Commission?
>
> MR. EUGENE STUART: That is correct.
> [Mr. Eugene Stuart is the attorney for the UAW.][101]

Caldwell also testified:

> We have been to every place in this government including at the highest levels to urge very strongly that the United States initiate a strong conversation with the Government of Japan and that to let this situation get to the point that we are right now is not in the interest of the Free World, the Government of the United States or the Government of Japan. . . . But the reason we are here is because we have been told that unless and until all of you on this Commission decide that injury has occurred, nothing more can be done under the law.[102]

POSTSCRIPT

On December 2, 1980, the House did pass a resolution that gave the president the authority to negotiate import restraints with the Japanese. This looms as a significant step toward imposing trade barriers because members of the Carter administration believed any limitation of imports by the president without congressional approval would constitute a violation of the Sherman Antitrust Act. A similar resolution was voted out of the Senate Finance Committee but never made it to a vote before the end of the session. While Congress debated about what to do, the Japanese government announced that they would "urge its car makers to excercise prudence in selling to the United States and take into account the current situation of the United States auto industry."[103]

After Ronald Reagan took office, he appointed another task force that was also unable to reach a consensus on whether to impose import restraints. In these discussions the State Department continued to oppose any kind of reduction in imports and argued that unless a program was carefully managed, any restraints imposed by the United States could spread—thus reducing American exports—and threaten the postwar progress in building up international trade. The Treasury, the Office of Management and the Budget, and the CEA also opposed import restraints, whereas the Departments of Transportation, Labor, and Commerce supported the negotiation of a VRA with the Japanese.[104]

In addition to this task-force study, Chairman John Danforth (R−Missouri) of the Senate Trade Subcommittee and ranking Democrat Lloyd Bentsen (D−Texas) also introduced a bill in Congress. This legislation would impose a formal quota of 1.6 million cars a year on Japan for three years. (In 1980, 1.9 million Japanese autos sold in the United States, and projections indicated this would increase to 2.1 million in 1981 if the United States did not impose import restraints.) This was not, however, as stringent as the quota Ford requested during the ITC hearings. Ford's total quota would have limited all imports to the United States (not just Japanese) to 1.7 million vehicles and Japanese imports to 930,000 units—over a 50 percent reduction.[105]

President Reagan decided not to support protectionist legislation nor to negotiate a formal, orderly marketing agreement with the Japanese. He did use the Danforth bill, however, as leverage with which to persuade the government of Japan to impose voluntary export quotas. Reagan warned the Japanese that unless imports of Japanese cars dropped significantly, and soon, Congress was likely to enact stringent import quotas, perhaps extending to other products—by large enough margins to override a presidential veto.[106]

This strategy proved ultimately successful. On May 1, 1981, the government of Japan announced a plan to limit auto exports to the United States to 1.68 million units for the fiscal year April 1, 1981, to March 31, 1982. The following year's shipments would be set at 1.68 million plus 16.5 percent of the growth in domestic car sales.[107] Japan also agreed to monitor exports in the third year to prevent a rapid increase in exports to the United States.[108]

These limits were less stringent than the quotas proposed in Congress or at the ITC hearings. When Japan agreed to the VRA, no clear indication existed of whether it would act as a binding constraint or whether it would provide financial relief for U.S. auto producers. Assuming that without export restraint the Japanese would have sold 2.1 million units in 1981 in the United States, the first-year limit would involve a reduction of 420,000 units. As the industry would probably only pick up about half of these sales because of the shortage in U.S. small-car production, the domestic producers as a group would sell only an additional 210,000 units. Although most of the producers saw this as a step in the right direction, industry analysts did not consider the increase in domestic sales big enough to make a substantial difference to their profitability.[109] Even with the Japanese VRA, the U.S. auto industry still faced serious financial problems because of its inability to produce an adequate supply of fuel-efficient cars. Auto industry analysts suggested that ultimately Detroit's prosperity would depend on whether it would be able to increase its productivity and design cars that would woo the American consumer away from attractive, high-quality imports. These analysts reminded the industry that limiting the number of imports would not necessarily turn the consumer back toward American cars.[110]

CONCLUSION

The agreement did, however, diffuse the movement in Congress to legislate import quotas on Japanese autos. Senator Danforth said that although he believed the restraint agreement lacked the strength he would have liked, he would agree to drop his bill. Yet the agreement was not restrictive enough to ensure domestic producers the leeway either to raise prices or to increase the sales of intermediate-sized cars substantially. Thus the VRA primarily functioned to provide a pragmatic political resolution to the trade dispute between the United States and Japan.

Technically, this agreement fell outside of the GATT legal framework because Japan voluntarily agreed to restrict exports.[111] Although the auto dispute never reached the GATT, the GATT framework constrained the outcome of the auto case in two respects. First, it required the United States to evaluate the industry's request for import restraint in the context of the escape clause. This allowed Congress to deflect political pressure from the industry aimed at legislating import quotas. This shield was important because while the VRA may have fallen outside of the GATT legal framework, legislated quotas would have been a violation of the agreement and thus would have threatened the foundations of the international trading system. In addition, if the industry had received a positive injury determination from the ITC, the VRA would probably have been much more restrictive than what was ultimately agreed upon.

The GATT also provided a multilateral perspective on an issue that was often cast in bilateral and sectoral terms. Ford Chairman Phillip Caldwell, in *Harvard Business Review*, described U.S. auto trade with Japan.

> In 1979, Japan sold $8 billion worth of its automobiles in the United States. Americans bought half of all exported Japanese cars. In contrast, the Japanese bought American cars worth only $200 million. The deficit in automotive trade with Japan represents one-third of the deficit the United States recorded in total trade with all countries.[112]

This description of auto trade with Japan seems to imply that the United States should maintain a balance of trade with Japan in automobiles. It does not take into consideration either the magnitude of the potential demand for American automobiles in Japan or the cost of excluding Japanese automobiles from the U.S. market. This perspective does, however, allow Caldwell to argue: "It is in our national interest to find a means of strengthening the U.S. auto industry [through import protection] during this period of extraordinary conversion and record investment requirements."[113]

U.S. membership in the GATT creates pressures for the government to take into account the economic benefits from trade in the process of deciding whether to protect a specific industry. Because the *national interest* is defined in terms of an open trading system, and not solely with respect to the balance of trade in a specific sector, GATT membership provides the United States with some criteria with which to evaluate industry requests for protection as well as with leverage to resist industry pressures. The implementation of trade restraints remains a continuing political temptation because import protection often appears to be a reasonable way of aiding an industry struggling to be competitive—even when imports do not constitute a significant part of the problem. Calhoun makes this point specifically in response to Ford's contention that the shift in demand from large to small cars is not relevant to the commission's analysis of injury. He noted:

> Moreover, where in both concept and in fact a shift in demand is distinguishable from a shift in imports, not to make it a factor in the consideration of causality transforms section 201 from an import relief provision to an industrial relief provision. Under such a view, whenever an industry is in decline because of internal structural changes or exogenous occurrences in the society independent of imports, an industry need only show that imports are increasing concomitant with its difficulty and it could receive relief. While one could make very good arguments supporting the need for an industrial policy which would provide assistance to worthy industries suffering generalized difficulty unassociated with imports, section 201 cannot be so construed.[114]

In their petitions both Ford and the UAW asked for this kind of industrial relief. The U.S. commitment to the GATT, however, provided the government with political leverage against the industry's demands and a competing view of the rationale for import protection. As a result, despite the industry's political importance it did not receive the protection it requested.

NOTES

1. U.S., Congress, House, Subcommittee on Trade of the Committee on Ways and Means, *Auto Situation: 1980* (Washington D.C.: Government Printing Office, 1980), p. 13.

2. This is calculated from table 29 of The United Automobile Workers, *Petition for Relief under Section 201 of the Trade Act of 1974 from Import Competition from Imported Passenger Cars, Light Trucks, and Utility Vehicles* before the United States International Trade Commission (Washington D.C., 1980), June 12, 1980, p. 195.

3. Ibid.

4. Ford Motor Company, *Petition for Relief from Increased Imports of Passenger Cars, Light Trucks, Vans, and Utility Vehicles under Section 201 of the Trade Act of 1974,* before the U.S. ITC, August 1, 1980. p. 4.

5. Edward Meadows "A Difference of Opinion," *Fortune Magazine,* August 11, 1980, p. 214.

6. Ibid.

7. Mira Wilkins, "Multinational Automobile Enterprises and Regulation: An Historical Overview," in *Government, Technology, and the Future of the Automobile,* ed. Douglas A. Ginsburg and William P. Abernathy (New York: McGraw-Hill, 1980) p. 228.

8. Ibid., p. 236.

9. Ibid., p. 255.

10. Ibid., p. 239.

11. Subcommittee on Trade, *Auto Situation,* p. 12.

12. Ibid., p. 53.

13. William Tucker, "The Wreck of the Auto Industry," *Harper's,* November 1980, p. 48.

14. Wilkins, "Multinational Automobile Enterprises and Regulation," p. 248.

15. Tucker, "Wreck of the Auto Industry," p. 51.

16. Ibid., p. 52.

17. The average fuel economy standards for passenger cars were 1978, 18 miles per gallon (MPG); 1979, 19 MPG; 1980, 20 MPG; 1982, 22 MPG; 1983, 26 MPG; 1984, 27 MPG; and 1985, 27.5 MPG. Subcommittee on Trade, *Auto Situation,* p. 77.

18. Ibid., p. 12.

19. U.S., Department of Transportation, *The U.S. Auto Industry* (Washington D.C.; Department of Transportation 1980), p. 35.

20. *Congressional Quarterly Weekly Report,* May 10, 1980, p. 1265.

21. Department of Transportation, *The U.S. Auto Industry,* p. 22.

22. The Department of Transportation study describes front-wheel drive as the elimination of the driveshaft and the rear axle and differential, thus allowing better use of the interior room of the auto for a given weight. Because the conversion to front-wheel drive requires the introduction of all new cars, including new engines and other components, it requires a longer lead time and is significantly more expensive than downsizing. Ibid., p. 25.

23. Ibid., p. iv.

24. U.S. International Trade Commission, *International Trade Commission Staff Report,* USITC Publication no. 1110 (Washington D.C.: I.T.C. 1980), p. A-43.

25. Department of Transportation, *The U.S. Auto Industry,* p. 84.

26. International Trade Commission, *International Trade Commission Staff Report,* p. A-31.

27. Subcommittee on Trade, *Auto Situation*, p. 14.

28. Department of Transportation, The *U.S. Auto Industry*, p. 35.

29. Edward Meadows, "A Difference of Opinion," *Fortune Magazine*, August 11, 1980, p. 213.

30. Subcommittee on Trade, *Auto Situation*, p. 19.

31. "Treasury Department Memo," December 26, 1979.

32. "U.S. Department of Labor Memo," January 21, 1980.

33. Adam Meyerson, "Made in U.S.A.?" *Wall Street Journal*, March 3, 1980, p. 16.

34. Subcommittee on Trade, *Auto Situation*, p. 40.

35. Sam Jameson, "UAW Chief Sets 3-Month Time Limit for Japan to Limit Exports or Face Curbs," Los Angeles *Times*, February 14, 1980, p. 2.

36. Ibid.

37. Mike Tharp, "UAW's Fraser Wins Pledge from Nissan and Toyota of Prudent Exports to the U.S.," *Wall Street Journal*, February 14, 1980, p. 3.

38. Ibid.

39. "Japan Asks Its Car Firms to Limit Exports to the U.S. and Start American Production," *Wall Street Journal*, February 13, 1980, p. 2.

40. Ibid.

41. Ibid.

42. A. E. Cullison, "Toyota, Nissan Refuse to Establish US Plants," *Journal of Commerce*, February 28, 1980, p. 19.

43. Masayoshi Kanabayashi, "Japanese Auto Makers' New Lament: In the U.S., Only Car Buyers Love Us," *Wall Street Journal*, February 15, 1980, p. 12.

44. Statement by Douglas Fraser before the Subcommittee on Trade of the House Ways and Means Committee (mimeo), March 7, 1980, p. 10.

45. Statement by Fred Secrest before the House Ways and Means Subcommittee on Trade, (mimeo), March 7, 1980, p. 9.

46. Statement by George Eads before the Subcommittee on Economic Stabilization of the Committee on Banking of the U.S. Senate (mimeo) April 3, 1980, p. 2.

47. Ibid.

48. Subcommittee on Trade, *Auto Situation*, p. 1.

49. Robert L. Simison, "Auto Union Plans to Take Imports War to U.S. Trade Unit, Bypassing Congress," *Wall Street Journal*, May 9, 1980, p. 5.

50. United Automobile Workers Union, *Petition for Relief under Section 201 of the Trade Act of 1974 from Import Competition from Imported Passenger Cars, Light Trucks, and Utility Vehicles before the United States International Trade Commission*, (Washington D.C.: 1980), p. 3.

51. The Congress designated the ITC to focus specifically on the effect of a particular import on the domestic U.S. industry and not to consider shifts in international comparative advantage as an explanation for why an industry is injured. Thus the decision-making process is inherently biased in favor of the domestic industry.

52. Kenneth Dam, *The GATT: Law and International Economic Organization* (Chicago: University of Chicago Press, 1970), p. 99.

53. United Automobile Workers Union, *Petition*, pp. 275–76.

54. Prehearing Brief of the Ford Motor Company, USITC Investigation TA-201–44, October 1, 1980, pp. 46–47.

55. "Summary of Ford's Section 201 Petition to the ITC," mimeographed, p. 3.

56. U.S., International Trade Commission, *Certain Motor Vehicles and Certain Chassis and Bodies Therefore*, USITC Publication no. 1110 (Washington, D.C.: 1980), p. 93.

57. Ford Motor Company, *Petition*, p. 2.

58. "On Eve of US Hearings on Auto Imports from Japan, All Parties Vie For Attention," *Wall Street Journal*, October 8, 1980, p. 2.

59. Ford, *Prehearing Brief*, pp. 28–29.

60. "Fact Sheet on the Auto Industry." (Undated mimeograph).

61. United Auto Workers Union, *Petition*, p. 88.

62. Ibid., p. 116.

63. Ibid., p. 180.

64. Ibid., p. 182.

65. Ibid., p. 201.

66. Ford Motor Company, *Petition*, p. 7.

67. Ibid., p. 42.

68. Ibid.

69. Ibid., p. 45.

70. Ibid., p. 48.

71. Ibid., p. 49.

72. *Prehearing Brief of the Ford Motor Company*, p. 29.

73. Ibid., p. 31.

74. *Prehearing Brief of the Nissan Corporation*, USITC Investigation TA-201–44, October 1, 1980, p. 33.

75. Ibid., p. 34.

76. International Trade Commission, *Certain Motor Vehicles*, p. A-71.

77. Ibid., p. A-43.

78. Ibid., p. A-68.

79. "Transcript of the International Trade Commission Hearings," pp. 144–45. (Undated mimeograph).

80. Ibid.

81. "Transcript of the ITC Hearings," p. 632. (Undated mimeograph).

82. Ibid., p. 632.

83. Ibid., p. 631.

84. Ibid., p. 617.

85. Ibid., p. 618.

86. This discussion is taken from the Statement of the General Motors Corporation submitted to the ITC on October 1, 1980. (mimeographed).

87. Ibid., p. 396.

88. Ibid.

89. General Motors memo, "Discussion of the Impact of Tariffs and/or Quotas," (undated mimeograph).

90. "Views of Chairman Bill Alberger," in International Trade Commission, *Certain Motor Vehicles*, p. 4.

91. Ibid., p. 28.

92. "Views of Commissioners George M. Moore and Catherine Bedell," in ITC, *Certain Motor Vehicles*, p. 167.

93. Ibid., p. 177.

94. "Views of Michael J. Calhoun," in ITC, *Certain Motor Vehicles*, pp. 81–82.

95. "Statement of Paula Stern," in ITC, *Certain Motor Vehicles*, p. 154.

96. Ibid., p. 161.

97. Ibid., p. 165.

98. Ian Hargreaves and David Buchanan, "US Vehicle Makers Lose Imports Fight," *Financial Times*, November 11, 1980.

99. Christopher Conte and Robert Simison, "UAW and Ford Requests for Curbs on Imports Are Rejected by Panel," *Wall Street Journal*, November 11, 1981, p. 3.

100. Ibid.

101. "Transcript of the ITC Hearings."

102. Ibid.

103. Clyde Farnsworth, "Tokyo to Urge Auto Export Restraint," New York *Times*, November 18, 1980, p. D1.

104. "An Auto Trade Dilemma for Reagan to Solve," *Business Week*, March 23, 1981, p. 42.

105. "Exhibit 19: Proposed Quota and Minimum Import Limits by Country," in Ford Motor Company, *Petition*.

106. "Delicate Dealing on Japanese Cars," *Business Week*, April 6, 1981, p. 27.

107. Christopher Conte and Urban C. Lehner, "Congressional Clash Averted," *Wall Street Journal*, May 4, 1981, p. 3.

108. This agreement applies only to passenger cars.

109. Conte and Lehner, "Congressional Clash," p. 3.

110. "A Bad Way to Aid Detroit," *World Business Weekly*, May 18, 1981, p. 63.

111. During the Tokyo Round negotiations of the GATT, inconclusive discussions were held on a safeguards code that would have made orderly marketing agreements (OMAs) and VRAs legitimate actions to take in response to a positive injury finding. That would mean that after appropriate hearings, findings, and notification a Contracting Party to the GATT could, under GATT law, selectively impose an OMA on one or a few countries while allowing imports from non-covered nations to be unrestrained. This discussion is taken from Morris Morkre and David Tarr, *Staff Report on Effects of Restrictions on U.S. Imports: Five Case Studies and Theory* (Washington D.C.: Federal Trade Commission, Bureau of Economics June 1980), p. 170.

112. Malcolm Salter, "The Automobile Crisis and Public Policy," *Harvard Business Review* 59 (January–February 1981): 78.

113. Ibid.

114. "View of Vice Chairman Michael Calhoun," in ITC, *Certain Motor Vehicles*, p. 72.

7

TELECOMMUNICATIONS
The Politics of Expansion

INTRODUCTION

This chapter addresses the international and domestic political conflict that resulted from the efforts on the part of the United States to expand multilateral trade in the telecommunications equipment market. Throughout its history the telecommunications equipment industry has been oriented to domestic markets, with exports and imports accounting for a small part of total output.[1] In 1975 U.S. imports constituted 1.7 percent of domestic consumption, whereas exports accounted for 3.6 percent of domestic production.[2] In large part this relatively small amount of trade among the United States, the EEC, and Japan in telecommunications equipment reflects public policy, which treats telephone operating companies as natural monopolies. A *natural monopoly* exists when the scale economies are so great that it is efficient for only one firm to produce the entire output for the industry. Natural monopolies pose the following dilemma for policymakers:

> If the industry's output is shared between several firms, then output will be produced at higher than minimum cost; if output is concentrated in a single firm, then the firm could use its market power to charge monopoly prices, distorting allocation of resources in the economy as a whole.[3]

In Europe and Japan telecommunications operating companies come under state ownership to prevent them from misusing their monopoly power. In the United States telephone operating companies are privately owned but regulated by the government to ensure that their policies reflect the "public interest."

Both government ownership and regulation of telecommunications services have resulted in the restriction of trade in telecommunications equipment. In Europe and Japan government procurement policies direct state-owned telecommunications operating companies to purchase equipment from domestic suppliers, thereby shielding them from foreign competition. In the United States regulatory policy protected AT&T's primary supplier, Western Electric, from foreign as well as domestic competition through prohibiting the attachment to the U.S. telecommunications system any equipment not owned by AT&T—that is, equipment supplied by "alien firms." Thus, while in Europe government procurement policies insulated the domestic telecommunications producers from foreign competition, in the United States government regulation provided this protection.

During the 1970s tension over trade in telecommunications equipment emerged as a result of the deregulation of the U.S. telecommunications industry. Changes in U.S. regulatory policy that allowed equipment not made by AT&T to be "plugged" into the system led to a sharp increase in the amount of equipment imported to the United States, especially from Japan. This liberalization of U.S. regulatory policy, however, was not accompanied by any changes in the government procurement policies of either Europe or Japan, which continued to exclude U.S. products. A congressional task force report on U.S.-Japanese trade found that in 1977 U.S. imports of network telephone and telegraph equipment from Japan amounted to $35 million, whereas U.S. exports to Japan totaled $4.5 million (mostly to U.S. military bases in Japan).[4] In response to this sectoral imbalance, business and labor groups pressured Congress to consider closing the U.S. telecommunications market to foreign suppliers. The U.S. government countered this pressure through attempts to pry open the Japanese telecommunications market.

The government procurement code negotiated at the Tokyo Round of the GATT (1978–80) provided the United States with leverage with which to gain access to state-controlled telecommunications procurement. Prior to this code, the GATT Article III exempted government procurement of goods and services from non-discriminatory treatment of foreign and domestic products. The government procurement code attempted to eliminate this discrimination and to allow foreign firms to compete for government procurement contracts on an equal basis with domestic firms.

This chapter focuses on the efforts of the United States to include Japan's telephone operating company, Nippon Telephone and Telegraph (NTT), under the entities covered by the government procurement code. The inclusion of NTT would mean that U.S. and other manufacturers in countries that are code signatories could submit bids for contracts with NTT, thus allowing the possibility for the sale of foreign telecommunications equipment to Japan.

The interest group politics framework helps to explain in this case why the issue of telecommunications trade was raised. The sectoral imbalance in telecommunications trade, especially with Japan, created incentives for the industry to pressure the U.S. government either to negotiate access to foreign markets for U.S. producers or to close the U.S. market. U.S. negotiators tried to increase access for American producers to foreign markets by way of the government procurement code. This potential increase in market access for U.S. goods became a crucial component of the U.S. package at the Tokyo Round.

This case also provides some support for the congressional autonomy framework in that Congress did not respond to industry pressures to close the American market to Japanese telecommunications equipment. Instead, Congress supported the STR in its efforts to pry open the Japanese market. Yet Congress also appeared to be under considerable pressure from the industry to obtain a meaningful agreement from Japan regarding NTT's procurement practices. Congress, in turn, put pressure on the STR negotiators to reach an agreement that would lead to substantive results. Without this industry pressure Congress may have been willing to accept a weaker agreement. The case indicates that while Congress does not act autonomously from industry pressures, it can use the GATT negotiations to deflect industry pressures for trade protection.

This case offers some support for the national autonomy framework in its use of threats to cut Japan entirely from the U.S. agreement under the government procurement code if Japan did not open NTT procurement to U.S. firms. The United States stood willing to forgo the economic benefits of cheaper Japanese goods if the Japanese offer did not meet U.S. expectations. The United States also acted autonomously in that the trade dispute over NTT's procurement practices was resolved through the negotiation of a bilateral "code-consistent" agreement between the United States and Japan outside of the multilateral code. Yet the ultimate objective of the use of this autonomy centered around increasing economic interdependence through a viable government procurement code. Thus while the United States acted autonomously during the course of the negotiations, this case does not indicate that national autonomy is the primary goal of U.S. trade policy.

This case, however, does illustrate the way in which the United States pursued a pragmatic trade policy in dealing with both domestic interest group pressures and the government of Japan. First, the case demonstrates that the interests of the domestic industry could not be ignored, although they also did not dominate the U.S. negotiating position. U.S. negotiators only accepted the Japanese offer when it provided real opportunities for U.S. firms to bid on NTT's procurement contracts for technically sophisticated products. Second, the case demonstrates the pragmatism of the U.S. negotiators. When it became clear that the government of Japan faced domestic political constraints that would not allow all of NTT's procurement to be included under the code, American negotiators were willing to accept a bilateral agreement.

Although the industry brought NTT to the attention of the STR negotiators, it did not have much influence in determining the form of the final agreement reached between the United States and Japan. The main difference between the industry and the government over NTT concerned the fact that the STR had expressed willingness to accept a bilateral agreement with Japan. The STR negotiators believed that this bilateral provided U.S. firms the opportunity to bid on high-technology equipment procured by NTT. In contrast, the majority of the industry took the position that including NTT entirely under the government procurement code was the only negotiating position that the United States should consider seriously. While this appears to be an unambiguous case of trade expansion, underlying the pragmatism of the STR negotiators seemed to be a belief that if U.S. firms did not obtain meaningful opportunities for increased telecommunications trade with Japan, Congress—under pressure from both factions of the U.S. industry—would seriously consider closing the U.S. market.

Providing background for the dispute, a description follows of the telecommunications industry and the equipment involved in a telecommunications system. Then the primary issues that emerged during the negotiation of the government procurement code are explored. These negotiations provided the United States with the opportunity to persuade Japan into liberalizing trade in telecommunications. The remainder of the chapter considers the relationship of NTT to its supplier companies and the problems this created during the bilateral negotiations between the United States and Japan over the government procurement code.

THE TELECOMMUNICATIONS INDUSTRY

The principle feature of a telecommunications network is the ability of one party to contact virtually any other party who subscribes to the telephone service. The telecommunications sector itself can be divided into those firms that produce equipment and those that operate telephone systems, known as *common carrier firms* or *operating companies*. In the United States the firms that provide telecommunications service and are the primary consumers of telecommunications equipment can be divided into the regulated and unregulated segments of the market. The regulated sector is composed of those common-carrier telephone companies whose rates are subject to state commission approval.[5] The unregulated sector consists primarily of businesses that purchase their own telecommunications systems. These include hotel and motel chains, utility companies, and banks.[6] Until 1983 when AT&T divested its operating companies, the regulated sector in the United States was dominated by AT&T and its 23 operating subsidiaries, which provided 82 percent of U.S. telephone service.[7]

Until the AT&T divestiture, both AT&T and the operating companies purchased the majority of their equipment from Western Electric, AT&T's manufacturing subsidiary. This acquisition of equipment was done on a cost-plus basis, a practice that helped to insulate Western Electric from market competition. A Western Electric document describes this mode of procurement:

> Western Electric prices its products on the basis of costs and not, as non-affiliated manufacturers do, on what the market will bear. There are two steps in the establishment of the price of each Western Electric product. The first is the calculation of the standard cost for the product. The second is the application of a factor to the standard cost of each item. This factor is called the product line price factor and is designed to provide for the recovery of all of Western's other expenses associated with the factors and for a reasonable return on investment.[8]

An OECD study of the telecommunications market found that competitive pricing also did not count as a crucial factor in European and Japanese telecommunications procurement. This study found that in EEC procurement practices price never constitutes the only factor, and sometimes it does not figure as the most important factor in the choice of supplier. Instead, once the choice of supplier is made, costs are audited and prices are set in such a way as to ensure a reasonable rate of return.[9] The contracts typically go to preferred suppliers and are allocated on the basis of historical market share. Rather than choose suppliers on the basis of competitive bidding procedures, the study indicated that the policy of the state-owned telecommunications companies has largely been to achieve noneconomic objectives in the supply field. To achieve the most important of these objectives—local production—the service companies have been willing to purchase equipment on terms favorable to domestic manufacturers, thereby protecting them from foreign competition.[10]

The main difference between the U.S. and state-controlled telecommunications industries is that although AT&T acts as the primary supplier in the United States, it is not the sole supplier of telephone services. Several other private corporations in the United States provide long-distance services, and a number of firms—including foreign firms—supply equipment to private end-users that hook into AT&T's central switching equipment.[11] Because of this, AT&T faces more potential competition than European firms from both other operating companies and other manufacturing firms. Conflict over trade in telecommunications equipment has resulted specifically from the ability of the unregulated sector of the U.S. market (the interconnect market)—as well as of those operating companies that do not have manufacturing affiliates (independent telephone companies)—to purchase either foreign or domestically produced equipment.

The largest increase in imports to the United States has resulted from the deregulation of the interconnect market by the Federal Communications Commission (FCC). This deregulation came about as the result of a decision made by the FCC that the terminal equipment market had to be entirely deregulated by March 1982 and that although equipment attached to the network would have to be certified by the FCC, service providers could not discriminate between the equipment they provide and that provided by other sources. Now that AT&T's former operating companies have become independent of AT&T, they too can choose their suppliers.

While competition (and imports) in the U.S. telecommunications equipment market increased as a result of changing U.S. regulatory policy, European and Japanese procurement practices have remained the same. The government procurement code, however, gave the United States an opportunity to try to force a change in the discriminatory procurement practices of the state-controlled telephone and telegraph companies in Europe and Japan. The U.S. government specifically used the negotiations over entity coverage for the government procurement code to prod the state-controlled Japanese telephone company, NTT, into accepting bids on equipment purchases from foreign suppliers. The following section discusses the negotiations over the government procurement code to provide the larger context in which the conflict over NTT's procurement practices took place.

THE GOVERNMENT PROCUREMENT CODE

The government procurement code was negotiated so that state-owned "entities" would accept bids from foreign suppliers on an equal basis with those submitted by domestic suppliers. Prior to the code the GATT agreement did not proscribe local sourcing by governments, and governmental agencies felt no international political pressure to buy goods from foreign firms.

Prior to the negotiation of the government procurement code, governments used their procurement policies to achieve domestic social and political goals through insulating domestic producers from foreign competition. These policies included efforts to:

1. Assist in easing balance-of-payments difficulties;
2. Ensure domestic sources of supply for national security needs or implement other security-related programs;
3. Promote the growth of certain industries, particularly those involving sophisticated technology;
4. Assist regions suffering from persistent unemployment or other economic problems; and
5. Bar the exportation of certain types of labor skills.[12]

Several pieces of legislation contributed to the formulation of the U.S. policy on government procurement. The Buy American Act, passed in 1933, mandated that U.S. government agencies give preferences to domestic suppliers. Since 1954 this preference has consisted of a 6 percent price differential, which could be raised to 12 percent if the low bidding firm is a small business or is located in an area of high unemployment.[13] In defense procurement this margin was set at 50 percent, which virtually guaranteed domestic sourcing.

In contrast to the United States, Europe and Japan do not have a formal system that discriminates in favor of domestic suppliers. They do, however, achieve the same result through administrative practices.[14] Both European and Japanese procurement officials typically will not buy a foreign product if the equivalent can be found locally at a reasonable price. A 1976 study by the U.S. comptroller general on OECD members' government procurement practices found that

> U.S. and other foreign-based companies, which attempt to sell to the German, French, Japanese, or British governments, have almost no chance of being awarded contracts unless the item is technically superior or not manufactured in those countries. All the sales representatives of U.S.-based firms we interviewed asserted that they had been unsuccessful in selling to those governments products which could be produced domestically.[15]

As a result of these procurement practices, in 1974 only 3 percent (1.3 billion) of the $44.6 billion in procurement (primarily from OECD countries) that the study analyzed was open to competition from foreign sources.[16] Owing to both the magnitude of government procurement and the small amount open to foreign firms, the agreement to consider bids submitted by foreign firms on an equal basis with domestic firms had the potential of opening up a significant amount of new opportunities for trade.

The problem that arises from local sourcing comes down to one of cost. The 12 percent preference given to American suppliers on government contracts is equivalent to a 12 percent tariff. While the individual firms that supply the government benefit from being insulated from foreign competition, local sourcing forces the taxpayers to absorb the increased costs resulting from forgoing the opportunity to purchase less expensive foreign goods. A British procurement official commented that "the policy of favoring British firms has at times increased costs and led to the purchase of products of lesser quality."[17]

The government procurement code attempted to take domestic political pressure off governments to buy only domestic goods by requiring them to entertain bids from foreign suppliers and to accept them if they were lower than those submitted by domestic producers. The agreement states that its goal is "to secure greater international competition and thus more effective use of tax revenues and other public funds through the application of commercial considerations when governments purchase for their own use."[18]

The United States stated at the outset of the Tokyo Round negotiations that the successful negotiation of the government procurement code stood as one of its primary objectives.[19] A congressional Budget Office study explained that the government procurement code would benefit the United States:

> Because most foreign governments control relatively more of their respective economies than does the US government, there is a widespread belief—unfortunately very difficult to establish quantitatively—that the opportunities for discrimination by foreign governments are much greater than the opportunities for such discrimination by the US government. Whatever their opportunities, foreign governments are widely seen as discriminating more aggressively in favor of domestic products than does the US government. If this were in fact the case, then a

multilateral opening of government procurement to international competition would clearly be in the U.S. interest.[20]

Within the United States, industry groups provided the initial impetus to negotiate the code. Western Electric, International Telephone & Telegraph, and General Electric all wanted to sell to government-controlled telephone, telegraph, and public utility firms abroad.[21] At the outset of the negotiations on the government procurement code, the EEC was the most tentative, as no EEC internal agreement existed over government procurement policies in telecommunications. Japan, initially, did not openly show any reluctance to the code, although later Japan's unwillingness to include NTT almost resulted in the collapse of the negotiations.

Once the negotiations began, a general consensus developed among the participants in the government procurement committee that the fundamental principle underlying the code should be nondiscrimination (national treatment) among members. An OECD study of members' procurement practices provided the basis for the major part of the background work for the Tokyo Round negotiations on government procurement. Although the OECD never reached an agreement on how to regulate government procurement, the GATT negotiating group did adopt many of the procedures proposed in these earlier negotiations.

The negotiations over the code can be broken down into two separate sets of issues. The first set deals with procedures that would help to ensure that foreign suppliers would not find themselves at a disadvantage either in the process of submitting bids or during the subsequent evaluation of the bids. The code attempted to achieve national treatment for foreign suppliers largely through several procedural obligations incurred by signatories to the code. These obligations required that those governmental agencies that were to be covered by the code use either open or selective tendering procedures.[22] The provision explicitly excluded negotiated contracts, which tend to be the most discriminatory.

In order to ensure that foreign firms are not put at a disadvantage in these requests for bids, the code also required that all potential suppliers receive the same information regarding the technical specifications of the products involved. The code further stated that time limits that specify when the bids must be received cannot be used to discriminate against foreign suppliers and that the rules for awarding a contract must be known in advance. This included information specifying whether the contract will be awarded to the lowest bidder, and if not, the criteria upon which the bids will be evaluated. After the contract has been awarded, the code further specified that the government of the unsuccessful tenderer can request the government agency that made the purchase to explain why a specific firm lost the contract. This information, however, could not be made public if it was thought to prejudice future tendering.

The second set of negotiations dealt with which government agencies (known as entities) to include under the code. These negotiations proved more difficult than those over the procedures. In deciding which entities to include under the code, the signatories attempted to obtain a balance of rights and obligations. This, however, involved a fair degree of difficulty because each government varied in size and the extent to which it played a significant role in its domestic economy. The signatories resolved the issue of entity coverage through a series of bilateral negotiations in which each signatory presented a list of entities to be covered by the code. After modifying these lists in light of other offers, the signatories compiled the final entity list, which was then generalized and open to all code members.

The traditional resistance of NTT to foreign products led to the belief primarily among U.S. business executives who had tried to sell to Japan that NTT would never allow itself to be included among Japan's list of entities. Although there was also some skepticism within the STR, the need to get an agreement on NTT procurement to balance the code and through this, balance the aggregate costs and benefits to the United States of the entire Tokyo Round, generated sufficient pressure from the United States to persuade the government of Japan to change NTT's procurement policies.

NIPPON TELEPHONE AND TELEGRAPH

In 1952 the Diet created NTT—a public corporation—to handle domestic communications.[23] NTT's activities, including determining wage rates and formulating the operating budget, are subject to approval by the Diet, although it maintains its own account independent from the national budget.[24] The Ministry of Posts and Telecommunications also scrutinizes the corporation. The law that established NTT, however, did not give the ministry specific supervisory control, thereby allowing the corporation a high degree of discretion over day-to-day activities, including procurement. As a result NTT developed a sense of superiority to the Ministry of Posts and Telecommunications, which has been enhanced since 1977 by virtue of its profitability. This superiority effectively insulated NTT from external political pressures during the early stages of the conflict between the United States and Japan over NTT's procurement practices.

When first faced with the prospect of being included under the government procurement code, NTT argued that it was not a government agency and therefore not subject to code coverage.[25] Although the government of Japan acknowledged that NTT did qualify as a public agency early in the negotiations, NTT's autonomy continued to pose problems.

NTT maintained control over its procurement by its policy only to buy from a few specified firms known as the "NTT family." These firms included Nippon Electric, Oki, Fujitsu, and Hitachi. The majority of NTT contracts have traditionally been negotiated on an individual basis with these suppliers without using any kind of competitive bidding procedures.[26] NTT has also subsidized a large amount of research and development (R&D) carried out by members of the NTT family, especially in the telephone exchange and transmission markets.[27]

Even when NTT did not negotiate contracts and did accept competitive bids, foreign manufacturers still suffered a disadvantage because NTT did not disclose publicly detailed specifications on the grounds that they were proprietary to NTT or to the company that developed the product. The ITC report on the interconnect market described this situation as a catch-22 because "although foreign firms are required to meet certain specifications for approval, it is NTT's policy not to divulge what the standards are."[28] Because NTT has had the sole responsibility for the procurement of equipment in the telephone exchange and transmission segments of the market, these policies have almost entirely insulated the

NTT family from any competition, foreign or domestic.[29] The elaborate certification procedures required by NTT for imported equipment also discouraged foreign producers from entering Japan's interconnect market. As a result of these stringent certification procedures, U.S. exports of private branch exchanges (PBXs) to Japan in 1974 amounted to 0.7 percent of the Japanese market.[30]

THE NETWORK OF INTERESTS: JAPAN, THE UNITED STATES, AND THE EUROPEAN ECONOMIC COMMUNITY

Two converging sets of pressures led to the bilateral conflict between the United States and Japan over including NTT under the government procurement code. During the Tokyo Round negotiations, the United States raised the possibility of including NTT under the government procurement code to bring the Japanese offer into a range that the United States could accept. Prior to these negotiations, however, the issue of NTT had also been raised in the context of a congressional debate over the U.S. deficit with Japan in telecommunications equipment. U.S. industry representatives considered NTT's refusal to purchase foreign equipment as justification for setting limits on imports of Japanese telecommunications equipment to the United States.

These two concerns—that is, the need for reciprocity in the government procurement code and the need to reduce the bilateral deficit with Japan in telecommunications equipment—corresponded to the concerns of two different factions in the U.S. telecommunications industry that emerged during the debate over NTT. Those firms with an interest in exporting to the Japanese market supported the U.S. negotiators in their attempts to obtain a meaningful offer under the government procurement code from the Japanese. Other firms more interested in insulating the U.S. market from Japanese competition looked upon the failure of the NTT negotiations as an opportunity to restrict Japanese imports.[31]

Although the firms hoping to close the U.S. market and those desiring to sell to Japan were interested in different outcomes from the negotiations, both factions lobbied the government to have all NTT procurement covered by the code.[32] The coalition, interested primarily in protection (which included the Communications

Workers of America), supported full code coverage because they believed it would be politically impossible for the Japanese to accept this request and thus lead to a breakdown in the negotiations over the code. Once the negotiations broke down, they would then be in a tenable position to ask Congress for some kind of import restraints on Japanese telecommunications equipment. The other group supported having NTT included among the entities fully covered by the code because, given the difficulty firms have encountered in trying to sell to Japan, they felt skeptical that anything less than full code coverage would result in actual sales.

Although the Japanese negotiating posture on NTT changed as the seriousness of the United States became more apparent, when the issue was first raised, NTT had strong domestic political support in favor of maintaining their traditional procurement relationships. Initially, the Ministry of Posts and Telecommunications supported the contention that NTT—although a government corporation—was not subject to direct government control and thus was exempt from the government procurement code.

NTT also had political support within the Japanese Diet from the Liberal Democratic party's (LDP's) communication division, which argued that NTT's system of negotiated contracts should be continued.[33] The communications division of the LDP took the position that NTT should not be forced to buy foreign-made equipment as long as the EEC did not include telecommunications procurement under the code. The LDP issued a statement worked out together with NTT that stressed that "even in the event that it becomes necessary to have NTT become subject to the government procurement code in order to facilitate a speedy conclusion to the GATT Tokyo Round, NTT's procurement of plant and equipment must follow the same pattern found in the EEC; they must not be subject to the provisions of the government procurement code which are based on the principle of competitive bidding."[34] This statement points out the apparent inconsistency from the perspective of the Japanese regarding U.S. policy on trade in telecommunications. Defenders of NTT were puzzled as to why the United States was pressuring Japan to include NTT under the code when the United States and the EEC had reached an agreement on entity coverage that did not include the European state-owned telephone operating company (PTTs).

The United States accepted the EEC offer, even though tele-

communications equipment was excluded, because it opened between $8 and $10 billion of procurement contracts. This came close
to the initial offer of the United States, which was between $10 and
$12 billion. In response to this exclusion of the telecommunications
operating companies, the United States did withdraw those agencies that were significant purchasers of telecommunications. The
Automated Data and Telecommunications Service of the General
Services Administration, which in 1980 allocated $807 million for
telecommunications products and services—became one of the
major cutbacks in the U.S. offer.[35] The U.S.-EEC agreement
prompted NTT to complain that Japan was being unfairly singled
out.

In response to this complaint the United States argued that
two factors figured in the decision to put pressure on NTT and not
on the European PTTs. First, U.S. negotiators made the assessment that since the EEC did not yet have in place an intracommunity
procurement policy in telecommunications, it would be virtually
impossible to include the PTTs under the code.[36] Second, the EEC
presented an acceptable offer to the United States without including the PTTs.

The combination of U.S. pressure to include NTT under the
code in conjunction with the U.S.-EEC agreement that did not
include telecommunications posed a serious domestic political
problem for Japan. Because the language of the code stated that
entity coverage must be generalized to all signatories, if Japan was
to include all NTT procurement under the code, the EEC would
also be able to bid on NTT's procurement contracts. The EEC,
however, had grounds to expect access to NTT because their PTTs
bought either from national firms or from local subsidiaries of
multi-national corporations (MNCs). Given the political difficulties of opening up NTT at all, the possibility of European telecommunications sales to Japan without reciprocity exceeded what Japan was politically able to offer.

HOW NTT WAS ISOLATED

The idea to negotiate for NTT coverage came initially from the
Industry Sector Advisory Committee (ISAC), although the STR
quickly picked up the idea because including NTT would substan-

tially improve the Japanese offer.[37] Once the STR adopted NTT as a target to be included under the code, it becomes difficult to differentiate the position of the STR from that of the industry. The congruence between the industry and the government with respect to NTT coverage gave the Japanese the impression that at first support for NTT coverage was limited to a few isolated government bureaucrats. An STR negotiator remarked that the Japanese would go to the Hill puzzled as to why the administration was pushing so hard for NTT coverage.[38]

The firm stance of the STR on NTT not only resulted from business pressure for increased trading opportunities. As well, the STR knew that Congress wanted the STR either to "get a good agreement or not come back with any agreement at all."[39] Congress understood that telecommunications was an area in which the United States was competitive and serious about trade expansion. In spite of the competitive strength of U.S. firms, Congress had come under increasing pressure to impose trade restrictions on Japanese telecommunications products. This pressure came from labor and those telecommunications firms concerned with insulating the U.S. market from Japanese competition.

A task force report by the House Subcommittee on Trade evidences this pressure for protection. The report describes U.S.-Japanese trade in telecommunications equipment as potentially creating a threat to American producers and jobs.

> It appears that the Japanese are using their protected home market to improve their telecommunications technology while exporting as much as they can as fast as they can into the open American market. Since telecommunications is one of the industries of the future this type of one-sided and unfair trade competition is particularly serious. There is growing concern that in telecommunications the United States may be facing job-displacing import competition when items which the United States markets competitively are denied access to export markets. This awareness will undoubtedly lead to demands for retaliation of import restrictions.[40]

The report further indicated that the subcommittee would "raise the issue of ways to encourage opening the Japanese telecommunications market during the drafting of the MTN implementing legislation on the government procurement code."[41] The main role of Congress in the NTT negotiations was to support the STR in their efforts to get a solid agreement with Japan on NTT.

This support involves two components. First, Congress had to make clear to the Japanese that it was backing the actions taken by the STR to persuade the Japanese government to change NTT's procurement practices. Second, this support had to pose a credible threat to close off a part of the U.S. market to Japanese imports either through prohibiting Japanese firms from bidding on U.S. government procurement contracts or through restricting telecommunications equipment imports. The seriousness of the belief within the administration that without an agreement on NTT Congress would place restrictions on Japanese imports prompted an interagency vote to exclude Japanese firms from being able to bid on U.S. government contracts.[42]

Once it became clear that the United States was serious about excluding Japan entirely from the code, the Japanese government began to put pressure on NTT to liberalize its procurement procedures. This policy shift was a result of a fear on the part of the Japanese that the United States would impose discriminatory measures on Japanese goods in the event that the negotiations failed. An STR official indicated that the Japanese were still very sensitive about being subject to discriminatory actions.[43] Timothy Curran wrote that for the Japanese government "whatever the merits of the case within the MTN context, it was believed that some sort of accommodation with the United States had to be worked out before Congressional protectionist pressure became too great."[44] As the pressure on NTT intensified, and the Japanese government became committed to trying to reach an agreement on NTT, the issue became defined as a bilateral U.S.-Japanese conflict.

Once NTT lost the political battle to retain its traditional method of procurement, it tried to reduce the impact any changes would have on its traditional suppliers by only offering to accept competitive bids on standardized and routine products. This strategy informed the first Japanese offer that included NTT purchases presented to the United States, March 28, 1979. This offer covered about $5 billion in government procurement opportunities. The United States rejected this offer both because the dollar amount was too low and because it did not cover the kinds of products the United States had expected. The United States, specifically, had hoped for between $8 and $10 billion in bidding opportunities, including central switching and phone equipment.[45] Although in this offer Japan included $2.3 billion of NTT expenditures, the items included consisted primarily of transmission equipment, that is, microwave relay systems and coaxial cables, computer paper, typewriters, and steel telephone poles, which were of little interest to the United States.[46] The Japanese justified their offer on the grounds that American companies could not meet the technical specifications of the Japanese telecommunications system.

In response to this list of products, Robert Strauss called the offer "totally inadequate."[47] He further stated that "he would not submit a bad agreement to the Congress because there were too many good things in our trade package to jeopardize it with something this patently unfair like the Japanese proposal on government procurement."[48] He also made clear that unless Japan proved willing to include sophisticated telecommunications equipment under the code, the United States would not accept Japan's offer. The United States argued that the inclusion of these NTT purchases was the only way in which they could put balance into the code.[49] The importance of NTT was further magnified because U.S. negotiators believed that the entire code would collapse without a successful bilateral agreement with Japan.

This Japanese offer reflected NTT's unwillingness to purchase sophisticated technology from foreign firms. Yet the U.S. negotiators had also failed to send a clear signal to Japan indicating exactly which products needed to be covered by the code to make Japan's offer adequate. Prior to this offer the STR had stressed primarily the dollar amount of products the United States was asking Japan to include under the government procurement code, as opposed to the specific products that were to be covered. The emphasis on the dollar amount—instead of on specific products— could have contributed to the uncertainty on the part of the Japanese with respect to which products they needed to include in their offer. The failure of the United States to specify which high-technology items to include may have contributed to the breakdown of the negotiations at this point.

It is not clear exactly why the STR did not specify to the Japanese the exact kind of equipment necessary for the United States to accept a Japanese offer. An industry representative did suggest that from the outset of the discussions between the STR and the industry's advisory committee, a consensus existed that the most promising segment of the Japanese market for U.S. firms was in digital switching equipment because NTT was just beginning to replace the older electromechanical switches with new computerized exchanges. Allowing U.S. firms to sell digital switches in the Japanese market would also help U.S. firms in third markets because it would discourage Japanese firms from subsidizing foreign sales with high profits possible in a sheltered domestic market. Because the U.S. industry was lobbying for all of NTT's procurement to be covered by the code, the STR negotiators may not have made clear to the Japanese exactly which products were necessary for NTT to include in order for the United States to accept an agreement.

After this breakdown in negotiations, the STR presented Japan with a list of products that the United States expected to be included in an acceptable offer for NTT. This list included switching equipment, transmission equipment, cables, data transmission equipment, telegraph equipment, and private branch exchanges (PBX). The STR still did not, however, rank order the different items to indicate which items were essential for the United States to accept an offer.[50]

Within a month the Japanese presented another offer to the United States. It covered $6.9 billion in government contracts, including $2.3 billion of NTT expenditures. Under this agreement NTT would accept bids for transmission systems, microwave relay systems, and coaxial cables. However, the offer excluded computers, central switching equipment, and telephone equipment. Strauss rejected this offer again because it would effectively shut out American products in precisely those areas in which the United States was most competitive.[51] To go ahead with an agreement required the support of at least some of the industry advisers, and the STR understood that the industry would not support an agreement unless it included high-technology items.

The question of how the United States determined the specific products to be covered by the agreement illustrates both the strengths of the ISAC committee system and some of the inherent weaknesses of the STR. Industry representatives pointed out two primary problems with the STR during these negotiations. First,

the negotiators did not understand the telephone system or procurement procedures for state-of-the-art telecommunications
equipment. As a result they did not know either the kinds of
products U.S. firms wanted to be included or the kinds of information and procedures U.S. manufacturers needed in order to make
competitive bids. The representative of the Electronic Industries
Association to the ISAC commented that he found most of the
meetings completely uninformative. Because of this he said that
some meetings were not well attended.[52] In contrast, a staff negotiator from the STR believed that the meetings with the telecommunications ISAC provided crucial information about the
industry. He also remarked that he needed an opportunity to sit
down with industry people and ask questions.[53] Second, some
industry representatives believed that the STR was primarily interested in negotiating an agreement that looked good but that in fact
did not create viable new trading opportunities for U.S. firms.

The following discussion of the final phase of the NTT negotiations focuses primarily on this belief that the objective of the
STR was to get an agreement that looked good—especially to
Congress—but that only secondarily concerned itself with creating
actual sales opportunities in Japan. At issue, once the Japanese
became serious about opening up NTT's procurement procedures,
was whether the conflict between Japan and the United States over
NTT could be resolved on a bilateral basis outside of the code. A
bilateral agreement would eliminate considerable domestic political problems for the Japanese government because it would avoid
raising the issue of EEC-Japanese telecommunications trade. The
STR negotiators found this problem worth avoiding.

U.S. industry, however, showed skepticism about the effectiveness of a bilateral agreement and questioned whether it would
have real meaning. Once the STR decided that the bilateral was the
only politically feasible solution, this industry skepticism was discounted. The United States ultimately signed an agreement with
Japan in which a bilateral that was "code consistent"—but not a
formal part of the government procurement code—covered the
sensitive high-technology equipment. The bilateral dimension of
the conflict ultimately dominated the remaining attempts to reach
a solution.

THE NEGOTIATIONS OVER THE BILATERAL

During summer 1980, six months before the code was to go into effect, the STR perceived that it had two options. First, it could accept the status quo—that is, agree to the last offer presented by Japan. An STR staff negotiator said, however, that they (the STR negotiators) both would not, and could not because of political pressures, do this. Second, they could modify the U.S. request to take into account the bilateral nature of the conflict. This would involve negotiating a separate bilateral that would cover the high-technology products in addition to including a part of NTT's routine procurement under the code. The STR decided this was a reasonable compromise because it would allow U.S. firms to bid on NTT's state-of-the-art equipment purchases, which was more important to the United States than demanding that NTT liberalize its procurement practices on a multilateral basis.

During the subsequent negotiations the STR presented the Japanese with a case study of a Department of Defense purchase of state-of-the-art equipment. The case study attempted to demonstrate that it was possible to purchase new technology in a manner consistent with the government procurement code. The Japanese responded that they had not understood how the code applied to R & D contracts and had originally believed that it was only suitable for off-the-shelf equipment.[54]

Although this response may have indicated a softening of the Japanese position, the United States still lacked confidence about the prospects for a successful conclusion to the negotiations. NTT continued to resist any proposals to alter its current procurement procedures, which were limited to negotiated contracts. Ultimately, however, NTT did agree to accept competitive bids for high-technology equipment in response to escalating government pressure. The Japanese government took a hard line on NTT once it became clear that the United States would accept code-consistent procedures, that is, not cover all of NTT under the code. After U.S. and Japanese negotiators had agreed to the bilateral, the STR presented this proposal formally to the ISAC as well as informally to the industry trade associations and the House Ways and Means Committee.[55]

During the course of these discussions a large segment of the industry indicated that they would prefer no agreement to a bilateral because they believed that a bilateral would not be strong enough to force the Japanese to change anything. This opposition reflected a general belief in the industry that without stronger international sanctions provided by the code Japan would not live up to the agreement. The industry was also uncertain about the kind of sanctions to which the United States could resort if NTT placed yet new barriers in the way of telecommunications trade.

In spite of industry opposition to the bilateral the STR continued to hold negotiations over procedures with the Japanese. U.S. negotiators remained convinced that the Japanese Diet would never agree to include sensitive items under the code. To accommodate U.S. business criticism, however, they did incorporate into the agreement a provision that would create a monitoring mechanism to ensure that the terms of the agreement were met. If evidence surfaced that NTT had continued to discriminate against U.S. firms, the provision provided that Japan would be excluded from U.S. government procurement contracts.

The inclusion of this monitoring mechanism sufficed to gain the acceptance of a core group of firms for the agreement.[56] Representatives of the industry's advisory committee indicated to the STR that they were generally supportive of the proposal. In addition, to ensure industry support, Rubin Askew, chief of STR at the time, consulted with individual executives as well as with members of the House Ways and Means Committee. Askew took the position that he was not going to go ahead with an agreement without a reasonable degree of support from the industry. In evaluating the reaction of the industry advisers, however, he discounted opposition to the bilateral for what he considered to be the wrong reason, that is, to establish a rationale for keeping Japanese imports out of the U.S. market.

Once Japan accepted the principle of code-consistent procedures, the STR negotiators felt confident that they had come upon the best possible agreement, given domestic political constraints in Japan. A determination on the part of the Carter administration to negotiate the agreement before leaving office enhanced this enthusiasm for the bilateral. At this point industry and labor groups had lost their ability to influence the shape of the agreement. Instead, the STR began to lobby individual firms that remained critical of the absence of full code coverage in an effort to solicit their support for the agreement. An industry representative remarked that even if the ISAC members had tried to oppose the agreement, they could not have stopped it from going through at this phase in the negotiations. He added, however, that if industry had not originally taken a hard line, the STR would have settled for a much weaker agreement.[57]

The United States and Japan signed the government procurement code agreement on December 19, 1980. At the signing Askew did not explicitly mention the bilateral dimension of the compromise and only alluded to the principle of "code consistency" in his remarks. He stated: "Under the terms of this three-year agreement the requirements of the government procurement code will be observed for all purchases by Japan's Nippon Telegraph and Telephone public corporation as well as for purchases by all of Japan's central government ministries and agencies covered by the code."[58]

THE AGREEMENT

The agreement reached between the United States and Japan divided NTT's procurement into three tracks:

1. Nontelecommunications equipment;
2. Off-the-shelf public telecommunications equipment that only needs minor modifications to adapt to Japan's network;
3. State-of-the-art telecommunications equipment developed specifically for NTT (this would also include R&D).

In addition to these three tracks they formulated a separate agreement in which Japan agreed to facilitate the sale of U.S. equipment in the interconnect market.[59]

The government procurement code covers the first track, which includes mainframe office computers, utility poles, and coaxial cables. The bilateral agreement consists of Tracks II and III. The essence of the compromise between the United States and Japan was that while Japan agreed to include sophisticated equipment in an agreement that contained obligations equivalent to those in the government procurement code, the United States agreed not to subject these obligations to an international dispute settlement mechanism. The major implication of this centered around the fact that the European telecommunications equipment manufacturers would have no access to a dispute settlement procedure to take issue with possible discrimination against their products by NTT.

The agreement states that for both Tracks II and III NTT will, "for each proposed procurement, invite applications from the maximum number of domestic and foreign suppliers consistent with the efficient operation of the procurement system."[60] To ensure that foreign—that is, U.S.—firms would not be discriminated against, the agreement stated that all firms that responded to a request for a proposal (RFP) issued abroad by the Japanese government would "be treated in a manner no less favorable than those domestic responding to the NTT-issued RFP's."[61]

The remainder of Attachment 1 of the agreement essentially obligates NTT to follow code-consistent procedures. NTT was required to:

1. Include information in the RFP with respect to the kind of product and the quantity required, the economic and technical requirements of the suppliers, the address and final date for submitting the proposal, and all the information necessary for obtaining procurement documentation;
2. Provide procurement documentation that includes information on where the applications are to be sent, a technical description of the product, and the criteria upon which the contract will be awarded;
3. Award contracts on the basis of the criteria stated in the procurement documentation.[62]

The agreement further provided for a dispute settlement mechanism, consisting of a panel of three arbitrators, one from each country and a third who is not a national of either the United States or Japan. Both the United States and Japan agreed that they would use their best efforts to implement the findings of the panel.[63] In the event that the recommendations go unimplemented, the agreement stipulates that "each Party may take appropriate measures to reestablish reciprocity in the field of government procurement."[64] This suggests that the United States would retaliate by withdrawing trade concessions if a satisfactory solution was not reached. As a further safety valve, Askew and Dr. Saburo Okita also agreed to review the progress of the agreement after three years to determine if it should be expanded or perhaps abandoned.

This dispute settlement mechanism in conjunction with the transparency provision for NTT's procurement procedures stood out as the crucial aspect of the agreement from the perspective of the STR. The STR aimed its primary objective toward giving U.S. firms an opportunity to compete in the Japanese market while not coercing Japan into buying U.S. products.

INDUSTRY AND LABOR REACTION

By the time the United States and Japan signed the agreement, the Electronic Industries Association (EIA) took the position that if the bilateral was in fact equivalent to code coverage, it should be given a chance. A press release of the communications division of the EIA stated:

> The U.S. Trade Representative believes the current agreement is the equivalent of full coverage of NTT by the Government Procurement Code, and in fact in some cases is better than coverage by the code. While this well may be the case, the text of the agreement is complex, and the carrying out of the various stipulations of the agreement will be complicated, relying heavily on the good faith of the Japanese. It should be noted that because of the perceived heavy reliance on good faith, many are skeptical about the implementation of the agreement.[65]

John Sodolski, vice-president of the EIA, indicated that this skepticism proved more representative of the membership of the EIA than widespread support for the agreement. Sodolski, however, being one of the most outspoken opponents of the agreement, believed that it would only serve to allow the Japanese to protect their market for another three years while still being allowed to export to the United States.[66] Another industry representative who supported Sodolski's interpretation of the agreement suggested that the STR staff may have led Askew to believe that there was less opposition to the bilateral than actually existed.

While Sodolski believed that the United States should have held out for full code coverage, the president of the EIA was anxious for the agreement to look like a success since the association had been closely involved in the negotiations. Thus, rather than criticizing the agreement, the EIA concluded, "While the U.S. telecommunications manufacturing industry would have preferred an even stronger instrument, the communications division of the EIA pledges to attempt to insure the workability and productiveness of the agreement negotiated between the U.S. and Japan in the NTT matter."[67]

The labor group most affected by the negotiations, the Communications Workers of America (CWA), also criticized the agreement. John Morgan, an assistant to the president of the union, argued that the EEC should not have been cut out of the benefits the United States received from the bilateral and that all government procurement should be on a multilateral basis. He also believed the dispute settlement mechanism was inadequate and that Japan would be able to continue to protect its market. Even after the United States and Japan signed the agreement, the CWA continued to take the position that anything less than full code coverage was a political failure on the part of the United States. In a letter to Askew, CWA president Glenn Watts contended, "The agreement, with its very complex and ambiguous procedures, will most probably be ineffective in opening the Japanese telecommunications market to United States producers."[68]

EPILOGUE

In spite of this criticism the STR believed that there was no way to know whether the bilateral would be effective until it was tried, and remained willing to go ahead with the agreement. Some indication that it might work was given by a member of the GATT staff who argued that one cannot assume that countries will sign an agreement they have no intention of following and that to a large extent the success of both the government procurement code and the separate U.S.-Japanese agreement will depend on whether U.S. firms submit bids on NTT contracts.[69]

NTT's new president, Hisashi Shinto, said that he was committed to change the course of NTT management and that although opening NTT's procurement practices would not be easy, he was not encountering any resistance. He said, "So far I don't feel any resistance, but unless I move very rapidly, everybody would want to stand still."[70]

Both the EIA and the CWA stressed the importance of the monitoring mechanism to determine whether NTT was backing up its commitments with actual purchases or had a reasonable justification for choosing a domestic supplier. Evidence of sales would then be a major part of the criteria used to decide whether the United States either terminates or decides to renew the bilateral when it expires after three years. Sodolski, however, expressed some doubt about the institutional memory of the STR and feared that the decision to renew the agreement would be based on political considerations that may not include the success of U.S. firms with respect to selling high-technology equipment to NTT.

CONCLUSION

The NTT case is somewhat deceptive because initially it appeared to be a case in which the United States sought to obtain increased access to the Japanese telecommunications market. The unified position of the telecommunications industry in favor of full code coverage for NTT further reinforced this interpretation of the motivation behind the U.S. negotiating position. This unity, however, obscured a basic split within the industry between those firms that supported full code coverage because they believed the Japanese would not be able to accept it politically, thereby providing them with a rationale for restricting imports of Japanese telecommunications equipment, and those that believed that without the sanctions provided by the government procurement code NTT would not be compelled to honor any bilateral commitments regarding its procurement practices.

This split introduced a high level of complexity into the negotiations between the U.S. industry representatives and the STR negotiators. These negotiations proved complex because different firms in the industry wanted the STR to pressure Japan into accepting full code coverage with the expectation of different outcomes. The STR's lack of understanding of the technology of the telecommunications equipment market further aggravated the tension between the STR and the industry. This lack of understanding led to the breakdown of the negotiations over NTT because the STR negotiators never specified the specific kind of equipment U.S. firms were most interested in trying to sell in Japan and what the minimum acceptable Japanese offer was.

As long as the STR kept full code coverage as its basic negotiating position, the negotiations remained deadlocked. Faced with the possibility in summer 1980 that the government procurement code would go into effect without including a bilateral between the United States and Japan, the STR decided, however, to change its negotiating strategy.[71]

This change involved two considerations. First, the STR was determined to get an agreement with Japan over the issue of government procurement. Second, the STR was beginning to focus more on the bilateral nature of the trade dispute. The STR sought to protect the political viability of the government procurement code because it provided a large percentage of the increased export opportunities for the United States that came out of the Tokyo Round negotiations. Because trade negotiations are based on balancing increased access to export markets against increased potential imports, the loss of the government procurement code could have resulted in a change of the dominant perception in Congress that the United States in aggregate terms was benefiting from the Tokyo Round agreements.

Thus, the STR negotiators were willing to change the U.S. negotiating position in part because they did not want to risk congressional scrutiny of a Tokyo Round package, which did not include the government procurement code. As a result, the STR stood willing to compromise to reach an agreement with the Japanese. The compromise, however, could not be over the sophistication of the equipment NTT would open to competitive bidding. If NTT only partially liberalized its procurement policies, Congress would probably have objected to exclusion of U.S. firms from the most interesting and lucrative contracts.

But the STR was willing to compromise on the question of

including NTT formally under the government procurement code. Because NTT's procurement policies had become primarily a bilateral trade dispute between Japan and the United States, the STR decided it was willing to accept a bilateral resolution to the conflict. The constraints posed by Japanese domestic politics—which made it impossible for the Japanese government to agree to include NTT under the code without a reciprocal agreement from the EEC— made this change in negotiating position necessary. It was clear, however, that the EEC was not ready to do this. While including NTT under the code would have been the most progressive solution in terms of liberalizing trade, the telecommunications equipment sector proved too sensitive politically for this kind of an agreement.

Ironically, although the U.S. industry supported the multilateral expansion of telecommunications trade, the STR did not accept it. The STR did not accept the industry's position because after the negotiations over NTT failed several times, they decided that including NTT under the code was not a politically viable option. Instead, the two options they faced were:

1. Negotiating a bilateral agreement with Japan that would cover all of NTT's procurement and be code consistent; or
2. Closing the U.S. market to Japanese imports.

Given this revised array of choices, in spite of industry opposition the STR pursued and ultimately reached a bilateral agreement with Japan to open NTT's procurement to U.S. firms. The letter exchanged between Askew and Okita over this agreement indicated that they hoped this step would be a beginning to the progressive liberalization of trade in telecommunications and that ultimately the EEC would open its telecommunications procurement so that the most important publicly owned telecommunications service companies would be included under the code.

Although the conflict over the government procurement code was resolved on a bilateral basis, it did provide Congress with an alternative to the imposition of trade restraints on Japanese telecommunications equipment. Because of this the political energies of the industry were channeled toward increasing opportunities for trade expansion and away from lobbying to protect the American market. Unlike the previous two cases the pragmatic resolution to this conflict involved negotiating increased market access for U.S. firms. This outcome was the least costly to U.S. consumers yet provided increased employment opportunities and the potential of higher profits for U.S. firms through increased foreign sales.

NOTES

1. Organization for Economic Cooperation and Development (OECD), *Study of the Telecommunications Equipment Sector,* DSTI/IND/IAQ/8.1.3 (I), mimeographed (Paris: OECD, 1981), p. 9.

2. Ibid., p. 11.

3. Ibid., p. 19.

4. U.S., Congress, House, Subcommittee on Trade of the Ways and Means Committee, *Task Force Report on United States-Japan Trade,* 95th Cong., 2nd Sess. (Washington D.C.: Government Printing Office, 1979), p. 33.

5. Long-distance rates are regulated by the FCC.

6. U.S., International Trade Commission, *A Baseline Study of the Telephone Terminal and Switching Equipment Industry,* USITC Publication no. 946. (Washington D.C.: USITC, 1979), p. 8.

7. Until 1970 the Bell system also had a monopoly on long-distance telephone service. (The FCC regulates long-distance telephone service.) General Telephone and Electronics is the second-largest American service company and makes up the largest share of the market independent of the Bell system measured in terms of telephones in service. (In 1977 there were 1,556 independent operating companies in the United States.)

8. OECD, *Study,* p. 37.

9. Ibid., p. 37.

10. Ibid., p. 29.

11. Microwave Communications Incorporated (MCI) was the first company to request the FCC to allow it to interconnect with the Bell system. Initially, the FCC turned down this request under pressure from AT&T. In 1969, however, it permitted the creation of "specialized common carriers" on an experimental basis. This decision allowed MCI and other long-distance transmission carriers to hook up to local telephone networks. William Shepard and Clair Wilcox, "Regulation of Communications," *Public Policies toward Business* (Homewood, Ill.: Irwin Series in Economics, 1979), p. 361. Other suppliers of long-distance telephone service in the United States include MCI, Southern Pacific Communications Co. (Sprint), Western Union's Metro I, and International Telephone and Telegraph's (ITT) City Call I & II. The interconnect equipment industry is composed of large, experienced, established telephone equipment manufacturers such as ITT, General Telephone and Electronics (GTE), and a host of relative newcomers such as

Rolm, Tele/Resources, Digital Telephone Systems, and Chestel. It also includes such foreign-based companies as Nippon Electric and Oki of Japan. This discussion is taken from Arthur D. Little Decision Resources, "Impact: The Outlook for the US Telephone Equipment Industry," (Cambridge, Mass.: ADL, June 1980), (mimeographed) R800601, p. 10.

12. U.S. Congress, Senate, Finance Committee, *Agreements Being Negotiated at the Multilateral Trade Negotiations in Geneva,* Prepared by U.S. International Trade Commission, 96th Cong., 1st Sess., 1979, no. 6 pt. 3, pp. 202−3.

13. William Cline, Noboru Kawanabe, T.O.M. Kronsjö, and Thomas Williams, *Trade Negotiations in the Tokyo Round: A Quantitative Assessment* (Washington D.C.: Brookings Institution, 1979), p. 189.

14. Ibid., p. 190.

15. Report to the Congress by the Comptroller General of the United States, *Governmental Buy-National Practices of the United States and Other Countries,* (Washington D.C.: Government Printing Office, 1976), p. 39.

16. Ibid., p. 11.

17. Ibid., p. 41.

18. Report by the Director General of the GATT, *The Tokyo Round of Multilateral Trade Negotiations* (Geneva: General Agreement on Tariffs and Trade, 1979), p. 137.

19. Interview with GATT official, Geneva, February 1981 (not for attribution).

20. U.S., Congressional Budget Office, *The Effects of the Tokyo Round of Multilateral Trade Negotiations on the US Economy: An Updated View,* (Washington, D.C.: Government Printing Office, 1979), pp. 25−26.

21. Interview with William Edgar, Department of State, July 1981.

22. *Open tendering procedures* are those under which all interested parties may submit a tender. Under *selective tendering* only those suppliers qualified in advance are invited to submit a bid. Countries using selective tenders, however, have to publish rules with respect to how suppliers can become qualified. Report by the Director General of the GATT, *Tokyo Round,* p. 138.

23. NTT is one of three Japanese public corporations. The other two are the Japanese National Railways Corporations and the Japan Monopoly Corporation. Prior to U.S. occupation these three corporations were government departments, which McArthur separated from their former ministries and set up as independent public corporations. This discussion is taken from Chalmers Johnson, *Japan's Public Policy Companies* (Washington D.C.: American Enterprise Institute, 1978), p. 38.

24. Ibid., p. 39.

25. It is interesting to note in this context that Johnson argues that the *kosha* ("public corporations, which includes NTT") are the most public of the *tokshu hojin* (a term that refers to both public corporations and public-private enterprises). Ibid., p. 38.

26. Comptroller General of the United States, *United States-Japan Trade: Issues and Problems,* ID-79−53 (Washington D.C.: General Accounting Office, 1979), p. 68.

27. The General Accounting Office study on U.S.-Japanese trade found that about 96 percent of NTT's procurement is carried out on a negotiated basis, largely from NTT family members. General Accounting Office, p. 66.

28. International Trade Commission, *Baseline Study*, p. 33.

29. NTT is the only operating company for domestic communications in Japan.

30. International Trade Commission, *Baseline Study*, p. 33.

31. Without specifying which firms, an STR staff negotiator described that the telecommunications industry could be split into three groups with respect to NTT: those seriously interested in making the code work, those on the fence, and those who wanted to close the U.S. market. Interview with David Shark, STR negotiator, January 1981 in Washington D.C.

32. If NTT were covered by the code, foreign firms would be able to bid on all NTT procurement contracts. It does not ensure, however, that U.S. or other foreign firms would win these bids.

33. Timothy Curran, "Politics and High Technology: US-Japan Negotiations over the Nippon Telephone and Telegraph Company, 1978–1979," mimeographed (Prepared for the U.S.-Japan Economic Relations Group, Washington, D.C., 1980) p. 45.

34. Ibid., p. 46.

35. Edward Goldstein, "Doing Business under the Agreement on Government Procurement," *St. John's Law Review* 55 (1980):1. p. 84.

36. The EEC is, however, moving in the direction of European competition in telecommunications procurement. Their approach is to use the transition to electronic technology to insist on the interoperability of equipment between member states. The compatibility between the systems in different member countries would then make procurement technically feasible—although still politically difficult because of the vested interests of the current national suppliers. This discussion is taken from, "EEC, GATT Codes Mean Tougher Competition for Government Tenders," *Business Europe*, March 23, 1979. The United States eventually hopes to force open the EEC market once this intra-European liberalization has taken place. Interview with Richard Heimlich, senior STR negotiator, Washington D.C., August 1980.

37. A State Department official explained that not only was NTT targeted by industry but also industry pressure on the government from both telecommunications manufacturers and heavy electrical machinery producers was instrumental in the decision on the part of the United States to negotiate the government procurement code. Interview with William Edgar, Department of State, August 1980.

38. Interview with David Shark, Office of the Special Trade Representative, Washington D.C., August 1980.

39. Ibid., January 1981.

40. U.S., Congress, House, Subcommittee on Trade of the Ways and Means Committee, *Task Force Report on United States-Japan Trade*, p. 33.

41. Ibid., p. 33. This implementing legislation is required because the adoption of the government procurement code involves a change in U.S. law in order

to waive the buy-America preference for code signatories.

42. The Council on Economic Advisors voted against this proposal and stated that they instead preferred a policy that would subject Japanese firms to a 20 percent preference. Council on Economic Advisors memo, May 1, 1979. (mimeographed).

43. Interview with Richard Heimlich, assistant STR for Industrial Trade Policy, Washington, D.C., August 1980.

44. Curran, "Politics and High Technology" p. 41.

45. The study by the Comptroller General on U.S.-Japanese trade stated that the factors that went into determining this amount were relative gross domestic products levels, the relative amount of government intervention in the private sector, and the absolute size of the government sector. Comptroller General of the United States, *United States-Japan Trade*, p. 77.

46. CEA memo, May 7, 1979.

47. *International Herald Tribune*, March 30, 1980.

48. *International Herald Tribune*, March 31, 1979.

49. Interview with David Shark, Office of the Special Trade Representative, Washington D.C., July 1980.

50. Curran, "Politics and High Technology," p. 60.

51. Ibid., p. 65.

52. Interview with John Sodolski, vice-president, Electronic Industries Association, Washington D.C., February 1981.

53. Interview with David Shark, Office of the Special Trade Representative, Washington D.C., February 1981.

54. Ibid., February 1981.

55. These trade associations included the EIA, which represents telecommunications equipment manufacturers; Computer and Business Equipment Manufacturers' Association, dominated by IBM; and the Semi-Conductor Industry Association.

56. The following account is based primarily on an interview with David Shark; see Shark, February 1981.

57. Sodolski, February, 1981.

58. "Statement of Rubin Askew," Washington, D.C., December 19, 1980 (mimeographed).

59. This agreement was issued in the form of a joint statement in conjunction with the statement on NTT procurement procedures.

60. "NTT Procurement Procedures," Attachment I, p. 1., December 19, 1980 (mimeographed).

61. Ibid., p. 1.

62. Ibid.

63. "NTT Procurement Procedures," Attachment II, "Procedures of Non-binding Arbitration," December 19, 1980 (mimeographed).

64. Ibid.

65. Electronic Industries Association, "News Release," December 19, 1980.

66. Sodolski, February 1981.

67. Electronic Industries Association, "News Release."

68. Letter from Glenn Watts, CWA president to STR Askew, December 19, 1980.

69. Interview with GATT staff, Geneva, March 1981 (not for attribution).

70. "Japan: The Doors of NTT Begin to Creak Open," *Business Week*, May 4, 1981, p. 67.

71. The government procurement code was scheduled to go into effect January 1981.

8

BEYOND DOMESTIC INTERESTS

This book has examined the role that multilateral agreements have played in the making of U.S. international trade policy. We have explored how U.S. adherence to the GATT regime acts as a constraint on domestic sectoral interest group pressure for protection from foreign imports. At the outset four alternative explanations were offered for the way in which U.S. international trade policy is formulated. The first explanation emphasizes the dominant role of domestic pressure groups in the determination of trade policy. The second stresses the autonomous decision-making power of Congress. The third explanation focuses on state competition in international trade relations and argues for the central role of national policy autonomy in determining all foreign policy decisions, including trade. Each of these explanations can account for some aspects of each case. Yet, each offers an incomplete explanation for the ultimate action taken by the government.

The following discussion reviews those aspects of each case that support these explanations. It then proposes that the ultimate policy outcomes can be explained best by taking into account the international trade regime. The policy that conforms to the norms, rules, and procedures of the international trade regime can best be described as pragmatic liberalism. Pragmatic liberalism suggests that policy is based on an international political agreement that promotes the liberalization of international trade while remaining sensitive to the need of member states to mitigate the adjustment costs imposed on domestic industries and to respond to powerful domestic interest groups.

In addition to demonstrating the role that the GATT regime has played within the three cases, the chapter briefly explores some of the implications this membership has for U.S. industrial policy. Finally, the GATT is linked to the broader issue of U.S. international economic policy. Threats to multilateralism come not only from the illegal imposition of import restraints. They can also come from foreign policy decisions, which have the potential of triggering retaliatory measures on the part of our trading partners. While domestic pressure groups that attempt to place limits on imports do not seem to threaten the GATT framework, other foreign policy actions can. This point is illustrated in a discussion of the decision taken by the Reagan administration to prohibit foreign firms producing under American licenses from selling prod-ucts used for the construction of the Siberia-to-Europe natural gas pipeline. This decision constitutes a threat to the GATT frame-work equal to that of the unilateral imposition of trade restraints. Thus future research must look beyond protectionist attempts to threaten the stability of the trading regime to the broader question of how trade sanctions are used to achieve foreign policy goals.

INTEREST GROUP PRESSURES AND TRADE POLICY: SCHATTSCHNEIDER'S VIEW

E. E. Schattschneider's study focuses on the vulnerability of Con-gress to interest group pressures for trade restraint.[1] The 1930 Tariff Act, which provides the empirical basis for his analysis, was formulated when Congress had neither the benefit of counter-vailing interest group pressures nor the knowledge of both the international and domestic consequences of restrictive tariffs. The findings in each of the three cases examined here suggest that Congress still plays an important role in the trade policy process and that sectoral pressure groups still have considerable influence over Congress.

Of the three industries the textile and apparel industry ap-pear to have the most complete hold on Congress. The textile and apparel industry derives its influence in Congress from its ability to argue convincingly that these industries together employ vast numbers of low-skilled workers for whom adjustment to new employment is especially difficult. Evidence of this includes the ability of this coalition to push a bill through Congress that would exempt textile and apparel products from tariff cuts at the Tokyo Round negotiations. After President Carter vetoed this bill, the coalition again demonstrated its political muscle by blocking legislation that would extend the subsidy-countervailing duty waiver. The EEC considered this measure as essential for the successful conclusion of the Tokyo Round. But the bill to extend the subsidy-countervailing duty waiver only passed Congress after negotiators from the Office of the Special Trade Representative had worked out an agreement with the industry. The textile and apparel white paper, however, did not include the main policy changes requested by the industry, that is, the imposition of a global quota and the reduction of the rate of quota growth to match the rate of growth of the American textile and apparel market.

The auto industry, represented primarily by the UAW Union and Ford Motor Company, also had some success in pressing Congress to consider legislation authorizing the president to negotiate import restraints on Japanese autos. This legislation, although passed by the House in 1980, never came up for a vote in the Senate. In 1981 Senator John Danforth (R-Mo.) introduced a bill that would impose a formal quota of 1.6 million Japanese cars a year for three years; it never came up for a vote in either the Senate or the House. The political momentum for legislated quotas was diffused after Japan agreed to impose a VRA.

In the telecommunications case no legislation was introduced into Congress designed to restrict the imports of Japanese telecommunications equipment. Congress, however, did play an important, if indirect, role in ensuring that the STR negotiators obtained a meaningful agreement from the Japanese to liberalize NTT's procurement policies. The STR negotiators believed that if the United States did not extract meaningful concessions over NTT's acceptance of bids from U.S. firms, the industry would complain to Congress. The likely outcome of these complaints would have been that the United States would not have signed the government procurement code with Japan, thereby threatening to unravel the balance of reciprocal trade benefits embodied in the Tokyo Round agreements. In addition, the intent of some of the leadership in the EIA, one of the major industry trade associations, was to use the inability of the United States to obtain access to the Japanese market as justification for Congress to impose restraints on the importation of Japanese telecommunications equipment.

Although evidence exists in each of the cases of the ability of the industry to persuade Congress to consider restrictive legislation, the outcomes in each case were not a direct result of interest group politics. The inability of interest groups to obtain desired outcomes raises the question of whether the transactional model stands as a more useful explanation of why interest groups failed to directly influence the policy process.

THE TRANSACTIONAL MODEL: THE BASIS FOR CONGRESSIONAL AUTONOMY

Bauer, Pool, and Dexter suggest two reasons why protectionist interest groups remain unsuccessful in their attempts to influence policy outcomes.[2] First, they believe that all issues in American politics involve countervailing interest group activity. Second, their analysis led them to conclude that the interests of a representative's constituency are not well defined, and thus members of Congress can respond primarily to those pressures they would otherwise support and elude those with which they do not agree. Bauer, Pool, and Dexter further suggest that the reluctance of Congress to pass restrictive trade legislation indicates the ability of Congress to act autonomously from interest group pressures.

The textile case, while providing the strongest evidence of the validity of the pressure group analysis, offers the least evidence for this second explanation. Congress, however, did appear to be autonomous to the extent that it allowed the executive branch to strike a deal with the industry and did not legislate quotas. This parallels the history of the U.S. multilateral trade agreements that cover textile and apparel products. The STA, the LTA, and the MFA were all negotiated by the executive branch.

In the auto case there was more evidence that Congress was able to consider aspects of a restrictive import policy aside from those raised by the industry. The debate over the 1980 legislation authorizing the president to negotiate an orderly marketing agreement (OMA) with Japan did not offer much evidence of countervailing interest group activity. Yet there was considerable opposition to the bill based on the inflationary impact that auto import restraints would have on the economy.[3] The auto case also demonstrates the autonomy of Congress in its ability to steer the industry to the ITC, thereby insulating itself for a period of time from direct political pressures.

In the telecommunications case the United States had two possible courses of action. First, the United States could use the government procurement code as leverage to force NTT to accept bids from U.S. firms. The second would be to limit Japanese telecommunications imports to the United States. A representative of the EIA indicated that his preference was for a restricted U.S. market over increased export opportunities. To the extent that Congress showed willingness to support the government procurement code negotiations in spite of the industry's preference for trade restraints, it acted autonomously.

THE STATE AS AN AUTONOMOUS ACTOR

Both Albert Hirschman and Stephen Krasner argue that autonomy is a crucial component of state strength in the international political system.[4] Thus for the United States to act in its national interest, we would expect it to maximize its decision-making discretion vis-à-vis its trading partners. The sovereignty of the state acts as the predominant motivating force behind these actions. Policies that maximize political power in the international system, macroeconomic stability, national economic growth, and social stability ensure state sovereignty. According to this view, the achievement of these goals in turn depends on the mobilization of domestic economic resources and shielding the domestic economy from the effects of external economic changes. Each of the cases also offers partial support for this perspective.

In the textile white paper the U.S. government agreed to renegotiate bilateral agreements with Hong Kong, Taiwan, and Korea to reduce the flexibility provisions in these bilateral agreements, thereby decreasing the possibility of import "surges" in sensitive categories. In the negotiations between the industry and the STR, industry representatives had argued that the current agreement allowed potentially destabilizing increases in imports. The STR subsequently agreed with this view. In the aftermath of the white paper, U.S. negotiators requested revisions of previous agreements, although none of the countries involved were willing to make any changes. To induce Hong Kong to accept these changes, U.S. negotiators had to offer concessions in other categories of textile and apparel products.

The United States acted autonomously in the auto case. To resolve the question of Japanese auto imports, the United States compelled Japan to agree to a VRA to limit Japanese exports to the United States to 1.68 million units for the fiscal year April 1, 1981, to March 31, 1982. Without the VRA the Japanese were expected to sell about 2.1 million automobiles in the United States during this period. This action is consistent with at least two of the national policies that Krasner suggests all states must pursue in order to enhance state strength in the international political arena: social stability, and aggregate national economic growth. To the extent that the VRA allows U.S. auto firms to rehire unemployed autoworkers, the agreement will enhance social stability. In addition, if the VRA provides American auto firms relief from foreign competition, U.S. firms may face reduced financial constraints in their retooling efforts, thereby enhancing profitability. This in turn could contribute to national economic growth.

Evidence of autonomous action on the part of the United States in the telecommunications cases is related to the issue of reciprocal market access in a specific product. Both U.S. industry officials and STR negotiators contended that the United States had a legitimate right to request access to the Japanese telecommunications market. They formulated this negotiating posture in response to the rapid increase in U.S. imports of telecommunications equipment from Japan, triggered by industry deregulation. Failing agreement with the Japanese, the United States had every intention of excluding Japan from the opportunity to bid on $17 billion of U.S. government procurement contracts. In addition, Japan would also run the risk that failure in the negotiations would trigger increasing momentum in Congress to consider restrictions on high-technology items.

PRAGMATIC LIBERALISM IN U.S. INTERNATIONAL TRADE POLICY

Although the three explanations examined above can partially account for the political pressures involved in each case, the results can best be explained by a perspective that takes into account actor perceptions of the benefits of international collaboration. The outcomes in all three cases were consistent in that the final decision in each involved adherence to the norms, rules, and procedures of the multilateral trade regime. The textile and apparel case offers strong evidence that the United States is pursuing a policy in which both multilateral agreements and a commitment to social stability come into play. In spite of the recognition on the part of the government of its political strength and the need to address its policy recommendations, the industry could not extract an agreement from the government that would involve violating the terms of the MFA.

Specifically, the industry wanted two policy outcomes that were inconsistent with the MFA. First, the industry lobbied for a global quota that would involve a departure from existing U.S. textile policy by requiring the reduction of existing quotas to accommodate new suppliers. U.S. textile and apparel policy has been to negotiate each quota individually on the basis of MFA regulations without regard to total U.S. textile and apparel imports. The industry hoped that a global quota on all U.S. imports of textile and apparel products would force negotiators to tighten existing bilaterals and negotiate new agreements with exporters not yet covered by the current arrangement. Second, it wanted the final agreement to tie the rate of increase of each quota negotiated under the bilateral agreements to the rate of growth of the U.S. market. This policy proposal would violate the 6 percent increase per year stipulated by the MFA since U.S. market growth has been very low.

Some months after the white paper had been negotiated, industry representatives expressed strong disappointment that the government had not implemented these changes in policy. At the same time, a U.S. government official in the Office of Textiles (located in the Department of Commerce) contended that there was a need for some government intervention in textile and apparel imports to provide for more certainty in the adjustment process so that communities would not be devastated by the loss of employment. The changes in the bilateral agreements that were made with Korea, Hong Kong, and Taiwan essentially sought to prevent surges—not to prevent the orderly growth of imports. Yet to the extent that these new bilaterals decreased the ability of exporters to respond to changes in fashion, U.S. textile and apparel manufacturers gained a competitive edge over imports. Although sustaining social stability served as the rationale for the renegotiation of the bilaterals, the new constraints imposed on major exporters to the United States reduced the competitive pressures on domestic producers. Thus the new agreements may have helped to keep noncompetitive producers in business, thereby creating a wealth transfer from consumers to producers.

The final auto decision also reflected a commitment to both multilateralism and domestic social stability. The United States demonstrated its commitment to multilateralism through the request made by Congress that the UAW and Ford go to the ITC for an injury hearing. The criteria for the determination of injury are based on Article 19 of the GATT.[5] Ultimately, the ITC found that imports did not constitute the most substantial cause of injury and on this basis could not recommend import relief. Although the government did negotiate a voluntary escape clause agreement with Japan to limit Japanese exports to the United States to 1.68 million units for 1980/81, this figure amounted to substantially less than the initial request made by both Ford and the UAW at the ITC hearings. While the VRA with Japan was negotiated for three years with the allowance of an increase each year of 16.5 percent of the growth in U.S. domestic car sales, the Ford petition had requested that total imports be limited to 1.7 million units for five years. This would have involved a reduction of Japanese imports to below 1 million units, as the remainder of the quota would be made up of imports from Western Europe. The VRA, however, proved sufficient to diffuse the political pressure on Congress to legislate quotas not totally insulating the American auto industry from foreign competition. To the extent that the reduction in Japanese exports to the United States reduced the quantity of cars on the U.S. market sufficiently to allow domestic producers to raise their prices, the VRA did facilitate a wealth transfer from consumers to producers of automobiles.

Unlike the textile and apparel and auto cases, the issue in the telecommunications case did not directly involve proposed legislation for import restraints; nor did it involve arguments that some trade restraint was necessary to enhance social stability. Instead, the government procurement code provided a framework within which to negotiate increased access for U.S. firms to foreign markets. This indirectly helped to promote social stability through the creation of jobs in the export sector to replace some proportion of those jobs lost in other sectors that were no longer competitive with imports. The existence of the government procurement code helps to explain why the political energies of the industry were diverted away from efforts to persuade Congress to restrict foreign imports. Because in this case the potential for increased profitability came from expanded access to the Japanese market, the agreement reached between the United States and Japan did not impose costs on U.S. consumers.

INDUSTRIAL POLICY IN THE UNITED STATES

The telecommunications case illustrates how the GATT regime can be used to create new export opportunities for American firms. The U.S. policy of pragmatic liberalism, however, which relies on the creation of new export opportunities, consists of a fragmented set of decisions. These decisions include policies that simultaneously provided increased market access for American exports through a commitment to multilateralism while at the same time legitimizing limited trade restraints to promote domestic social stability in regions of the country that depend upon declining industries for their economic base. This disjointed trade policy has not posed a political threat to the multilateral trade framework. But pragmatic liberalism poses problems in its implicit economic prescriptions vis-à-vis both imports and exports. Specifically, U.S. trade policy has created economic problems because it condones import restraints without attention to the question of industrial adjustment. It also expands export opportunities without encouraging American firms to incorporate production for export into their central business strategy.

Although pragmatic liberalism may be descriptive of U.S. postwar trade policy, as a policy prescription it will only create, not alleviate, problems that result from the increasing enmeshment of the United States in the international economy. The United States will increase its chances to become competitive on an international scale only if it develops a trade strategy that fuses both import policy and export policy into a coherent whole.[6] If the United States would formulate both import and export programs in a way that would create incentives for U.S. firms to respond to international competition, the United States would then have the basis for a coherent industrial policy. This would include policies aimed at promoting the restructuring of declining industries and alleviating the transition costs of moving the factors of production (primarily labor) from declining into growth industries.

Pragmatic liberalism has led to the proliferation of VRAs as well as other bilateral agreements designed to shelter domestic producers from foreign imports.[7] These policies have been promoted on the grounds that they help to sustain social stability in regions of the country in which declining industries are located. This concern with social stability, however, has directed attention of policymakers away from the long-run consequences of the failure of American industry to adjust to foreign competition. The result of this policy has been to increase the cost of goods insulated from foreign competition, thus threatening the competitive position of other U.S. industries that depend on these sheltered goods as inputs. To promote economic growth, the United States needs to augment its import policy through the addition of incentives for industries either to restructure or to shift into growth sectors. This long-run strategy for adjustment would involve phasing out products in which an industry is no longer competitive while expanding investment in those goods in which the United States has the potential of regaining a comparative advantage. It would also require measures that compensate labor in declining sectors. This would include:

> generous job training [for workers displaced by foreign competition], help in relocating, new industries within their regions in which they easily can gain employment at wages as high as they had before, generous unemployment compensation, and insurance against bad health.[8]

In conjunction with these policies, the government would also aid in restructuring declining industries. This may involve providing guaranteed loans to allow firms to salvage competitive parts of the declining industry through "carefully targeted rationalizations, new investments in plants, machinery, and research and development, and funds to help develop foreign markets."[9]

While U.S. industrial policy would encourage industries in the process of restructuring to pursue export opportunities in foreign markets, there is also a need to direct the attention of internationally competitive industries toward the potential for export expansion. In spite of the commitment on the part of the United States to multilateralism, American firms have not taken advantage of this increased access to foreign markets. *Business Week* reports:

> Right now, exports are seen not only as peripheral to the profits of most U.S. corporations but as marginal to the well-being of the nation as a whole. Mesmerized by the big domestic U.S. market, corporations do not generally even think about exports as an integral part of their operations, while Washington has, until recently, relegated trade policy to fifth place in determining economic policy for the country.[10]

Policies the government could pursue that might stimulate exports of U.S. firms include increasing the funds of the Export-Import Bank to be used to finance foreign sales, provide export insurance coverage for foreign exchange losses and foreign inflation, and expand its current programs (administered by the Commerce Department) for direct marketing assistance to help exporters to find customers and to promote products.[11] These policies would encourage American firms to take advantage of the multilateral trade regime bolstered by the GATT. To remain entrenched in a policy of pragmatic liberalism may be politically acceptable—that is, the GATT may be sufficiently resilient to accommodate protectionist policies, which result from this political pragmatism. Yet it may also contribute to the eventual industrial decline of the United States, as more and more industries are faced with import competition and little effort is made by U.S. industries to adopt a competitive posture in the international economy.

Critics of industrial policy claim that "creating a U.S. industrial policy will not guarantee international competitiveness or eliminate the side effects of the global economy. In American politics . . . an omniscient, centralized structure is all too likely to result in protection for our declining industries and the destruction of incentives to switch resources into more promising sectors."[12] This criticism assumes that political incentives exist only to benefit declining industries and neglects the economic, political, and social costs involved in the transfer of resources from declining into competitive sectors of the U.S. economy. If the United States would adopt an industrial policy, political incentives would come into play for competitive industries to participate in the trade policy debate.

Both the current ad hoc U.S. policy of pragmatic liberalism and a new industrial policy in the United States would impose costs on the U.S. economy. An industrial policy's advantage stems from the fact that these costs could be weighed against one another instead of weighing the certain and known costs of protection against the unknown and possibly devastating costs of doing nothing. Trade protection is politically expedient not because it is costless but because these costs are not always apparent to those groups that bear them. While an industrial policy aimed at shifting resources into internationally competitive sectors of the economy would be costly because labor and capital are not perfectly mobile, these costs should in principle be more short-term than the costs involved in trade protection. These costs should be short-term because they would be incurred to facilitate industrial transition rather than to maintain noncompetitive producers over an indefinite length of time. Thus an industrial policy in the United States would offer a political alternative to trade protection and help to change the political calculus of trade by offering incentives to competitive industries to become politically engaged.

U.S. FOREIGN POLICY AND INTERNATIONAL TRADE

U.S. policies that embargo the sale of specific products to achieve foreign policy goals also discourage American firms from pursuing an export-oriented market strategy. The most recent U.S. embargo has involved the prohibition of sales by U.S. firms (and their foreign subsidiaries) of equipment to be used in the construction of the Siberia-to-Europe natural gas pipeline. The United States implemented this embargo ostensibly for three reasons: first, to signal to the Soviet Union its displeasure with the imposition of a military government in Poland; second, to prevent European dependence on Soviet energy sources; and finally, to prevent Soviet diversion of its foreign exchange earnings to military buildup.

While this political strategy appears unlikely to slow construction of the pipeline, Caterpillar Trac or Company recently announced that it is laying off 2,000 employees owing to the loss of foreign contracts. If the pipeline construction is completed on schedule in spite of the embargo, this may indicate that economic embargoes impose greater economic cost on the United States through the reduction of export opportunities than they impose on the adversary, which is only faced with the problem of finding alternative suppliers. To make it more difficult for the Soviet Union to locate alternative suppliers, the United States also attempted to prohibit European corporations manufacturing under U.S. licenses from selling oil and natural gas equipment to the Soviets.[13] This decision to embargo all pipeline technology threatened to trigger European retaliation against U.S. exports. The basis for this retaliation was the Europeans' contention that the loss of sales due to the embargo will reduce employment when Europe can least afford a loss of jobs.

Retaliation against U.S. exports in response to the embargo poses a threat to the stability of the GATT framework, much the same as the illegal imposition of U.S. import restraints. Thus the future stability of the GATT may be contingent upon other foreign policy decisions that affect the international economic environment. An analysis of the pipeline case indicates that in addition to domestic pressures for protection foreign policy decisions outside the GATT framework could undermine the evolving structure of multilateral agreements. This may in turn contribute to the conditions that could again lead to the international economic chaos of the 1930s.

Both the GATT regime and the U.S. decision to embargo pipeline technology and equipment make up important components of the international political environment of business. The U.S. decision to participate in the GATT and the decision to impose an embargo are both political decisions and constitute international economic policies that American firms may hope to influence but ultimately have to live with. Both serve as constraints on the political power of American business in their attempts to influence the policy process in these issue areas. The GATT regime, however, has evolved into a political agreement among states based on a consensus over the norms, rules, and procedures to be used for both expanding trade and for resolving economic conflict. This consensual regime provides a more stable political environment for business than the unilateral U.S. decision on the embargo. In contrast to the GATT, the embargo threatens to undermine the stability of the international political consensus, thereby creating increased uncertainty and thus a higher level of business risk in international trade.

The political decisions analyzed in this study indicate that U.S. enmeshment in the international economy will continue to increase in the future. Obstacles to this increase seem more likely to come from the use of international economic sanctions as foreign policy tools than from domestic pressures for protection. A decision on the part of the United States to support an international economic policy based on consensus rather than on unilateral action would provide a relatively stable international political environment within which American business could operate. In addition, this policy would also help to maintain the stability of the international economic order. This direction would allow increased international economic growth and contribute to the stability of the international political system.

NOTES

1. E. E. Schattschneider, *Politics, Pressures, and the Tariff* (Hamden, Conn.: Archon Books, 1963).

2. Raymond Bauer, Ithiel de Sola Pool, and Lewis Anthony Dexter, *American Business and Public Policy: The Politics of Foreign Trade* (Chicago: Aldine, 1972).

3. This view is expressed in the comments of one opponent to the bill, Representative William Frenzel, who argued that "if import curbs were adopted, they would result in a terrible cost to consumers and potentially high costs to other producers." *Congressional Quarterly Almanac*, 1980, p. 303.

4. Albert O. Hirschman, *National Power and the Structure of Foreign Trade* (Berkeley: University of California Press, 1980) and Stephen D. Krasner, *Defending the National Interest: Raw Materials Investments and U.S. Foreign Policy* (Princeton, N.J.: Princeton University Press, 1978).

5. Article 19, "the escape clause," allows for the temporary imposition of trade restraints if the industry in question can demonstrate that imports are a substantial cause of injury.

6. This, however, is unlikely given the current fragmented structure of the American government and the ideological commitment to the diffusion of power at both the federal and state levels of government.

7. The imposition of these restraints has admittedly been made easier owing to the monopoly power of the United States in international markets.

8. Robert Reich, "Playing Tag with Japan," *New York Review of Books*, June 24, 1982, p. 40.

9. Ira C. Magaziner and Robert B. Reich, *Minding America's Business: The Decline and Rise of the American Economy* (New York: Harcourt Brace Jovanovich, 1982), p. 210.

10. "What Caused the Decline: A Failure to Sell Abroad," *Business Week* (Special Issue on the Reindustrialization of America), June 30, 1980, p. 13.

11. This discussion is based on the analysis of American industrial policy by Magaziner and Reich in *Minding America's Business*.

12. Arthur Denzau, "Will an Industrial Policy Work for the United States?" Center for the Study of American Business Formal Publication no. 57 (St. Louis: Washington University, September 1983), p. 16.

13. "Shaken Alliance: Economic Battles Push US-Europe Close to the Danger Point," *Wall Street Journal*, July 15, 1982, p. 1.

BIBLIOGRAPHY

Allen, William. *International Trade Theory: Hume to Ohlin.* New York: Random House, 1969.

Arthur D. Little Decision Resources. "Impact: The Outlook for the U.S. Telephone Interconnect Equipment Industry." Cambridge, Mass., June 1980.

"Auto Union Plans to Take Imports to US Trade Unit, Bypassing Congress," *Wall Street Journal,* May 9, 1980, p. 5.

Baldwin, Robert E. "The Political Economy of Postwar U.S. Trade Policy." Bulletin no. 1976—4. New York: Center for the Study of Financial Institutions, 1976.

Bange, Kenneth. "Voluntary Export Restrictions as a Foreign Commercial Policy." Ph.D. dissertation, Michigan State University, 1967.

Bauer, Raymond A., Ithiel de Sola Pool, and Lewis Anthony Dexter. *American Business and Public Policy: The Politics of Foreign Trade.* Chicago: Aldine, 1972.

Beckett, Grace. *The Reciprocal Trade Agreements Program.* New York: Columbia University Press, 1941.

Blackhurst, Richard, Nicolas Marian, and Jan Tumlir. "Adjustment, Trade and Growth in Developed and Developing Countries," *GATT Studies in International Trade.* no. 6. General Agreement on Tariffs and Trade: Geneva, September 1978.

———. "Trade Liberalization, Protectionism and Interdependence." *GATT Studies in International Trade.* no. 5. General Agreement on Tariffs and Trade: Geneva, November 1977.

Brenner, Steven Robert. "Economic Interests and the Trade Agreements Program: 1937—1940: A Study in Institutions and Political Influence." Ph.D. dissertation, Stanford University, 1977.

Bronz, George. "The Tariff Commission as a Regulatory Agency." *Columbia Law Review* 61 (1961): 1, pp. 463–489.

Brown, William Adams, Jr. *The United States and the Restoration of World Trade.* Washington D.C.: Brookings Institution, 1950.

Cairncross, Frances., ed. *Changing Perceptions of Economic Policy.* New York: Methuen, 1981.

Cline, William, Noboru Kawanabe, T. O. M. Kronsjö, and Thomas Williams. *Trade Negotiations in the Tokyo Round: A Quantitative Assessment.* Washington D.C.: Brookings Institution, 1978.

Conte, Christopher, and Robert Simison. "UAW and Ford Requests for Curbs on Imports Are Rejected by Panel." *Wall Street Journal*, November 11, 1980, p. 3.

Cooper, Richard N. "Economic Interdependence and Foreign Policy in the Seventies." *World Politics* 24 (January 1972): 159–81.

———. *The Economics of Interdependence: Economic Policy in the Atlantic Community.* New York: McGraw-Hill for the Council on Foreign Relations, 1968.

Cox, Robert W., and Harold Jacobson, eds. *The Anatomy of Influence: Decision Making in International Organizations.* New Haven, Conn.: Yale University Press, 1972.

Curran, Timothy, "Politics and High Technology: US-Japan Negotiations over the Nippon Telephone and Telegraph Company 1978–1979." Prepared for the U.S.-Japan Economic Relations Group, Washington D.C., 1980. Mimeographed.

Curtis, Thomas B., and John Robert Vastine. *The Kennedy Round and the Future of American Trade.* New York: Praeger, 1971.

Curzon, Gerard. *Multilateral Commercial Diplomacy: The General Agreement on Tariffs and Trade and Its Impact on National Commercial Policies.* London: Michael Joseph, 1965.

Dam, Kenneth W. *The GATT: Law and International Economic Organization.* Chicago: University of Chicago Press, 1970.

Denzau, Arthur. "Will an Industrial Policy Work for the United States?" Center for the Study of American Business Formal Publication no. 57, Washington University, St. Louis, September 1983.

Destler, I. M., Haruhiro Fukui, and Hideo Sato. *The Textile Wrangle.* Ithaca, N.Y.: Cornell University Press, 1979.

Diebold, William J. "The End of the ITO." *Essays in International Finance.* no. 16. Princeton: Princeton University Press, October 1952.

———. *New Directions in Trade Policy.* New York: Council on Foreign Relations, 1941.

Evans, John W. *The Kennedy Round in American Trade Policy: The Twilight of the GATT?* Cambridge, Mass.: Harvard University Press, 1971.

"On Eve of US Hearings on Auto Imports from Japan, All Parties Vie for Attention." *Wall Street Journal*, October 8, 1980, p. 2.

Farnsworth, Clyde. "Carter Acts to Speed Car Import Study." *New York Times*, July 9, 1980, p. D4.

———. "Panel Briefs Reagan on Auto Aid." *New York Times*, March 3, 1981, pp. D1.

———. "Pressure Mounting on Trade Packages: Lobbyists Pursue Special Waivers." *New York Times*, March 25, 1979, pp. IF, 4F.

———. "Tokyo to Urge Auto Export Restraint." *New York Times*, November 18, 1980, p. D1.

Finlayson, Jock A., and Mark Zacher. "The GATT and Regulation of Trade Barriers: Regime Dynamics and Functions." *International Organization* 35 (Autumn 1981): 561–602.

Ford Motor Company. *Petition for Relief from Increased Imports of Passenger Cars, Light Trucks, Vans, and Utility Vehicles under Section 201 of the Trade Act of 1974*, Before the USITC. August 1, 1980.

———. *Prehearing Brief of the Ford Motor Company*. USITC Investigation TA-201–44, October 1, 1980.

Gardner, Richard N. *Sterling and Dollar Diplomacy in Current Perspective: The Origins and the Prospects of Our International Economic Order*. New York: Columbia University Press, 1975.

General Agreement on Tariffs and Trade. *Report by the Director General of the GATT: The Tokyo Round of the Mulitlateral Trade Negotiations*. Geneva: General Agreement on Tariffs and Trade, 1979.

Ginsburg, Douglas H., and William J. Abernathy, eds. *Government, Technology, and the Future of the Automobile*. New York: McGraw-Hill, 1980.

"GM Shakes Up the Auto Industry." *Wall Street Journal* May 26, 1982, p. 30.

Goldstein, Edward. "Doing Business under the Agreement on Government Procurement." *St. John's Law Review* 55 (1980): pp. 63–91.

Haas, Ernst B. "Why Collaborate? Issue Linkage and International Regimes." *World Politics* 32 (April 1980): 357–405.

———. "Words Can Hurt You; or, Who Said What to Whom About Regimes." *International Organization* 36 (Spring 1982): 207–44.

Hayes, Michael T. *Lobbyists and Legislators: A Theory of Political Markets*. New Brunswick, N.J.: Rutgers University Press, 1981.

———. "The Semi-Sovereign Pressure Groups: A Critique of Current Theory and an Alternative Typology." *Journal of Politics* 40 (February 1978): 134–61.

Hirschman, Albert O. *National Power and the Structure of Foreign Trade*. Berkeley: University of California Press, 1980.

Hornsby, Michael. "EEC and America Set for a Confrontation over Duties." *Times* (London), October 17, 1979.

Hudec, Robert E. *The GATT Legal System and World Trade Diplomacy.* New York: Praeger, 1975.

Hunsberger, Warren. *Japan and the United States in World Trade.* New York: Harper & Row for the Council on Foreign Relations, 1964.

Jackson, John H. *World Trade and the Law of GATT: A Legal Analysis of the General Agreement on Tariffs and Trade.* New York: Bobbs-Merrill, 1969.

Jacobson, Harold. *Networks of Interdependence: International Organizations and the Global Political System.* New York: Alfred A. Knopf, 1979.

Jameson, Sam. "UAW Chief Sets 3−Month Time Limit for Japan to Limit Exports or Face Curbs." Los Angeles *Times*, February 14, 1980, p. 2.

"Japan Asks Its Car Firms to Limit Exports to the US and Start American Production." *Wall Street Journal,* February 13, 1980, p. 2.

"Japan: The Doors of NTT Begin to Creak Open." *Business Week,* May 4, 1981, p. 67.

Johnson, Chalmers. *Japan's Public Policy Companies.* Washington D.C.: American Enterprise Institute, 1978.

Johnson, Harry G. "Technological Change and Comparative Advantage: Advanced Country's Viewpoint." *Journal of World Trade Law* 9 (January−February 1975): 1−13.

Kelly, William B., ed. *Studies in United States Commercial Policy.* Chapel Hill: University of North Carolina Press, 1963.

Kindleberger, Charles P. *The World in Depression: 1929−1939.* Berkeley: University of California Press, 1973.

Krasner, Stephen D. *Defending the National Interest: Raw Materials Investments and U.S. Foreign Policy.* Princeton, N.J.: Princeton University Press, 1978.

———. "State Power and the Structure of International Trade." *World Politics* 28 (April 1976): 317−48.

———. "Structural Causes and Regime Consequences: Regimes as Intervening Variables." *International Organization* 36 (Spring 1982): 185−206.

———. "The Tokyo Round: Particularistic Interests and Prospects for Stability in the Global Trading System." *International Studies Quarterly* 23 (December 1979): 491−539.

Larsen, Dale. "Costs of Import Protection in the United States." May 10, 1979. Mimeographed.

Lipson, Charles. "The Transformation of Trade: The Sources and Effects of Regime Change." *International Organization* 36 (Spring 1982): 417−56.

Lowi, Theodore. "American Business and Public Policy: Case Studies and Political Theory." *World Politics* 16 (July 1964): 677–93.

Magee, Stephen P. "International Trade." Working Paper no. 79-10, University of Texas at Austin, Bureau of Business Research, 1979.

———. "The Welfare Effects of Restriction on U.S. Trade." *Brookings Papers on Economic Activity*, 9th issue (1972): 645–708.

Meadows, Edward. "A Difference of Opinion." *Fortune*, August 11, 1980, pp. 213–14.

Meier, Gerald M. *International Economics: The Theory of Policy*. New York: Oxford University Press, 1980.

Mintz, Ilse. *U.S. Import Quotas: Costs and Consequences*. Washington D.C.: American Enterprise Institute, 1973.

Morkre, Morris, and David Tarr. *Staff Report on Effects of Restrictions on U.S. Imports: Five Case Studies and Theory*. Washington D.C.: Federal Trade Commission, June 1980.

Munger, Michael. "The Costs of Protectionism: Estimates of the Hidden Tax of Trade Restraint." Center for the Study of American Business Working Paper no. 80, Washington University, St. Louis, July 1983.

Olson, Mancur. *The Logic of Collective Action: Public Goods and the Theory of Groups*. Cambridge: Harvard University Press, 1971.

Organization for Economic Cooperation and Development. "Study of the Telecommunications Equipment Sector." DSTI/IND/IAQ/8.1.3. (I). Paris: OECD, 1981. Mimeographed.

Pastor, Robert. *Congress and the Politics of U.S. Foreign Economic Policy: 1929–1976*. Berkeley: University of California Press, 1980.

Reich, Robert B., "Making Industrial Policy." *Foreign Affairs* 60 (Spring 1982): 852–81.

———. "Playing Tag with Japan." *New York Review of Books*, June 24, 1982, pp. 40–44.

Reich, Robert, and Ira C. Magaziner. *Minding America's Business: The Decline and Rise of the American Economy*. New York: Harcourt Brace Jovanovich, 1982.

Ricardo, David. *Principles of Political Economy and Taxation*. London: George Bell and Sons, 1891.

Ruggie, John Gerard. "International Regimes, Transactions, and Change: Embedded Liberalism in the Postwar Economic Order." *International Organization* 36 (Spring 1982): 379–416.

Salter, Malcolm. "The Automobile Crisis and Public Policy." *Harvard Business Review* 59 (January–February 1981): 73–82.

Schattschneider, E. E. *Politics, Pressures, and the Tariff: A Study of Free Private Enterprise in Pressure Politics as Shown in the 1929–1930 Revision of the Tariff*. Hamden, Conn.: Archon Books, 1963.

Schumpeter, Joseph. *Capitalism, Socialism, and Democracy.* 5th ed. London: Allen and Unwin, 1976.

Shonfield, Andrew, ed. *International Economic Relations of the Western World, 1959–1971: Volume 1: Politics and Trade.* London: Oxford University Press, 1976.

Shepard, William, and Clair Wilcox. *Public Policies toward Business.* Homewood, Ill.: Irwin Series in Economics, 1979.

Simison, Robert. "Car Wars: Protectionism Battle over Imports of Autos May Head for Congress." *Wall Street Journal,* February 15, 1980, pp. 1, 12.

Smith, Adam. *An Inquiry into the Nature and Causes of the Wealth of Nations.* Edited by Edwin Cannan. Chicago: University of Chicago Press, 1976.

Smith, Charles. "Japan May Liberalize Telecommunications Purchasing." *Financial Times* (London), February 20, 1979.

"The Reindustrialization of America." *Business Week.* New York: McGraw-Hill, June 30, 1980, pp. 55–142.

Tasca, Henry Joseph. *The Reciprocal Trade Policy of the United States: A Study in Trade Philosophy.* Philadelphia: University of Pennsylvania Press, 1938.

Truman, David B. *The Governmental Process: Political Interests and Public Opinion.* New York: Alfred A. Knopf, 1951.

Tucker, William, "The Wreck of the Auto Industry." *Harper's,* November 1980, pp. 45–60.

Tumlir, Jan. "International Economic Order: Rules, Cooperation, and Sovereignty." In *Issues in International Economics,* edited by Peter Oppenheimer. Boston: Oriel Press, 1980.

———. "National Interest and International Order." *International Issues,* no. 4. London: Trade Policy Research Centre, 1978.

———. "National Sovereignty, Power, and Interest." *ORDO,* 31, 1–26. New York: Gustav Fischer Verlag, 1978.

United Automobile Workers Union. *Petition for Relief under Section 201 of the Trade Act of 1974 from Import Competition from Imported Passenger Cars, Light Trucks, and Utility Vehicles before the United States International Trade Commission.* Washington D.C., 1980. Mimeographed.

"Unreliable Supplier: U.S. Trade Restrictions in Recent Years Are Said to Cost Billions in Lost Business." *Wall Street Journal,* May 26, 1982, p. 56.

U.S., Comptroller General. *Government Buy-National Practices of the United States and Other Countries.* Washington D.C.: General Accounting Office, 1976.

———. *United States—Japan Trade: Issues and Problems.* ID-79—53. Washington D.C.: General Accounting Office, September 21, 1979.

U.S., Congress, Congressional Budget Office. *The Effects of the Tokyo Round of Multilateral Trade Negotiations on the U.S. Economy: An Updated View.* Washington D.C.: Congressional Budget Office, July 1979.

U.S., Congress, House, Subcommittee on Trade Policy of the House Committee on Ways and Means. *Auto Situation: 1980.* Washington, D.C.: Government Printing Office, 1980.

———. *Compendium of Papers on U.S. Foreign Trade Policy.* Washington D.C.: Government Printing Office, 1957.

———. *Task Force Report on United States-Japan Trade.* Washington D.C.: Government Printing Office, 1979.

U.S., Congress, Senate, Committee on Finance. *Agreements Being Negotiated at the Multilateral Trade Negotiations in Geneva.* 96th Cong. 1st Sess. U.S. International Trade Commission Study no. 332—101, MTN Studies, no. 6. Washington D.C.: Government Printing Office, 1979.

———. *Multilateral Trade Negotiations: International Code Agreed to in Geneva Switzerland.* Washington D.C.: Government Printing Office, 1979.

U.S., Department of Transportation. *The U.S. Auto Industry 1980: Report to the President from the Secretary of Transportation.* DOT-P-1081—02. Department of Transportation, Washington D.C., 1981.

U.S. International Trade Commission. *A Baseline Study of the Telephone Terminal and Switching Equipment Industry.* USITC Publication no. 946. Washington D.C., 1979.

———. *Certain Motor Vehicles and Certain Chassis and Bodies Therefore.* USITC Publication no. 1110, Washington D.C., 1980.

———. *The History and Current Status of the Multifiber Arrangement.* USITC Publication no. 850. Washington D.C., January 1978.

Vernon, Raymond, "America's Foreign Trade Policy and the GATT." *Essays in International Finance.* no. 21. Princeton: Princeton University Press, 1954.

———. *Business and the State: Changing Relations in Western Europe.* Cambridge, Mass.: Harvard University Press, 1974.

Vernon, Raymond, ed. *The Technology Factor in International Trade.* New York: Columbia University Press, 1970.

Wilkins, Mira, and Frank Ernest Hill. *American Business Abroad: Ford on Six Continents.* Detroit: Wayne State University Press, 1964.

———. *The Maturing of the Multinational Enterprise: American Business Abroad from 1914 to 1970.* Cambridge, Mass.: Harvard University Press, 1974.

INDEX

"Administration's Program for
  Textiles." *See* "Proposed
  Presidential Textile Program"
Agricultural Act of 1956, 103
Alberger, William, 153
American Apparel Association, 94
American Business and Public Policy, 32
American Textile Manufacturers
  Association, 102
American Textile Manufacturers'
  Institute, 94
Apparel industry. *See* Textile industry
Arab oil boycott, 130–131
Askew, Rubin, 134, 187, 189, 193
AT&T, 169–171
Autarky, 45
Auto industry
  and agreement with Japanese,
    158–160
  and Congress, 134–139
  development of
    in 1930s, 128–129
    in 1950s, 129
    in 1960s, 129
    in 1970s, 129–132
    after World War II, 129
    decline in, 132–134
  and downsizing, 131–132
  and executive branch, 134–139
  and Ford petitions
    and causality, 142–143
    defense of, 125–126, 141
    filing of, 139–140
    and quotas, 141–142
  and ITC proceedings
    decision of, 153–156
    and Ford Motor Company,
    146–147
    hearings of, 150–152
    and importers, 148
    staff report of, 149
    stages of, 143–144
    and UAW, 144–145
  layoffs in, 131–133
  overview of, 125–128
  postscript of, 156–168
  and UAW, 139–143
Autonomy
  of Congress, 30–32
  political, 45–46
  in state strength, 203–204

Bauer, Pool, Dexter study
  and interest groups, 22
    protectionists, 202
  and Schattschneider's position, 30
  and textile industry, 94
  transactional model of, 31–32

Bauer, Raymond. *See* Bauer, Pool, Dexter study
Bedell, Catherine, 153–154
Bentsen, Lloyd, 157
Blumenthal, W. Michael, 111
Brandis, Buford, 101
Brock, William, 88

CAFE, 131, 137
Caldwell, Phillip
  and auto trade with Japan, 159
  and ITC proceedings, 143
  testimony of, 150–151, 155–156, 159
Calhoun, Michael, 154, 160
Carson City Silver Dollar Bill, 108
Carter, Jimmy, 87, 108
Caterpillar Tractor Company, 211
CEA
  and auto import restraints, 138,157
  and textile industry, 110
  and textile program, 112–116
  and trade policy, 87–88
Chrysler, 132
Classical pluralism, 33
Common carrier (telecommunications) firms, 169
Communications Workers of America, 190–191
Congress
  and auto industry, 134–139
  autonomy of, 30–32
  and tariffs, 63
  and trade policy, 34
Consumers, 26–29
Contracting Parties, 81
Corporate average fuel economy, 131, 137
Cotton Textile Committee, 105
Council of Economic Advisors. *See* CEA
Culbertson, William, 63–64
Curtis, Thomas, 82
Curzon, Gerard, 74
Curzon, Victoria, 74
CWA, 190–191

Danforth, John, 157–158, 201
Dent, Frederick, 84
Department of Transportation study, 131–133
Dependence on trade, 47
Dexter, Lewis. *See* Bauer, Pool, Dexter study
Dillon Round 78–79
Distributive policy, 32–33
DOT study, 131–133

Eads, George, 138–139
Economic interdependence, 45–46
EEC
  and Dillon Round, 78–79
  and injury clause, 86
  and subsidy-countervailing duty waiver, 108–110
  and Trade Expansion Act, 79
EIA, 189–191
Electronic Industries Association, *See* EIA
Emergency Tariff Act of 1921, 62
Energy Policy and Conservation Act, 130–131
Escape clause
  allowances of, 140, 142
  and trade agreements program, 76–77
  and trade policy, 13
  and UAW petition, 139–140
European Economic Community. *See* EEC
Executive Branch, and auto industry, 134–139
Export restraint on
  in Siberia-to-Europe pipeline, 200

FCC, 171
Federal Communications Commission, 171
Feketekuty, Geza, 111
Ford Motor Company
  and fairness in auto trade, 137
  in ITC proceedings, 146–147
  and large-car market, 131–132

and petitions to ITC, 139–143
and small-car inventories, 130
Fordney-McCumber Tariff Act of 1922,
63
Foreign policy, 210–212
Fraser, Douglas, 136–137, 139, 150

Gardner, Richard, 70–71
GATT
and auto case outcome, 159–160
and collaboration of states, 45–46
commitment of U.S. to, 11
cornerstones of, 74
creation of, 4
framing of, 72
and future trade policy, 209
and impairment, 75
and import protection, 14
influence of on trade policy, 4
and international regime, 5, 55–57
and market disruption, 103
membership to, 73
and MFN clause, 74
and national interest, 12–13
norms of 4, 6
and NTBs, 82–83
and nullification, 75
principles of, 5–6
and quotas, 74
rounds of, 71–72. *See also* Dillon
Round; Kennedy Round; Tokyo
Round
rules of, 7
secretariat services of, 73
signing of, 71
stability of, future, 211–212
and tariff concessions, 140, 142
and tariff negotiations, 73
and textile industry, 95, 97, 101–102
and trade policy, 16
and TSB, 106–107
General Agreement on Tariffs and
Trade. *See* GATT
General Motors, 130–132, 152
Geral, Arthur, 98–99
Governmental Process: Political Interests

and Public Opinion, The, 23
Government procurement code,
171–175
Grey, Rodney, 93

H.R. 9937, 108
Haas, Ernst, 46
Hayes, Michael
and interest groups, 22–23, 35–36
and trade policy, 33–38
Heckscher, E., 5–6
Hirschman, Albert
and imports, 46–47
neomercantile position of, 44–45
and political costs, 48
and state strength, 46–48, 203
House Subcommittee on Trade, 134,
139
Hull, Cordell, 65

Imports
competition of, 8–9. *See also* Auto
industry; Telecommunications
industry; Textile industry
Hirschman's view of, 46–47
Japanese
in auto industry, 125, 157–158
in textile industry, 101–102
restraint on
in auto industry, 126, 156–160
in textile industry, 97–100
and Trade Act of 1974, 142
Industry Sector Advisory Committee,
179
Injury, 81
Interest groups
assumptions about
Bauer's, Pool's, and Dexter's,
22, 30–32
Olson's 23–24
Schattschneider's, 27–29
basis of, economic 23–26
conflictual, 35–38
consensual, 35–38
model of, 32–33
Schattschneider's view of, 200–202

and tariffs, 21, 26
and textile industry, 93–94
International regime, 55–57
International trade. *See* Trade policy
International Trade Commission. *See*
    ITC
International Trade Organization. *See*
    ITO
ISAC, 179
ITC
    and case of auto industry, 57
    and escape clause hearings, 8
    proceedings for auto industry
        decision of, 153–156
        and Ford Motor Company,
            146–147
        hearings of, 150–152
        and importers, 148
        staff report of, 149
        stages of, 143–144
        and UAW, 144–145
ITO
    Charter, 69–71
    design of, 68–69
    opposition to, 70
    role intended for, 14
    and trade policy, 68–71

Kelly, William, 62, 65
Kennedy, John, 79
Kennedy Round, 82
Krasner, Stephen
    and autonomy of state, 203
    and definition of regime, 5
    neomercantile position of, 44–45
    and state strength, 49–52

Larsen, Dale, 10
League of Nations Convention on the
    Abolition of Import and Export
    Prohibitions and Restrictions, 64
Logic of Collective Action, The, 23
Long-Term Arrangement. *See* LTA
Lowi, Theodore, 22, 32–35
LTA, 94, 104–105

Magee, Stephen, 6, 10
Market disruption, 103, 105
Memorandum of Disapproval, 108
MFA, 8, 94, 105–106
MFN, 63–64
Ministry of International Trade and
    Industry. *See* MITI
Mintz, Ilse, 10–11
MITI, 136–137
Monopoly, natural, 165
Moore, George, 153–154
Most-favored nation. *See* MFN
MTN
    and ITO, 60
    ratification of, 109–110, 116
    and tariff cuts, 115, 118
    textile tariffs in, 96
Multifiber Arrangement. *See* MFA
Multilateral trade negotiations. *See*
    MTN
Multilateralism, 6, 13
Multi-national corporations. *See* MNCs
Munger, Michael, 10
MNCs, 179

National interest
    and Congress, 2
    definition of, evolving, 12
    Hirschman's view of, 46–48
    and international regime, 55–57
    Krasner's view of, 49–52
    and open trading system, 160
    overview of, 43–45
    and political autonomy versus
        economic interdependence,
        45–46
    Tumlir's view of, 52–54
*National Power and the Structure of
    Foreign Trade*, 44
National power policy, 46
Nippon Telephone and Telegraph. *See*
    NTT
Nissan Motor Company, 136–137, 148
Nondiscrimination, 6, 13, 74
Nontariff barriers. *See* NTBs
NTBs

in auto industry, 133
and Trade Act of 1974, 82–83, 85
NTT
   activities of, 175–176
   agreement with, 187–189
   creation of, 175
   family, 176
   and government procurement code,
      177–179
   isolation of, 179–184
   and negotiations over bilateral,
      185–187

OECD
   and telecommunications industry,
      170, 172–174
   and textile industry, 98–100
Office of Management and the Budget,
   157
Office of Textiles, 205–206
Office of the Special Trade
   Representative. See STR
Ohlin, Goran, 5–6
Okita, Saburo, 189, 193
Olson, Mancur, 11, 23–25
OMA, 147, 203
   Operating companies, 169
Orderly Marketing Agreement. See
   OMA
Organization for Economic
   Cooperation and Development.
   See OECD

Pastor, Robert, 34
Peril point, 77–79
Political autonomy, 45–46
Political coalitions. See Interest groups
Pool, Ithiel DeSola. See Bauer, Pool,
   Dexter study
Postes, Telephone, and Telegraph. See
   PTT
Potter, David, 152
Power concept, 47
Pragmatic liberalism
   notion of, 3–4
   and political agreement, 199–200

in trade policy, 205–207
Pressure response model, 31
Progressive liberalism, 6
"Proposed Presidential Textile
   Program"
   creation of, 111–112
   final draft of, 117–118
   first draft of, 112–115
   options added to, 115–117
   and Tokyo Round, 8, 96
PTTs, 178–179

Quantitative restrictions. See Quotas
Quotas
   in auto industry, 126–127
   and balance-of-payments shortage,
      74
   and GATT, 74
   opposition to, 64
   on textile imports from Japan, 102

Reagan, Ronald, 157–158, 200
Reciprocal Trade Agreements Act of
   1934
   extension of, 72
   significance of, 68
   stipulations of, 65–68
   and tariffs, 21–23
   and trade policy, 13–14, 65
Reciprocity, 6, 13
Regulatory policy, 32–33
Reich, Robert, 15
Restrictions. See Quotas
Ricardo, David, 5
Roosevelt, Franklin Delano, 65–66
Ruggie, John, 3

Schattschneider, E.E.
   and interest groups, 26–29
      pressures of, 200–202
   and trade policy, 21
   and Smoot-Hawley Tariff Act, 65
Secrest, Fred, 126, 133–134, 138
Sherman Antitrust Act, 157
Shinto, Hisashi, 191
Short-Term Arrangement. See STA

Smith, Adam, 5
Smoot-Hawley Tariff Act
  and auto industry, 129
  and logrolling in Congress, 64
  Schattschneider's analysis of,
    27–29, 65
Snapback clause, 114, 117
Sodolski, John, 189–190
Special Trade Representative. See STR
State-owned telephone operating
  companies, 178–179
"State Power and the Structure of
  International Trade," 44
State strength
  and autonomy, 203
  definition of, 43
  Hirschman's view of, 46–48
  Krasner's view of, 49–52
  Tumlir's view of, 52–54
Stern, Paula, 150–152, 154–155
STR
  and cases of textile and
    telecommunications industries, 56
  and Japanese investment in U.S.,
    134–135
  and negotiations over bilateral,
    185–187
  and NTT, 179–184
  and textile industry, 108, 110–111,
    204
  and Trade Expansion Act, 80
  and trade policy, 56–57, 88
Strauss, Robert, 110–112, 182

Tariff Act of 1930, 200
Tariff Commission
  creation of, 62
  and escape clause relief, 77
  and negotiation of tariffs, 36
  and peril point, 78–79
  and Trade Expansion Act, 79–81
Tariffs
  negotiable, 21–22
  nonnegotiable, 21
  and peril point, 78

and Reciprocal Trade Agreement Act
  of 1934, 21
and Smoot-Hawley Tariff Act, 27–29
Telecommunications industry
  agreement of, 187–189
  description of, 169–171
  in Europe, 166
  future of, 190–191
  and government procurement code,
    171–175
  and impact of NTT case, 191–194
  in Japan, 166. See also NTT
  and network of interests, 177–179
  and NTT
    creation of, 175–176
    and government procurement
      code, 176–177
    isolation of, 179–184
    and negotiations over bilateral,
      185–187
  overview of, 165–169
  and reaction of industry and labor,
    189–190
Textile industry
  and import restraint, 97–100
  overview of, 93–97
  and textile white paper
    impact of, 121–122
    implementation of, 119–121
    and negotiation of tariffs,
      107–110
    publication of, 118–119
    and STR, 109–111
    and textile program of
      administration, 111–118
  trade policy in
    in 1930s, 101
    in 1950s, 101–103
    in 1960s, 104–105
    in 1970s, 105–106
    and market disruption, 103, 105
    problems of, 100–101
    and TSB, 106–107
Textile program. See "Proposed
  Presidential Textile Program"

Textile Surveillance Board, 106–107
Textile white paper
  and negotiation of tariffs, 107–110
  and STR, 109–111
  and textile program of
    administration
      creation of, 111–112
      final draft of, 117–118
      first draft of, 112–115
      implementation of, 119–121
      options added to, 115–117
      publication of, 118–119
Theory of comparative advantage,
  5–6, 43
Tokyo Round
  codes of, 85–87
  and extension of duty waiver, 110
  and government procurement code,
    166–167
  and NTBs, 85
  reorganization plan of, 87–88
  and telecommunications imports,
    8–9
  and textile imports, 8–9
  and textile program, 96–97
Toyota, 130, 136
Trade Act of 1974
  and import restraints on autos, 142
  and negotiation of textile tariffs, 108
  in trade policy, 82–85
Trade Agreements Act 1934, 30
Trade agreements program
  escape clause of, 76–77
  peril point of, 77–79
  provisions of, 75–76
Trade Expansion Act of 1962, 79–81
Trade policy
  1922–1934
    and MFN clause, 63–64
    and new tariff legislation, 61–63
    and quotas, 64
    and Reciprocal Trade
    Agreements act of 1934, 65–68
      and Smoot-Hawley Tariff Act,
      64–65

beyond domestic interests
  and foreign policy, 210–212
  and industrial policy, 207–210
  overview of, 199–200
  and pragmatic liberalism,
    205–207
  and Schattschneider's view,
    200–202
  and state strength, 203–204
  and transactional model,
    202–203
cases of. See Auto industry;
  Telecommunications industry;
  Textile industry
collaboration in, international
  Hirschman's view of, 46–48
  Krasner's view of, 49–52
  overview of, 43–45
  and political autonomy versus
  economic interdependence,
    45–46
  Tumlir's view of, 52–54
domestic interests of
  and Congress, 30–32
  and consumers, 26–29
  and interest groups, 23–26
  an interest group model,
    32–33
  overview of, 21–23
  principal-agent perspective of,
    33–39
explanations of, 1–4
and GATT, 4, 71–75
and ITO, 68–71
and Kennedy Round, 82
and national interest, 2
politics of
  case of, 7–9, 14–15
  domestic dimension of, 1–4
  and GATT, 4–7
  international dimension of, 1–4
  study of, 11–16
  and trade protection versus
  adjustment, 9–11
in retrospect, 59–61

and Tokyo Round, 85–88
and Trade Act of 1974, 82–85
and trade agreements program,
    75–79
and Trade Expansion Act of 1962,
    79–81
Trade protection, 9–11
Trade Renewal Act of 1958, 77
Transactional model of political
    influence, 31, 202–203
Treasury Department
    and auto import restraints, 157
    and flexibility provisions, 119–121
    and Japanese investment in U.S., 135
    and textile program, 112–116
    and trade policy, 87–88
Truman, David, 23, 25–26
TSB, 106–107
Tucker, William, 130
Tumlir, Jan, 45, 52–54

UAW
    and import relief, 8
    in ITC proceedings, 143–145

and petition to ITC, 139–140
United Auto Workers. See UAW

Vanik, Charles, 118–119, 129, 139
Vernon, Raymond
    and GATT influence, 75
    and product life cycle approach, 6, 8
    and Smoot-Hawley Tariff Act, 64
Volkswagen, 130
Voluntary restraint agreement. See
    VRA
VRA
    GM suggestion for, 152
    impact of, 158–159
    implementation of, 126–128
    request for, by Secrest, 138

Waiver extension, of subsidy-
    countervailing duty, 108–110,
    118–119
Wilcox, Clair, 69–70
Wolff, Alan, 111, 112, 116–117

Young, Howard, 150